OXFORD MONOGRAPHS ON LABOUR LAW

General Editors: PAUL DAVIES, KEITH EWING, MARK FREEDLAND

EU Intervention in Domestic Labour Law

OXFORD MONOGRAPHS ON LABOUR LAW

General Editors: Paul Davies, Cassel Professor of Commercial Law in the London School of Economics; Keith Ewing, Professor of Public Law at King's College, London; and Mark Freedland, Fellow of St John's College, and Professor of Employment Law in the University of Oxford.

This series has come to represent a significant contribution to the literature of British, European and international labour law. The series recognizes the arrival not only of a renewed interest in labour law generally, but also the need for fresh approaches to the study of labour law following a period of momentous change in the UK and Europe. The series is concerned with all aspects of labour law, including traditional subjects of study such as collective labour law and individual employment law, but it also includes works which concentrate on the growing role of human rights and the combating of discrimination in employment, and others which examine the law and economics of the labour market and the impact of social security law and of national and supranational employment policies upon patterns of employment and the employment contract. Two of the authors contributing to the series, Lucy Vickers and Diamond Ashiagbor, have received awards from the Society of Legal Scholars in respect of their books.

Titles already published in this series

Freedom of Speech and Employment
LUCY VICKERS

*International and European
Protection of the Right to Strike*
TONIA NOVITZ

The Law of the Labour Market
SIMON DEAKIN AND
FRANK WILKINSON

The Personal Employment Contract
MARK FREEDLAND

The European Employment Strategy
DIAMOND ASHIAGBOR

Towards a Flexible Labour Market
PAUL DAVIES AND MARK
FREEDLAND

EU Intervention in Domestic Labour Law

PHIL SYRPIS

OXFORD
UNIVERSITY PRESS

OXFORD
UNIVERSITY PRESS

Great Clarendon Street, Oxford OX2 6DP

Oxford University Press is a department of the University of Oxford.
It furthers the University's objective of excellence in research, scholarship,
and education by publishing worldwide in

Oxford New York

Auckland Cape Town Dar es Salaam Hong Kong Karachi
Kuala Lumpur Madrid Melbourne Mexico City Nairobi
New Delhi Shanghai Taipei Toronto

With offices in

Argentina Austria Brazil Chile Czech Republic France Greece
Guatemala Hungary Italy Japan Poland Portugal Singapore
South Korea Switzerland Thailand Turkey Ukraine Vietnam

Oxford is a registered trade mark of Oxford University Press
in the UK and in certain other countries

Published in the United States
by Oxford University Press Inc., New York

British Library Cataloguing in Publication Data

Data available

Library of Congress Cataloging in Publication Data
Syrpis, Phil.
    EU intervention in domestic labour law / Phil Syrpis.
    p. cm.—(Oxford monographs on labour law)
Includes bibliographical references and index.
ISBN 978-0-19-927720-9
    1. Labor laws and legislation—Economic aspects—European Union countries.
2. Labor laws and legislation—Social aspects—European Union countries.
3. Freedom of movement—European Union countries.   4. Free trade—European
Union countries.   5. Labor courts—European Union countries.   6. Law—European
Union countries—International unification.   I. Title.   II. Title: European Union
intervention in domestic labour law.   III. Title: EU intervention in domestic labor law.
    KJE2855.S97 2007
    344.2401—dc22   2007014690

Typeset by Newgen Imaging Systems (P) Ltd., Chennai, India
Printed in Great Britain
on acid-free paper by
Biddles Ltd., King's Lynn

ISBN 978–0–19–927720–9

1 3 5 7 9 10 8 6 4 2

For my father, George, and in memory of my mother, Vasso

General Editors' Preface

An important aspect of the coverage of a modern series of labour law monographs is that of EU law, as it bears upon the employment relationship and the functioning of the labour market. The Editors are therefore very pleased to have the opportunity to build upon existing success in this respect by recommending for publication in the series this work of Dr Phil Syrpis. It represents a pithy and tightly-argued contribution to the theoretical understanding of EU employment and labour market law, and in particular of the *rationales* for EU intervention in the domestic employment law of the Member States.

The singularity of the theoretical approach which Dr Syrpis has taken to this large subject relates mainly to the way he sets up and explores not just the antithesis (or at least tension) between economic and social rationales, but also (or instead) the more complex interaction between the integrationist, the economic, and the social rationales. He has understood, and succeeds very well in demonstrating, that none of these rationales would produce a single trajectory of development for EU employment law, even if any one clearly prevailed over the other two.

Because these different rationales have both interacted and mutated in the course of Community political processes over the years, the challenge for the author is to craft an analysis which is both fine and subtle, especially at and in relation to a time when the Community, recently much enlarged, seeks to re-group following the set-back to the European Constitution in June 2005. In an accomplished work, Dr Syrpis has very clearly met that challenge, and we are delighted to add the resultant work to our series, the high standard of which we feel it will surely be judged to maintain.

Paul Davies, Keith Ewing, Mark Freedland

London
December 2006

Preface

This book examines the rationales for, and techniques of, EU intervention in domestic labour law. It aims to provoke the reader into thinking about the roles that the EU does, and should, play in this field. I argue that there are three rationales on which EU intervention may plausibly be said to be premised. These are termed integrationist, economic, and social. While these three rationales are, in important respects, distinct, they do not point clearly towards particular policy prescriptions. Nevertheless, an understanding of each of the three rationales, coupled with an understanding of the relationship between them, helps to explain the chequered history of EU labour law and enables one to point towards various alternative ways forward for the EU in this contentious field.

My analysis of the three rationales for EU intervention in domestic labour law indicates that there are two fundamental questions to be answered. The first concerns the extent to which the integrationist rationale calls for the elimination of disparities between the labour law rules of the Member States. The second concerns the nature of the relationship between the economic and the social rationales.

I suspect that my treatment of the first question will generate the most controversy. According to some conceptions of the integrationist rationale, including those which seem to have been adopted by the Court of Justice, disparities between national rules, including national labour law rules, are inherently problematic. These conceptions of the integrationist rationale lead one to the conclusion that an objective of EU intervention must be the elimination of these problematic disparities between national labour law regimes. But there are other conceptions of the integrationist rationale, including those which seem to have been adopted by the political institutions in the labour law field, which are less hostile to diversity. If these conceptions are accepted, disparities between national labour law regimes are, within certain bounds, tolerated and even encouraged. My argument is that it is necessary to choose between these alternative conceptions of the integrationist rationale, and, in the course of the book, I outline the reasons why I believe that the logic of market integration does not commit the EU to the view that disparities between national labour law regimes should be eliminated.

Thus, while integration may impose certain constraints on national autonomy in the labour law field, it does not demand harmonization. This creates a space within which the institutions may focus on the economic and social rationales for intervention. The relationship between the economic and the social rationales determines what might be termed the normative compass for the European project.

I argue that the social can contribute to the economic, but that it is also important in its own right. A clear commitment to the social rationale enables the institutions to resist the temptation systematically to privilege the economic over the social, and is able to contribute to the enhanced legitimacy of the EU.

Many of the ideas in the book were first explored in my D Phil thesis, whose focus was on the worker participation law of the European Communities, and which was completed, under Paul Davies' supervision, in 2000. My ideas have developed since, in particular during the time I spent as a Jean Monnet Fellow at the European University Institute in Florence in 2002. I would like to take this opportunity to thank my supervisor Paul Davies; my D Phil examiners, Mark Freedland and Simon Deakin; Gráinne De Búrca, Christian Joerges, and Silvana Sciarra at the EUI; and the editors, Gwen Booth, the referees and reader at OUP, for their encouragement and support.

I also owe thanks to many friends and colleagues, at Jesus College, Cambridge; Wadham College, Oxford; the EUI; and, in particular, at the University of Bristol. Patrick Capps, Jeffrey Hackney, Richard Huxtable, Andrew Johnston, Claire Kilpatrick, Harry McVea, Matthijs Punt, Paul Skidmore, and Stephen Watterson all deserve particular mentions. Most of all, however, I would like to thank my family. My parents, to whom this book is dedicated, have provided unstinting support to me throughout my life. My twin boys, Alex and Kris, born in January 2004, did all they could to delay the publication of the book. There is no doubt in my mind that were it not for the efforts of Tonia Novitz, to whom I owe an enormous intellectual and personal debt, it would never have been completed.

Phil Syrpis

Bristol
January 2007

Contents

Table of Cases

Table of EU Material

OTHER EU MATERIALS

List of Abbreviations

General

BEPGs	Broad Economic Policy Guidelines
CEEP	European Centre of Enterprises with Public participation and of Enterprises of General Economic Interest
ECHR	European Convention on Human Rights (Convention for the Protection of Human Rights and Fundamental Freedoms)
ESCB	European System of Central Banks
EEA	European Economic Area
EES	European Employment Strategy
EMI	European Monetary Institute
EMU	Economic and Monetary Union
ETUC	European Trade Union Confederation
ILO	International Labour Organization
OCA	Optimum Currency Area
OECD	Organization for Economic Cooperation and Development
OMC	open method of coordination
SMEs	small and medium-sized enterprises
TeCE	Treaty establishing a Constitution for Europe
TEU	Treaty on European Union
UNICE	The Confederation of European Business

Publications

CML Rev	Common Market Law Review
ELR	European Law Review
ILJ	Industrial Law Journal
JCMS	Journal of Common Market Studies
LQR	Law Quarterly Review
MLR	Modern Law Review
OJLS	Oxford Journal of Legal Studies

1

Introduction

Introduction

This book is relatively short. It does not purport to be an exhaustive account of European intervention in the labour law arena. Instead, it aims to provoke the reader into thinking about the roles that the European Union (or EU) does, and should, play in this field. There is, in my view, all too little theoretical work focusing on the rationales for EU intervention in particular sectors of the economy. As a result, many people misunderstand the contribution that the EU is, or might be, able to make. Europhiles and Eurosceptics alike tend to have unrealistic expectations of what 'Europe' can achieve.

The relationship between the EU and domestic labour law is complex. EU intervention serves a variety of objectives and takes a variety of different forms. This book discusses the goals for 'Social Europe' and the tasks needed to reach those goals. On the institutional level, it examines the capacities of different modes to handle specific governance tasks.[1] The aim is to acquire a sense of the proper functions of the EU in the labour law field. My contention is that it is only possible to achieve this through an exposition of the plausible rationales for EU intervention, and an examination of means through which the objectives associated with each of the rationales may best be realized.

The EU has profoundly affected the nature of UK labour law. Labour lawyers in the UK have long been aware of the need to monitor developments at the European level. They have become used to the range of ways in which the EU acts, and have spent time and energy poring over the pronouncements of the European courts. The nature of EU intervention has changed significantly with time, but notwithstanding or perhaps because of this fact, questions have continued to be asked about the appropriateness or legitimacy of particular interventions.

In 1996 Mark Freedland observed that 'there is no single clear or accepted policy agenda for employment law in the European Union'.[2] Little has changed in the

---

[1] Thus the book adopts the approach suggested in D Trubek and L Trubek, 'Hard and Soft Law in the Construction of Social Europe: the Role of the Open Method of Co-ordination' (2005) 11 European Law Journal 343, 344. It does not, however, engage in an empirical analysis of the relative capacity of particular governance strategies.

[2] M Freedland, 'Employment Policy' in P Davies *et al* (eds), *European Community Labour Law: Principles and Perspectives; Liber Amicorum Lord Wedderburn* (Clarendon, Oxford 1996) 275, 278.

intervening years. Given the contestability which attaches to both labour law and the EU, this should not come as a surprise.

First, a few words about labour law. There are a number of actors who have an interest in the rules governing the world of work, most notably employers and workers. On many issues their interests conflict, though on others, they may converge. There are many, from all parts of the political spectrum, who argue that the setting of labour standards should be left to free negotiation between employers and workers, or their respective representatives. Decisions by public authorities to intervene in the determination of workers' terms and conditions of employment tend to be controversial. If and when it occurs, labour market regulation may serve a variety of objectives; for example, the protection of the worker, the reduction of unemployment, or the generation of economic efficiency. The labour law traditions in the Member States of the EU are very different, creating further problems for any putative supranational regulator in Europe.

Next, the EU. Ever since the European Economic Community was formed by the Treaty of Rome in 1957, the European project has been controversial. The states involved in the project—at the outset six, now twenty-seven—are on a remarkable journey, but it is one with no obvious destination. One part of the project has involved the creation of a common, single, or internal market, but there is little agreement over what market-making must or may entail. There is, moreover, little agreement over the extent to which the European project must or may involve something beyond mere market-making, and if so what that something extra should be. Successive treaties have fudged this issue, reflecting nothing more sinister than a divergence of views among key actors. It is difficult to assess the extent to which Member States are committed to common goals, and if so, what those goals are. The ongoing debate surrounding the Treaty establishing a Constitution for Europe has shown that any consensus about the future of Europe is fragile, or perhaps even illusory. The hopes and aspirations of some correspond to the fears of others. The result is confusion.

In this book, I give as clear and coherent an account as I can of the ways in which the EU has influenced domestic labour law. The main focus is on the rationales on which EU intervention may plausibly be premised. I categorize these as integrationist, economic, and social.[3] I aim to show what a commitment to each of these rationales entails, paying close attention both to the level at which intervention occurs and the nature of such intervention. The intention is to use an analysis of a specific policy area—labour law—to suggest a variety of ways in which it may be possible to conceptualize the EU's role and to provide some

---

[3] cf the 'market integration', 'market management', and 'social citizenship' models adopted by Fitzpatrick, in B Fitzpatrick, 'Straining the Definition of Health and Safety' (1997) 26 ILJ 115, 116–19. See further J Kenner, 'Citizenship and Fundamental Rights: Reshaping the European Social Model' in J Kenner (ed), *Trends in European Social Policy* (Dartmouth, Aldershot 1995).

insights into the implications of the various shifts in policy-making technique. This introductory chapter defines the scope of the project and introduces the important themes with which the rest of the book will deal.

What is EU Intervention in Domestic Labour Law?

This book is concerned with actions taken at the European level, within the framework of the organization now known as the European Union,[4] which have an impact on domestic labour law. I examine not only the interventions of the political institutions (including those of the social partners acting under Articles 138 and 139 EC), but also those of the legal institutions.[5]

As we shall see, the case law of the Court of Justice relating to the establishment and functioning of the market in Europe creates the framework for labour law. The Court's analysis of what I term the integrationist rationale, has a huge impact not only on the interventions of European-level political institutions in the labour law field, but also on the freedom of Member States to create and maintain their chosen labour law regimes. Thus, as well as considering the body of rules adopted at the EU level, directly concerned with the employment relationship,[6] this book also examines those interventions of the political and legal institutions which do not appear to be directed towards regulation of the employment relationship but which nevertheless have an impact on domestic labour law, including interventions associated with the establishment and functioning of the market in Europe.

It may be useful at this stage to make it clear that the book does not deal systematically with interventions in domestic labour law by other international organizations such as the ILO, WTO, and Council of Europe. And, although attention is paid to the likely effectiveness of particular interventions, there is no concrete analysis of the impact which EU measures have on the various national systems.

---

[4] I refer to the broad European Union (or EU), rather than the European Community (or EC), throughout this book; except in those instances in which it remains meaningful to distinguish between the two (eg when referring to the different objectives of the Community and the Union; or when considering the impact of the principle of subsidiarity on the competence of the Community).

[5] I distinguish between the interventions of 'courts' or 'legal institutions' (ie the Court of Justice and the Court of First Instance) and the interventions of 'political institutions' (ie the European Council, the Council of Ministers, the European Parliament, the Commission, the social partners acting under the social dialogue procedure, and a range of other advisory committees) at the European level.

[6] I refer to these as European Union (or EU) labour law. Other writers use the terms EU (or EC) social policy, or EU (or EC) employment law, to refer to the same body of rules. I have chosen to avoid those terms because of the risk of confusion. Social policy may be thought to have a much wider ambit (see eg T Hervey, *European Social Law and Policy* (Longman, London 1998)); while employment law may be thought to refer only to measures adopted under the Employment Title of the EC Treaty.

The Three Rationales for EU Intervention

It is tempting to believe that the primary rationale for EU labour law must be social. However, this would be misleading: 'The founding fathers of the Community—and the same applies to the Council and the Commission in Brussels—never sought, or at all events never sought as their first aim, to reform the lot of the man who sells his labour.'[7]

The main argument advanced in this book is that there are three separate rationales upon which European intervention in domestic labour law may plausibly be said to be based. These are termed integrationist, economic, and social. The three rationales are reflected in the Preamble to the Treaty on European Union (Maastricht Treaty), in which the Heads of State and Government stated that they were 'determined to promote economic and social progress for their peoples, within the context of the accomplishment of the internal market'. This statement is typical of the approach of the institutions, who too often claim that tensions between the various rationales for EU labour law do not exist. In contrast, I argue that the three rationales are, in important respects, distinct. A strong commitment to, for example, the social rationale, is likely to lead to a very different set of interventions at EU level in the labour law field from those which would flow from a commitment to the integrationist rationale.

I do not, however, argue that any of the three rationales point clearly towards particular policy prescriptions. As chapter 2 makes clear, each of the three rationales is internally contested. Unsurprisingly, institutional understandings of what each of the three rationales may or must entail have altered over time. Moreover, the relationship between the three rationales has also changed as the policy priorities of key actors have evolved. My contention is simply that the three rationales are useful as analytical categories. An understanding of each of the three rationales, coupled with an understanding of the changing relationship between the three rationales, not only helps to explain the chequered history of EU labour law, but also enables one to point towards various alternative ways forward for the EU in this contentious field. At this stage I devote just a single paragraph to each of the three rationales. Full explanations appear in chapter 2.

Where the EU acts for integrationist reasons, it acts with the aim of establishing, or improving the functioning of, the European market. The integrationist rationale is concerned with market-constituting measures, ie measures necessary either to create a European market, to convert various national markets into one European market, or to enable the European market to function as a single, integrated unit. There has been a long-running debate, albeit one which has seldom risen to the surface since the 1950s, surrounding the need for EU intervention in

---

[7] GF Mancini, 'Labour Law and Community Law' (1985) 20 Irish Jurist 1, 1.

the labour law field in the context of the establishment and functioning of the market in Europe. A newer debate surrounding the extent to which EU labour law is required or desirable in the context of Economic and Monetary Union is also developing. Some advocate total harmonization of national social policies. At the other extreme, others argue that the cause of integration calls for no intervention in the social sphere; for many it is axiomatic that social advantages will flow automatically from the completion of the common or internal market, perhaps via the process of regulatory competition, without the need for intervention at the European level. In between, there are many other positions, with calls for minimum standard setting, for coordination, and for various forms of managed diversity. The integrationist rationale is the most complex of the three and the one which is least well understood. As a result, large parts of chapters 2, 4, and 5 are devoted to a detailed exposition of the integrationist rationale and of the implications which various conceptions of the integrationist rationale may have in the labour law field.

Under the economic rationale, the EU takes action to improve the performance of the European economy, for example by reducing unemployment, enhancing efficiency, or improving Europe's international competitiveness. Since Maastricht, combating unemployment and encouraging non-inflationary growth have become central aims of the EU, and under the so-called 'Lisbon Strategy', launched in 2000, action has been taken at both Member State and European level to realize those aims. The nature of the relationship between economic objectives and labour standards is controversial. There is an 'uneasy compromise between those who argue that excessively high labour standards result in costs which blunt the competitive edge of companies and those who believe that productivity is the key to competitiveness and that high labour standards have always formed an integral part of a competitive labour market'.[8] The EU appears to be leaning towards the latter view. However, many, particularly in the business lobby, remain sceptical of the claim that high social standards, particularly those imposed on business by a public regulator, are able to improve competitiveness. Others fear that social objectives will inevitably be sacrificed on the altar of economic efficiency where economic objectives are allowed to infiltrate, and even dominate, labour law discourse. In this book, the relationship between the economic and social rationales for EU labour law is subjected to close analysis.

Interventions based on the social rationale aim to improve the position of workers. While the economic rationale calls for measures which improve the performance of the European economy, the social rationale is concerned with the distribution of the benefits derived from improved economic performance.[9] The social rationale can be conceptualized in a variety of ways. It may, for example, be

---

[8] E Szyszczak, 'Future Directions in European Union Social Policy Law' (1995) 24 ILJ 19, 22. See also Commission White Paper, 'European Social Policy—A Way Forward for the Union' COM (94)333, 27 July 1994, 23.

[9] 'While everyone would like to have a larger pie, everyone would also like to have a larger share of that pie'; B Langille, 'Eight Ways to think about International Labour Standards' (1997) 31(4) Journal

argued that workers should be protected either from employers or from the vagaries of the market, or that they should be afforded certain rights, perhaps stemming from their status as EU citizens. Although the most fundamental rationale for the very existence of labour law at the national level is to defend the interests of the weaker party in the employment relationship, who is almost invariably the worker, social objectives form no more than a part of the rationale for EU labour law. I discuss the importance the social rationale through the EU's history and consider the social benefits which interventions of different types are able to produce.

Competence Questions

These then are the three rationales for EU labour law which will be considered in depth in the course of this book. But is it appropriate that action to achieve integrationist, economic, and social goals should be taken at European level? The EU is a multi-centred democracy. Concerns about the legitimacy of the different centres are growing. International units of governance such as the EU, which are still trying to carve out a role for themselves on the world stage, are especially sensitive to legitimacy challenges. It is, I argue, important that they are able to demonstrate that they are able to 'add value' to policy-making processes. There are a number of possibilities here. The EU may enable or facilitate Member States' achievement of given goals. Alternatively, it may act as a forum in which relevant actors are better able to identify, or align, their policy priorities. Debates about the allocation and exercise of competence within the EU are complicated because of the fact that it is not possible or indeed desirable to draw clear lines between the respective spheres of influence of the European institutions and the Member States.

Europe only has the competence to act in so far as it is granted this power in the Treaties, by its constituent Member States.[10] According to the first paragraph of Article 5 EC (first introduced at Maastricht) the Community 'shall act within the limits of the powers conferred upon it by this Treaty and of the objectives assigned to it therein'. The EC Treaty imposes two important constraints. First, Community action must find a legal basis within the Treaty, and second, it must be in conformity with the principles of subsidiarity and proportionality.

The competence of what was then the European Economic Community to act in the labour law field and to influence the employment relationship was not clearly established under the Treaty of Rome of 1957. The expectation, following the Spaak and Ohlin reports of the 1950s, was that social advantages would flow from the establishment and functioning of the common market, and that EU

of World Trade 27, 33. The economic rationale is concerned with the size of the pie; the social, with ensuring that workers get to eat it. To pursue the analogy too far, integrationist policies are those which bind the pie together.

[10] See A Dashwood, 'The Limits of EC Powers' (1996) 21 ELR 113, 114.

level action in the social field would not be required in order to achieve social benefits. This does not mean that social objectives were abandoned, or that the Treaty
of Rome espoused a neo-liberal agenda. Instead, the intention was 'not only to
preserve intact but hopefully to expand and strengthen Member States' powers of
economic intervention and social governance'.[11] Later Treaties did, however, give
the Community the power to intervene in the social field.[12] As a result of successive amendments to the Treaties, the EU has a secure, expanding, though still
restricted, competence to intervene in the social field.

EU action must also be in accordance with the principles of subsidiarity and
proportionality, twin principles which, at the very least, invite the institutions to
stop and think before exercising the competence which has been allocated to them
in the Treaties. The subsidiarity principle in Article 5(2) EC insists that the Community 'shall take action, only if and insofar as the objectives of the proposed
action cannot be sufficiently achieved by the Member States and can therefore, by
reason of the scale or effects of the proposed action, be better achieved by the
Community'. It has generated a mountain of academic comment and will be fully
discussed in chapter 3. The proportionality principle in Article 5(3) EC states that
any action by the Community 'shall not go beyond what is necessary to achieve
the objectives of this Treaty'. In order for the principle to be satisfied, it must be
shown that action at the European level is suitable for the purpose of attaining the
objective pursued, and that it does not go beyond what is necessary to achieve it.
Proportionality defines the permissible extent of European level action: 'Every
proposed measure must be scrutinised to see whether it could do its job in a way
that would be less obtrusive or burdensome for the Member States.'[13] The argument advanced in chapter 3 is that a vigorous application of the principles of subsidiarity and proportionality contributes to the legitimacy of the EU.

An Analysis of EU Interventions

Finally, the book considers the various ways in which the Union has acted in the
labour law field in order to achieve its stated objectives. In chapter 4, I analyse the
negative integration case law of the Court of Justice in the labour law field. In
chapter 5, I examine the variety of ways in which the political institutions have

---

[11] S Giubboni, *Social Rights and Market Freedom in the European Constitution—A Labour Law
Perspective* (CUP, Cambridge 2006) 16. The economic constitution of the EC is said to express and
reflect 'embedded liberalism'.

[12] P Davies, 'The Emergence of European Labour Law' in Lord McCarthy (ed), *Legal Intervention
in Industrial Relations: Gains and Losses* (Blackwell, Oxford 1992) 347. See also W Däubler (ed),
Market and Social Justice in the EC—the Other Side of the Internal Market (Bertelsmann Foundation,
Gütersloh 1991) 43: 'The Heads of Government no longer look upon social progress as an automatic
sequel to an opening of the market; instead they feel that separate measures are required in order to
improve working conditions, increase the standard of living and augment industrial safety.'

[13] Dashwood (n 10 above) 115.

responded, looking particularly closely at harmonization, minimum standard setting, and various more flexible interventions, including those under the open method of coordination. Particular attention is paid to the Posted Workers Directive and the Directive on services in the internal market,[14] to the Working Time Directive,[15] and to the integrated Broad Economic Policy and Employment Guidelines.[16] The key distinction between the various interventions of the political institutions is the extent to which they leave scope for national autonomy. One of the central questions which this book attempts to answer concerns the extent to which the EU's integrationist, economic, and social objectives demand that national autonomy be constrained, and if so, in what ways.

According to some conceptions of the integrationist rationale, including those which seem to have been adopted by the Court of Justice in much of its case law, disparities between national rules, including national labour law rules, are seen as inherently problematic. These conceptions of the integrationist rationale lead one to the conclusion that an objective of EU intervention must be the elimination of these problematic disparities between national labour law regimes; with the level at which harmonization is to occur being determined by the relationship between the economic and the social rationales. Other conceptions of the integrationist rationale are less hostile to diversity. If these conceptions are accepted, it becomes possible to see the role of the EU in the labour law field in an altogether different light. Disparities between national labour law regimes are, within certain bounds, tolerated and even encouraged. The task for the institutions is not to harmonize national regimes, but instead to contribute towards the realization of the economic and social objectives of the EU and its Member States.

A Map of What is to Follow

The structure of the book is simple. Chapter 2 explores the three rationales for EU intervention in labour law in greater depth. It considers what a commitment to each of the three rationales may or must entail and also attempts to tease out the

---

[14] Directive 96/71/EC of 16 December 1996 concerning the posting of workers in the framework of the provision of services [1997] OJ L18/1; Directive 2006/123/EC of 12 December 2006 on services in the internal market [2006] OJ L376/36.

[15] After amendment by Directive 2000/34/EC of 22 June 2000 amending Council Directive 93/104/EC concerning certain aspects of the organisation of working time to cover sectors and activities excluded from that Directive [2000] OJ L195/41, the Working Time Directive has now been consolidated; see Directive 2003/88/EC of 4 November 2003 concerning certain aspects of the organisation of working time (the Working Time Directive) [2003] OJ L299/9. Proposals to amend the Directive are currently before the Council of Ministers and European Parliament; see COM(2004)607 and COM(2005)246.

[16] Council Decision 2005/600/EC of 12 July 2005 on Guidelines for the employment policies of the Member States [2005] OJ L205/21; and Council Recommendation 2005/601/EC of 12 July 2005 on the broad guidelines for the economic policies of the Member States and the Community (2005 to 2008) [2005] OJ L205/28.

relationships between the three. Chapter 3 examines the principles governing the allocation and exercise of competence within Europe; the limits which the Treaty has imposed on the ability of the EU to realize integrationist, economic, and social objectives. The 'proper' competence of the EU is currently much-debated, and in the course of chapter 3 I employ the concept of legitimacy in order to explain how it may be possible to answer competence questions in the future, through the use of the principles of subsidiarity and proportionality. Chapters 4 and 5 examine the ways in which the institutions have intervened in the labour law arena. They deal with the negative integration case law of the Court of Justice and the various responses of the political institutions. Harmonization, minimum standard setting, and various other more flexible approaches are examined closely, as is the open method of coordination, with a view to assessing the extent to which these regulatory techniques are capable of meeting the EU's social, economic, and integrationist objectives, and answering questions about the proper competence of the EU. Chapter 6 concludes.

My argument is that, for a range of reasons developed in the course of the book, the integrationist rationale need not, and should not, be conceptualized so that disparities between national labour law regimes are regarded as problematic. Nevertheless, the integration project does impose certain constraints on national autonomy in the labour law field, and it is a legitimate function of the EU to ensure that national policy choices remain within permissible bounds. Moving beyond integration, it is important that the institutions focus on the development of what might be termed a normative compass for the European project, enabling a proper balance to be struck between the economic and the social. The Third Way rhetoric of the institutions suggests that the economic and the social are mutually reinforcing, and that there can be no conflict between the two. The reality is rather different, and there is some evidence that in their interventions, the political institutions have a tendency systematically to privilege the economic over the social. A clear commitment to the social rationale would help to ensure that the institutions were able to resist this tendency, and would contribute towards the enhanced legitimacy of the EU project.

2

The Three Rationales for EU Intervention in Domestic Labour Law

Introduction

This book is concerned with EU intervention in domestic labour law. An obvious starting-point is an examination of the objectives, goals, or aims which those involved in the policy-making process are attempting to advance. Given the number of actors, and the fifty-year time-frame, it is hardly surprising that there are a number of different, even conflicting, objectives which EU labour law has been said to serve. This chapter represents an attempt to categorize these various objectives into three broad rationales (ie fundamental bases or reasons) for EU intervention in domestic labour law.

My argument is that there are three distinct rationales upon which EU intervention in domestic labour law may be based; the integrationist rationale, the economic rationale, and the social rationale. I should state at the outset that I do not contend that any of the three rationales points clearly towards specific policy outcomes. In this chapter, I explore the three rationales, to see where a commitment to each of the rationales might lead. Part of the analysis rests on the Treaties. Close attention is paid to the competence which they afford the institutions to intervene in domestic labour law on the basis of each of the three rationales. Equally, part of the analysis looks beyond the Treaties. The Treaties are examined with a critical eye. I highlight the ways in which the Treaties make it difficult or impossible to achieve integrationist, economic, or social objectives. The variety of ways in which the Treaties influence the conceptualization of each of the rationales is also considered. The intention is to provide the reader with a framework which identifies various possible conceptions of the three rationales and follows them through to their logical conclusion.

I devote considerable attention to distinctions between the three rationales. It will become clear that there is considerable support not only in the Treaties but also in the academic literature for my chosen categorization. However, it will also become clear that there are occasions on which it is not possible to draw clear lines between the three categories. The rationales have a core and a periphery. The peripheries may overlap. It may, for example, be difficult or impossible to decide whether an intervention directed towards the reduction of unemployment should be classified as social or economic. Similarly, it may be difficult or impossible to distinguish between (integrationist) policies which aim to improve the functioning of the market within Europe and (economic) policies which aim to improve the performance of the European economy.

Notwithstanding this, I maintain that there are significant advantages to be derived from separating out the fundamental bases for EU intervention. It is important for commentators to know, for example, whether actors involved in the policy-making process intend that particular interventions improve the functioning of the market in Europe, or improve the position of workers. Of course, specific measures may be based on more than one of the three rationales. It may, for example, be argued that measures adopted in the employment policy field have both economic and social advantages. Nevertheless, paying distinct attention to the capacity of such measures to realize on the one hand economic, and on the other social, benefits is useful. It may enable one to ascertain which of the two rationales is, in reality, more important, and it may also assist in evaluating the fitness for purpose of particular interventions. Keeping the rationales distinct may also help to prevent the all-too-common gravitation towards normatively indeterminate policies.[1] Understanding the nature of the three rationales and the relationship between them helps both policy-makers and students of the policy-making process to understand the history of EU intervention in the social field and to identify possible ways forward.

This chapter considers what a strong commitment to each rationale entails. My analysis leads to a number of conclusions. One significant, but unsurprising, conclusion is that the three rationales are liable to lead the EU in very different directions. Integrationist, economic, and social analyses are apt to identify different phenomena as problems, and they therefore prescribe different solutions. Most of the chapter deals with the integrationist rationale. This is because it is the most complex of the three. In this chapter, I make two important points about the integrationist rationale. First, it is of a different order than the other two. Integration is pursued not for its own sake, but as a means through which other (economic and social) benefits may be realized. Second, contrary to the assumptions of many, the integrationist rationale may be about something more than, or indeed something other than, the elimination of disparities between the laws of the Member States. The all-too-common failure to appreciate this is liable to lead to serious

---

[1] M Freedland, 'Employment Policy' in P Davies *et al* (eds), *European Community Labour Law: Principles and Perspectives; Liber Amicorum Lord Wedderburn* (Clarendon, Oxford 1996) 275, 289–96. The editors of the *Common Market Law Review* describe the European Council's recent conclusion on the proposal for a directive on services in the internal market (discussed in ch 5 below) as 'yet another example of the perfect double speak with which the members of the highest institution of the EU try to suggest that adherence to conflicting goals in the Community is perfectly possible without sacrificing in any way the focus of the objectives'; Editorial Comments, 'The services directive proposal: Striking a balance between the promotion of the internal market and preserving the European social model?' (2006) 43 CML Rev 307.

misconceptions about the possible nature of the market-making endeavour in the social sphere. Although the social and economic rationales are much better understood, they may both be conceptualized in a variety of different ways.

The chapter reflects on the uneasy relationship between the two rationales. What will become apparent is that neither the economic nor the social rationale have been well developed in the EU context. The EU's commitment to economic and social progress is rarely spelled out in anything other than vague, general terms, and the tensions between various conceptions of the economic and the social rationale are insufficiently explored.

The Integrationist Rationale

Where European institutions act on the basis of the integrationist rationale, they act with the aim of establishing, or improving the functioning of, the European market. The integrationist rationale is concerned with market-constituting measures; measures necessary to create a European market, to convert national markets into one European market, or to enable the European market to function as a single, integrated unit.

There can be no doubt that integration is a key part of the European project. The Preamble to the Treaties refers to 'an ever closer union among the peoples of Europe'. The Treaty of Rome committed the States to the progressive establishment of the common market.[2] The Single European Act 1986 was primarily directed towards the completion of the internal market.[3] The Treaty on European Union (TEU or Maastricht Treaty) introduced provisions which paved the way for Economic and Monetary Union.[4] Improving the functioning of the market has, throughout the EU's history, been an important objective of both the Court of Justice and the political institutions. The Court of Justice, together with national courts, has taken the lead in relation to 'negative integration', striking down national measures which obstruct the establishment and functioning of the market. The Treaties also make provision for a 'positive integration' programme, affording the institutions specific competence to adopt measures on the basis of the integrationist rationale. Articles 94 and 95 EC give the institutions the competence to approximate laws and thereby contribute towards the establishment and improving the functioning of the market. There are also other legal bases, notably Articles 40, 42, 44, 46, 47, and 55 EC, and Article 308 EC, which have been used by the institutions to intervene in domestic labour law in order to further integrationist objectives. All these legal bases are discussed below.

---

[2] Art 7 EEC, now replaced.
[3] Art 14 EC. See also Commission White Paper on Completing the Internal Market, COM(85)310, 14 June 1985.   [4] Arts 4 and 98–124 EC.

The existence of the integrationist rationale is not called into question by the debate on whether integration is, or should be, at the top of the EU's normative pyramid. Conventional wisdom suggests that integration is the governing value for EC law—or that it was, at least until the passage of the TEU.[5] I disagree. My argument is that both integration and diversity are important values in today's EU, and that the legitimacy of the EU depends on the way in which the balance between the two competing values is struck. I do not believe that one should try to establish any normative preference between integration and diversity.[6] A normative orientation which is, in principle, agnostic as between integration and diversity, is now relatively uncontroversial. It has considerable academic support,[7] and was reflected in the ill-fated Treaty establishing a Constitution for Europe (TeCE). The spirit of the Treaty is best captured by the ambiguous phrase 'united in diversity'. In the Preamble to the Treaty, the Heads of State and Government stated that they were 'convinced that, while remaining proud of their own national identities and history, the peoples of Europe are determined to transcend their ancient divisions and, united ever more closely, to forge a common destiny'. This is altogether less suggestive of the primacy of integration than the 'ever closer union' formulation of previous Treaties. I emphasize that while this normative perspective does not detract from the fact that establishing and improving the functioning of the market in Europe remain important objectives of the Union, it does, as will become apparent in the course of this book, have significant ramifications for the operation of the integrationist rationale.

These ramifications are all the more pronounced because of the fact that there is little or no agreement over what action is required in order to establish the market in Europe, or to improve its functioning. For a start, there is scope for debate over what it means to 'create', 'open', 'build', 'constitute', 'construct', or 'establish' a market.[8] That much is obvious from the history of European integration. The Treaty of Paris establishing a European Coal and Steel Community adopts a different approach to the Treaty of Rome establishing a European Economic Community (EEC). Within the EEC, the Common Agricultural Policy was based on a fundamentally different

[5] In Opinion 1/91 [1991] ECR I-6079 (*Re EEA*) [17], the Court stated that 'the objective of all Community Treaties is to contribute together to making concrete progress towards European unity'.

[6] See also A Estella, *The EU Principle of Subsidiarity and its Critique* (OUP, Oxford 2002) 5.

[7] See eg G De Búrca and J Scott (eds), *Constitutional Change in the EU: From Uniformity to Flexibility?* (Hart, Oxford 2000). For particular illustrations, see C-D Ehlermann, 'Harmonisation for harmonisation's sake?' (1978) 15 CML Rev 4; C Harlow, 'Voices of Difference in a Plural Community' (Harvard Jean Monnet Working Paper No 03/00, 2000); and M Dougan, 'Vive la Différence? Exploring the Legal Framework for Reflexive Harmonization within the Single European Market' in R Miller and P Zumbansen (eds), *Annual of German and European Law, Volume 1 (2003)* (Berghahn, New York 2004) 113.

[8] 'The legal-economic philosophies of European market-building have witnessed seismic shifts from positive to negative integration, and back again, to novel and varied means of "European" re-regulation such as (national) mutual recognition and conjoined (supranational) standard-setting via ad hoc secondary vehicles of market governance such as committees and agencies'; M Everson, 'Adjudicating the Market' (2002) 8 European Law Journal 152, 156.

understanding of the workings of markets than most of the rest of the Treaty. Some economists see an opposition between the market and the state, and view regulation as an exogenous interference with the market mechanism. Others challenge the idea that markets are a separate realm, arguing that they are social constructs, embedded in social relations, constituted by law and social norms.[9] As for the creation of markets, there are those who argue that it is possible, and desirable, for market order to emerge spontaneously, but others who suggest that it is prudent, even necessary, for political institutions to intervene so as to ensure that markets are constituted and organized in particular ways.[10] Next, those who agree on the need for intervention, often disagree in fundamental ways over the sorts of intervention that might be required. It is not at all obvious, for example, whether the establishment of the market calls for harmonization of legal regimes within the market area, or whether there should be scope for regulatory competition between different legal regimes within a single market, and if so, whether that competition should be bounded by rules, and if so, what those rules should be. These disagreements inevitably spill over into the labour law arena. The Treaty does not identify whether labour law measures are required in order to ensure that the market becomes established and functions properly. Views differ. Some take the view that European labour law is 'an essential element in the creation of a single integrated market',[11] while others see a much reduced role for EU intervention in the social field. The latter group is itself split. Some are content to leave labour law to the market, while others believe that political intervention is necessary, but that it should occur at the national, rather than the European, level.

The Treaties make it clear that integration is pursued not for its own sake, but rather as a means for the achievement of other ends or a vehicle through which other benefits may be realized. Article 2 EC states that the Community's 'task' is:

... to promote throughout the Community a harmonious, balanced and sustainable development of economic activities, a high level of employment and of social protection, equality between men and women, sustainable and non inflationary growth, a high degree of competitiveness and convergence of economic performance, a high level of protection and improvement of the quality of the environment, the raising of the standard of living and quality of life, and economic and social cohesion and solidarity among the Member States.

This task is to be achieved 'by establishing a common market and an economic and monetary union and by implementing common policies'.[12]

---

[9] K Polanyi, *The Great Transformation* (Beacon Press, Boston 1944).

[10] M Egan, *Constructing a European Market* (OUP, Oxford 2001); A Supiot, 'The dogmatic foundations of the market' (2000) 29 ILJ 321.

[11] P Watson, 'Social Policy after Maastricht' (1993) 30 CML Rev 481, 513.

[12] Art 2 EC. Art 2 EU provides that one of the objectives which the Union sets itself is 'to promote economic and social progress and a high level of employment and to achieve balanced and sustainable development, in particular through the creation of an area without internal frontiers, through the strengthening of economic and social cohesion and through the establishment of economic and monetary union, ultimately including a single currency in accordance with the provisions of this Treaty'.

For the framers of the Treaty it was seen as axiomatic that, through the establishment of a common market, social and economic benefits would result. The Treaty of Rome was premised on theories which claimed that free international trade would bring about a removal of economic and social disparities between different regions.[13] There is now less faith in the operation of the market, and more of an acceptance of the need for intervention in the course of the market building endeavour.[14] But there is still profound disagreement over the nature of the intervention which might be required, and, of particular relevance to the present enquiry, no consensus over the need for, or nature of, intervention at European level in the social field.

This section is concerned with the extent to which EU intervention, by both political and legal institutions, is able to contribute towards the establishment and functioning of the market in Europe. It is worth warning readers that the section is both long and complex.

The two limbs of the market-making thesis which have received the greatest attention are the elimination of barriers to free movement and the elimination of distortions of competition. According to the Treaties,[15] the case law of the Court of Justice, and the consistent rhetoric of the political institutions, the most significant obstacles to the establishment and functioning of the market are barriers to the free movement of factors of production and distortions of competition.[16] Dashwood argues that the two types of approximation measures which can be shown to be contributing to the internal market mechanism, are those designed to remove 'disparities between national provisions that are liable to hinder freedom of movement';[17] or to remove 'disparities that are liable to create or maintain distorted conditions of competition'.[18] Essentially, and this is the way it is often put, 'disparities in national regulatory policies can hinder market access and restrict competition'.[19] Action to eliminate such disparities can, therefore, be said to be based on the integrationist rationale.[20]

Thus, it seems clear that there is scope for EU intervention where disparities between national labour law rules amount to either barriers or distortions. If these

---

[13] See S Giubboni, *Social Rights and Market Freedom in the European Constitution—A Labour Law Perspective* (CUP, Cambridge 2006) 42, commenting in particular on the Ohlin Report.

[14] Egan (n 10 above) 38: 'Free markets require more rules, many of which are increasingly framed at the supranational level'.

[15] Art 3(a), (c), (g), and (h) EC; and the prohibitions laid down in Arts 28, 39, 43, and 49 EC, and Arts 81, 82, 86, and 87 EC.

[16] The Treaty provides specific legal bases for the elimination of distortions of competition, but for various reasons Arts 96 and 97 (formerly 101 and 102) EC have been very little used and have played no role in the labour law field. I do not consider them further. See further P Collins and M Hutchings, 'Articles 101 and 102 of the EEC Treaty: Completing the Internal Market' (1986) 11 ELR 191.

[17] See eg Case C-350/92 *Spain v Council* [1995] ECR I-1985 [33].

[18] See eg Case C-300/89 *Commission v Council* [1991] ECR I-2867 [14] and [15]. A Dashwood, 'The Limits of EC Powers' (1996) 21 ELR 113, 120. [19] Egan (n 10 above) 5.

[20] See also M Kumm, 'Constitutionalising Subsidiarity in Integrated Markets: The Case of Tobacco Regulation in the European Union' (2006) 12 European Law Journal 503, 507.

terms are defined broadly, the need for EU intervention based on the integrationist rationale expands.[21] The next two subsections discuss the circumstances in which national labour law rules may amount to barriers to free movement and distortions of competition. My analysis suggests that neither the barrier to free movement nor the distortion of competition has a clear meaning. An obvious consequence is that the scope for EU intervention on the basis of this limb of the integrationist rationale is also unclear.

The other key conclusion which emerges from the discussion is that, at least according to some analyses, barriers to free movement and distortions of competition may arise as a result of something other than disparities between national provisions. First, it may not be national provisions which create the problem. Measures adopted at the EU level may infringe the free movement provisions of the Treaty;[22] and it may also be that rules contained in collective agreements, or even individual contracts of employment, may operate so as to undermine the market-building endeavour. Second, and crucial to the argument advanced in this book, it may not be the existence of disparities that is identified as problematic; instead it may, for example, be that the existence of an unacceptably low standard in one, several, or indeed all Member States creates an impediment to the establishment and functioning of the market. This is hugely significant. If the existence of disparities need not be regarded as problematic, courts need not subject national rules, including national labour law rules, to scrutiny just because they happen to be different to the rules in other States; and the political institutions need not intervene so as to eliminate disparities between national rules.

Having addressed the elimination of barriers to free movement and distortions of competition, this section goes on briefly to consider whether there are any other circumstances in which the EU can take action in the labour law field on the basis of the integrationist rationale. The question is simple. Can EU intervention contribute to the establishment and functioning of the market even though it does not eliminate barriers to free movement or distortions of competition? If the answer is yes, there must be scope for further intervention on the basis of the integrationist rationale. I suggest that the answer must be yes. One example relates to restrictions on national policy choices in the labour law field, imposed in the name of Economic and Monetary Union (EMU). Such interventions are on the periphery of the integrationist rationale. Nevertheless, they deserve to be included

---

[21] See G Bermann, 'Taking Subsidiarity Seriously: Federalism in the European Community and the United States' (1994) 94 Columbia Law Review 331, 356–7: 'Even a subject plainly reserved to the States is transformed into a Community matter to whatever extent the federal political [or, I would add, judicial] branches find that the cross-border mobility of goods (or, by parallel reasoning, workers, services or capital) would be advanced by bringing the various national rules on the subject into closer alignment with each other.'

[22] Case C-51/93 *Meyhui* [1994] ECR I-3879 [11]: 'It is settled law that the prohibition of quantitative restrictions and of all measures having equivalent effect applies not only to national measures but also to measures adopted by the Community institutions'.

here. An analysis of their likely contribution to the integration project, which should encompass an analysis of both the contribution EMU makes to integration and the contribution which the specific restriction on Member State choice makes to EMU, forms a useful part of an overall assessment of their utility, which must also involve consideration of the relationship between integrationist and other rationales for intervention.

Intervention to eliminate barriers to free movement

It is entirely uncontroversial that the existence of barriers to free movement affects the establishment and functioning of the market. EU intervention in the labour law field can be said to be based on the integrationist rationale where it can be shown to remove barriers to free movement. Two conditions must be met. First, the institutions must demonstrate the existence of a barrier to free movement. Second, they must show that their intervention eliminates, or contributes towards the elimination of, the barrier in question.

The schema established by the EC Treaty

The EU is able to eliminate barriers to free movement using either a negative or a positive integration strategy, or a combination of the two. Negative integration involves courts annulling or disapplying rules and practices which constitute barriers to trade. It does not involve the adoption of regulation at the EU level. Actions relying on the supremacy and direct effect of EC law can be brought by private parties, before national courts, challenging the legality of measures which infringe the free movement provisions of the Treaty (Articles 28, 39, 43, 49, and 56 EC).[23] The Treaty provisions have been interpreted expansively by the Court, starting with the free movement of goods,[24] and moving more recently, but no less decisively, to the other freedoms.[25] The courts' task in these cases involves two elements. First, the courts must determine whether particular measures constitute barriers to free movement. This involves assessing whether particular measures are problematic from the integrationist perspective. Second, if it is held that measures amount to barriers, the courts must assess whether they are justifiable. This involves the courts in a delicate balancing exercise, in which they have to weigh

---

[23] It is also possible, under Art 226 EC, for the Commission to bring actions directly before the Court of Justice against Member States whose laws or practices infringe EC law.

[24] Case 8/74 *Procureur du Roi v Dassonville* [1974] ECR 837 [5].

[25] The leading cases for each of the 'four freedoms' are Case 120/78 *Rewe-Zentral v Bundesmonopolverwaltung für Branntwein* [1979] ECR 649 (*Cassis de Dijon*), for goods; Case C-415/93 *Bosman* [1995] ECR I-4921, for workers; Case C-55/94 *Gebhard* [1995] ECR I-4165, for establishment; and Case C-76/90 *Säger* [1991] ECR I-4221 and Case C-384/93 *Alpine Investments* [1995] ECR I-1141, for services. The free movement of capital provisions were completely revised by the TEU. Art 56 EC was first held to have direct effect in Cases C-163, 165, and 250/94 *Sanz de Lera* [1995] ECR I-4821. Like the provisions dealing with the other freedoms, it has been interpreted broadly by the Court; see Case C-174/04 *Commission v Italy* [2005] ECR I-4933.

the European interest in integration against other legitimate objectives pursued at national, subnational, or enterprise level.[26]

There are three possible outcomes to consider in the context of cases brought under the free movement provisions of the Treaty. First, national rules and practices may be found not to hinder free movement. In this case, they escape the scrutiny of the courts, except as regards the primary definitional question.[27] Second, national rules and practices may be found to hinder free movement, and not to be justifiable. Where the courts deem a barrier unlawful, a step towards free trade is taken. In these cases the mutual recognition principle carries the day, with the result that the offending rules and practices may not be applied to imported factors of production.[28] Third, national rules and practices may be found to hinder free movement, but also to be justifiable. Member States may justify measures which are liable to hinder free movement either on the basis of express derogations provided for in the Treaty (for example Articles 30, 39(3) and (4), and 45 EC) or on the basis of a broader set of mandatory or imperative requirements in the general interest, devised in the *Cassis de Dijon* case, and developed in later cases.[29] Derogations from the free movement provisions of the Treaty also have to satisfy a proportionality test. National measures will infringe the proportionality principle unless they represent the least restrictive (of free movement) way to realize the State's legitimate objectives.[30] Where the courts uphold a restrictive rule, they are denying free trade and accepting the legitimacy of protection at national level.[31]

Positive integration involves the adoption of measures at EU level to eliminate barriers to trade. Since the development of what is termed the 'new approach to harmonization', ushered in by the Commission's White Paper on Completing the

---

[26] Egan (n 10 above) 89. For a full analysis of the approach of the Court at the justification stage in the labour law field, see ch 4 below.

[27] See eg Cases C-267 and 268/91 *Keck and Mithouard* [1993] ECR I-6097 [16], [17].

[28] See eg *Cassis de Dijon* (n 25 above). Note that the operation of the mutual recognition principle is not straightforward; Commission Report, 'Second Biennial Report on the Application of the Principle of Mutual Recognition in the Single Market' COM(2002)419, 23 July 2002; and K Armstrong, 'Mutual Recognition' in C Barnard and J Scott (eds), *The Law of the Single European Market: Unpacking the Premises* (Hart, Oxford 2002) 225.

[29] Note that, formally at least, if a State is successful in defending a measure under the doctrine of the mandatory requirements developed in *Cassis de Dijon*, Art 28 will be considered not to have been violated in the first place. Thus, formally at least, a measure which is justified on the basis of the mandatory requirements does not breach Art 28 EC, and does not amount to a quantitative restriction or a measure having equivalent effect. I wholeheartedly agree with Weiler that 'this is no more than formalist sophistry', brought about by the understandable reluctance of the Court to acknowledge that it had simply written into the Treaty a new open-ended derogation clause to complement Art 30 EC. As Weiler says, 'the material test of a violation of Article [28 EC] is the need of a Member State to come into court and defend its actions as justified in accordance with the doctrinal hoops of *Cassis*: legitimate policy, absence of extant harmonization, proportionality *etc*.' See J Weiler, 'The Constitution of the Common Market Place: Text and Context in the Evolution of the Free Movement of Goods' in P Craig and G De Búrca (eds), *The Evolution of EU Law* (OUP, Oxford 1999) 349, 366. cf G Davies, 'Can Selling Arrangements be Harmonised?' (2005) 30 ELR 371, 376–7.

[30] See eg Case 104/75 *De Peijper* [1976] ECR 613, and *Cassis de Dijon* (n 25 above).

[31] A McGee and S Weatherill, 'The Evolution of the Single Market—Harmonisation or Liberalisation' (1990) 53 MLR 578, 580. See also O Gerstenberg, 'Expanding the Constitution

Internal Market,[32] and very much influenced by the *Cassis de Dijon* case, the political institutions have concentrated their legislative efforts on those areas in which national regulation is liable to hinder free movement, but is also justified; that is, on those areas in which negative integration is not able to eliminate barriers to trade. Most commentators appear to agree that the institutions are right to focus their regulatory efforts on this area, thus allowing the courts' negative integration strategy based on the principle of mutual recognition to do most of the work as regards the elimination of barriers to free movement.[33] The impact which the principle of proportionality may have here is discussed in chapter 3 below.

The Treaties give the institutions the competence to act in a variety of ways in order to advance their positive integration programme. As we shall see in chapter 3, the powers of the institutions are limited. As stated in Article 5(1) EC, 'the Community shall act within the limits of the powers conferred upon it by this Treaty and of the objectives assigned to it therein'. Specific legal bases prescribe the permissible objectives of European level action. The Court of Justice is the ultimate arbiter of the legality of the acts of the political institutions, and has the task of ensuring that they do not exceed their powers. This section briefly examines the integrationist legal bases which have been used by the political institutions to intervene in the labour law field; in particular Articles 94 and 95 EC and Article 308 EC.

Under Article 94 EC, the Council 'shall, acting unanimously on a proposal from the Commission and after consulting the European Parliament and the Economic and Social Committee, issue directives for the approximation of such laws, regulations or administrative provisions of the Member States as directly affect the establishment or functioning of the common market'. Under Article 95(1) EC, introduced in the Single European Act 1986 in order to assist in the establishment of the internal market, 'by way of derogation from Article 94 and save where otherwise provided in this Treaty',[34] the Council 'shall, acting in accordance with the procedure referred to in Article 251 and after consulting the Economic and Social Committee, adopt the measures for the approximation of the provisions laid down by law, regulation or administrative action in Member States which have as their object the establishment and functioning of the internal market'.

Both Articles are means for the achievement of the EU's integrationist objectives. Article 95 EC builds on Article 94 EC in that it makes it easier for the Council to adopt integrationist measures, by providing for voting by qualified majority rather

Beyond the Court: The Case of Euro-Constitutionalism' (2002) 8 European Law Journal 172, 178–9: 'EC law, rather than being a mere synonym for economic freedoms, becomes, through the Court's emphasis on the possibility of a justification for overriding the interest in free trade by a public interest taking precedence over the fundamental economic freedoms, a device of enhancing democratic deliberation about risk and its control within the Member States.'

[32] COM(85)310 (n 3 above).

[33] cf G Davies (n 29 above), who argues that Art 95 EC has, and should have, a broader remit than Art 28 EC.

[34] As Art 95 EC expressly derogates from Art 94 EC, if a measure falls within the scope of Art 95, then it is Art 95 which should be used in preference to Art 94; *Spain v Council*, (n 17 above) [29].

than by unanimity.[35] However, Article 95(2) EC provides that paragraph 1 does 'not apply to fiscal provisions, to those relating to the free movement of persons nor to those relating to the rights and interests of employed persons'; a phrase which clearly limits the relevance of Article 95 EC in relation to labour law measures.

One other difference between the two Articles is that Article 94 EC refers to the common market, whereas Article 95 EC refers to the internal market. The common market was not defined in the Treaty of Rome. In Article 14 EC, introduced by the Single European Act 1986, it was said that the internal market 'shall comprise an area without internal frontiers in which the free movement of goods, persons, services and capital is ensured in accordance with the provisions of this Treaty'. This definition elicited a range of responses. There appears to be broad agreement that the internal market 'encompasses far less than' the common market, but disagreement over the desirability of the change. Pescatore has criticized the Single European Act 1986 for substituting the well-balanced and complex notion of a 'common market' with the one-sided notion of an 'internal market' based on an arbitrary selection of the Treaty objectives, ignoring essential features such as the rules on competition,[36] economic policy, commercial policy, and taxation.[37] Dashwood on the other hand, refers to the common market as a 'notoriously open-textured concept', and seems to prefer the term 'internal market'.[38] I have the privilege of being able to sidestep the debate.[39] While there may be differences between the relative scope of the common and internal markets,[40] they are not relevant to the scope of the integrationist rationale. For example, it is not possible to argue that an approximation measure is incorrectly based on Article 95 EC for the reason that it affects the establishment and functioning of the common, rather than the internal, market. The integrationist rationale is concerned with both the establishment and functioning of the European market, and with both freedom of movement and undistorted competition. For my purposes at any rate, 'between the concepts of the common and internal market no substantial differences exist'.[41]

The Articles seem to be limited in two ways. First, they only afford the political institutions the competence to approximate laws, regulations, and administrative

---

[35] Art 95 EC refers to 'the procedure referred to in Article 251'. Art 251 EC describes the complex 'codecision' procedure involving the Commission, the European Parliament, and the Council, under which unanimity in the Council is not required.

[36] Pescatore is wrong on this point. In *Commission v Council* (n 18 above) [14], the Court held that a precondition for the internal market was the existence of conditions of competition which were not distorted. See further R Barents, 'The Internal Market Unlimited: Some Observations on the Legal Basis of Community Legislation' (1993) 30 CML Rev 85, 104; S Crosby, 'The Single Market and the Rule of Law' (1991) 16 ELR 451, 457; and D Chalmers, 'The Single Market: From Prima Donna to Journeyman' in J Shaw and G More (eds), *New Legal Dynamics of European Union* (Clarendon, Oxford 1995) 55, 62.

[37] P Pescatore, 'Some Critical Remarks on the Single European Act' (1987) 24 CML Rev 9, 11.

[38] Dashwood (n 18 above) 123.

[39] Chalmers refers to debates about the differences between the common and internal markets as 'arcane'. D Chalmers *et al, European Union Law* (CUP, Cambridge 2006) 466.

[40] My agnosticism is based on the lack of a consensus over the scope of the 'common market'.

[41] Barents (n 36 above) 104–5; *Commission v Council* (n 18 above) Opinion of AG Tesauro, 2887–9.

provisions, and do not give them the power to approximate, for example, enterprise practice.[42] As we shall see, enterprise practice may, at least according to some analyses and in some contexts, create an impediment to the establishment and functioning of the market. Such an obstacle could not be eliminated through the adoption of measures under Articles 94 or 95 EC. Second, they give the institutions the specific power to approximate laws. This suggests that measures which do not approximate, or harmonize,[43] the laws of the Member States cannot be properly based on Article 94 and 95 EC. However, what has been termed 'minimum harmonization' has been a feature of European policy under Article 94 EC since the 1970s, including in the labour law arena, and it now seems impossible to question the legality of minimum standard setting, or of some other flexible forms of EU legislation, under these Articles, on the grounds that 'approximation' *stricto sensu* is not involved.[44]

The free movement provisions also give the political institutions specific competences to act in order to help achieve free movement goals.[45] The Treaty clearly recognizes that the intervention of the political institutions may be required in order to realize the free movement of workers, freedom of establishment, and the freedom to provide services.

The last of the integrationist legal bases is Article 308 EC. It reads as follows: 'If action by the Community should prove necessary to attain, in the course of the operation of the common market, one of the objectives of the Community and this Treaty has not provided the necessary powers, the Council shall, acting unanimously on a proposal from the Commission and after consulting the European Parliament, take the appropriate measures.'

---

[42] Measures which are not laid down by law, regulation, or administrative action 'clearly fall outside the ambit of Article 100 [now Art 94 EC]'; G Close, 'Harmonisation of Laws: Use or Abuse of the Powers under the EEC Treaty?' (1978) 3 ELR 461, 470. See also Case C-210/03 *Swedish Match* [2004] ECR I-11893 [33].

[43] It seems that the terms approximation and harmonization 'are entirely interchangeable'; Dashwood (n 18 above) 120. See also PJ Slot, 'Harmonisation' (1996) 21 ELR 378; D Vignes, 'The Harmonisation of National Legislation and the EEC' (1990) 15 ELR 358, 361; and I Pernice, 'Constitutional, Federal and Subsidiarity Aspects' in I Pernice (ed), *Harmonization of Legislation in Federal Systems* (Nomos Verlagsgesellschaft, Baden-Baden 1996) 10–11. cf S Simitis and A Lyon-Caen, 'Community Labour Law: A Critical Introduction to its History' in P Davies *et al* (eds), *European Community Labour Law: Principles and Perspectives; Liber Amicorum Lord Wedderburn* (Clarendon, Oxford 1996) 1, 4.

[44] Dashwood maintains that for measures such as the European Company Statute, in which EU level legislation is used to create a new property form rather than to align national laws, Arts 94 and 95 cannot be used; Dashwood (n 18 above) 120.

[45] See Arts 40, 42, 44, 46, 47, and 55 EC. To give just two examples, Art 40 authorizes the Council to 'issue directives or make regulations setting out the measures required in order to bring about freedom of movement for workers', and Art 44 gives the Council the power to act 'in order to attain freedom of establishment as regards a particular activity'. Article 44(2)(g), which has been used to intervene in domestic labour law, gives the Community institutions the power to coordinate 'to the necessary extent the safeguards which, for the protection of the interests of members and others, are required by Member States of companies or firms ... with a view to making such safeguards equivalent throughout the Community'.

Article 308 EC is a broad legal basis. Plainly, it is not limited to the achievement of integrationist objectives but can be used in order to attain any of the objectives of the Community, albeit only 'in the course of the operation of the common market'.[46] It 'may be used as the legal basis for a measure only where no other provision of the Treaty gives the Community institutions the necessary power to adopt the measure in question'.[47] Its importance has therefore declined since the adoption of the TEU, in which the competence of the political institutions was extended.[48] Article 308 EC may be used to eliminate those obstacles to the establishment and functioning of the market which cannot be eliminated by legislation based on other Treaty Articles. Where, for example, barriers to free movement which affect the functioning of the market are caused not by disparities between national law rules, but by disparities between the practice of enterprises, the use of Article 308 EC may be called for.

The free movement provisions of the EC Treaty

The integrationist rationale affords the EU the opportunity to intervene in domestic labour law to the extent that domestic labour law provisions constitute barriers to free movement. It is therefore of crucial importance to be able to determine whether or not a particular provision constitutes a barrier to free movement. This section examines the case law of the Court of Justice in relation to the free movement provisions of the Treaty.

The case law of the Court has been neither consistent nor convincing. At least in part as a result of this, the proper scope of the relevant Articles is much debated in the literature. There are many excellent accounts examining constitutional, historical, economic, comparative, and institutional dimensions.[49] It is not at all obvious whether the free movement provisions are intended to, or should, catch only protectionist (or discriminatory) practices; whether they are intended to, or should, have a broader scope and catch all restrictions on free trade, regardless of whether they are discriminatory; or what may qualify as a restriction on free trade. This section does not attempt to follow the twists and turns of the Court's case law. Instead, it examines the two key tests used by the Court in its assessment of the existence of barriers to free movement.

---

[46] See Dashwood (n 18 above) 123–4, and T Hartley, *The Foundations of European Community Law* (5th edn, OUP, Oxford 2002) 107–11. Dashwood suggests amending Art 308 EC so that 'in the course of the operation of the common market' is replaced by 'an objective directly affecting the establishment or functioning of the internal market'. This would identify Art 308 even more strongly with the attainment of integrationist objectives. Note, however, that the reference to the operation of the common market was deleted from Art I-18, the functional successor of Art 308 EC in the Treaty establishing a Constitution for Europe. For comment, see S Weatherill, 'Better Competence Monitoring' (2005) 30 ELR 23, 32–7.   [47] Case 45/86 *Commission v Council* [1987] ECR 1493 [13].
[48] Early judgments on the scope of Art 308, eg Case 8/73 *Massey-Ferguson* [1973] ECR 897, are too broad.
[49] See in particular M Maduro, *We, The Court: The European Court of Justice and the European Economic Constitution* (Hart, Oxford 1998); K Armstrong and S Bulmer, *The Governance of the Single European Market* (MUP, Manchester 1998); Weiler (n 29 above); and C Barnard and S Deakin, 'Market Access and Regulatory Competition' in Barnard and Scott (n 28 above) 197.

In any case before it, the Court first has to decide whether a particular rule or practice creates an impediment to the establishment or functioning of the market. A curiosity of the free movement case law is the continuing uncertainty over whether private, as well as public, action is, and should be, caught by the free movement provisions. The classic position—that the free movement provisions were addressed to States,[50] while the competition provisions were addressed to undertakings— led to gaps in the application of EU law.[51] Notwithstanding this, the free movement of goods provisions have been interpreted so as to catch only public action.[52] On the other hand, the *Bosman* case made it clear that Article 39 EC on the free movement of persons 'not only applies to the action of public authorities but extends to rules of any other nature aimed at regulating gainful employment in a collective manner'.[53] *Angonese* went further, stating explicitly that 'the prohibition of discrimination on grounds of nationality laid down in Article 39 of the Treaty must be regarded as applying to private persons as well'.[54] It is far from clear whether the so-called horizontal scope of Article 39 EC will be extended to non-discriminatory measures which hinder the free movement of persons, or whether the case law under Article 39 will also extend to Articles 43 and 49 (and perhaps even Article 28) EC.[55] The arguments are finely balanced. Whatever the legal position, it seems obvious to me that barriers to free movement, at least given the approach in the *Dassonville* line of cases, may arise not only as a result of national laws, but also as a result of enterprise practices. Were, for example, several large supermarket chains to adopt a 'Buy British' policy, there would be a significant negative effect on trade in goods sold by importers.

Leaving the thorny issue of horizontal application to one side, I now focus on the tests used by the Court to assess the existence of barriers to free movement. An expansive interpretation of the free movement provisions was first signalled in *Dassonville*, a case concerned with the interpretation of Article 28 EC. The Court of Justice held that 'all trading rules enacted by Member States which are capable of hindering, directly or indirectly, actually or potentially, intra-Community trade' fall within the scope of Article 28 EC.[56] Under the *Dassonville* line of authority,

---

[50] Acts of the Community institutions may also breach the free movement provisions; *Meyhui* (n 22 above) [11]: 'It is settled law that the prohibition of quantitative restrictions and of all measures having equivalent effect applies not only to national measures but also to measures adopted by the Community institutions.'

[51] See J Baquero Cruz, *Between Competition and Free Movement: The Economic Constitutional Law of the European Community* (Hart, Oxford 2002).

[52] Art 28 EC applies to the activities of quasi-public bodies (see eg Case 222/82 *Apple and Pear Development Council* [1983] ECR 4083). Moreover, the State may, in certain circumstances, also be held responsible for the action of private bodies, where it has failed to take measures to stop barriers to trade from emerging (see eg Case C-112/00 *Schmidberger* [2003] ECR I-5659).

[53] Case C-415/93 *Bosman* [1995] ECR I-1141 [82]; Case 36/74 *Walrave and Koch* [1974] ECR 1405.   [54] Case C-281/98 *Angonese* [2000] ECR I-4139.

[55] See S Van den Bogaert, 'Horizontality: The Court Attacks?' in Barnard and Scott (n 28 above) 123; and the Court of Appeal's reference to the Court of Justice in *Viking* [2006] 1 CMLR 27 (CA).

[56] Case 8/74 *Procureur du Roi v Dassonville* [1974] ECR 837 [5].

which applies not only to the free movement of goods but also to the other free-doms, the key question appears to be whether the trading rules in question affect access to markets in other Member States. Following the *Dassonville* case, restric-tions on the provision of services which affect access to markets in other Member States have been held to be capable of hindering intra-Community trade.[57] Sim-ilarly, rules which directly affect workers' access to employment markets in other Member States have been held to be capable of impeding freedom of movement for workers.[58]

The implications of the *Dassonville* case and its progeny are stark. Under the *Dassonville* test, the existence of discrimination against imports is not relevant to the question of whether a barrier to trade exists.[59] Access to markets can be said to be affected by almost any difference in national labour law regimes. Once it has been held that domestic labour law rules amount to barriers to free movement, there is an onus on Member States to justify those rules according to EU law criteria. States must show that domestic rules serve legitimate objectives and satisfy a proportional-ity test (ie States must show that they do not impose any greater restriction on free movement than is necessary for the achievement of the legitimate objectives).

However, this approach which, to repeat, maintains that a barrier to free move-ment exists wherever access to markets in other Member States is, or might be, affected, has not been followed in all cases. First, there are a number of cases in which the Court has accepted that there may be a *de minimis* test. The Court has, albeit on rare occasions, held that where the purpose of a national rule is not to regulate trade and the restrictive effects which it might have on free movement are 'too uncertain and indirect', the rule is not to be regarded as being of a nature to hinder trade between Member States.[60]

Second, there is an important strand of the Court's case law, albeit one which is limited to the assessment of 'national provisions restricting or prohibiting certain sell-ing arrangements' under Article 28 EC, in which the Court has employed a rather different test. It is well known that in the *Keck* case, the Court of Justice decided that, so long as they do not discriminate against imports, national provisions

---

[57] Case C-384/93 *Alpine Investments* [1995] ECR I-1141 [38].

[58] *Bosman* (n 53 above) [103].

[59] Case C-412/93 *Leclerc-Siplec* [1995] ECR I-179, Opinion of AG Jacobs: 'If an obstacle to inter-State trade exists, it cannot cease to exist simply because an identical obstacle affects domestic trade'. See also Case C-244/04 *Commission v Germany* [2006] ECR I-885 [30]: 'it is settled case-law that Article 49 EC requires not only the elimination of all discrimination on grounds of nationality against service providers who are established in another Member State, but also the abolition of any restriction, even if it applies without distinction to national providers of services and to those of other Member States, which is liable to prohibit, impede or render less advantageous the activities of a ser-vice provider established in another Member State, where he lawfully provides similar services'.

[60] See Case C-379/92 *Peralta* [1994] ECR I-3453 [24], and Cases C-140/94 to 142/94 *Comune di Bassano* [1995] ECR I-3257 [29]. Weatherill has argued that only those laws which impose a 'direct or substantial hindrance' to market access should come within the scope of the free movement provisions of the Treaty; S Weatherill, 'After *Keck*: Some Thought on how to Clarify the Clarification' (1996) 33 CML Rev 885, 896–7.

restricting or prohibiting certain selling arrangements fall outside the scope of the free movement provisions.[61] In the *Keck* case, the Court of Justice confirmed the legitimacy of national control of selling arrangements,[62] making it clear that it was not problematic from the perspective of the integrationist rationale. In order to reach this conclusion, the Court adopted new reasoning. The Court did not argue that rules relating to selling arrangements fall outside the scope of the free movement provisions because they are not capable of hindering trade, because they do not affect access to markets in other Member States, or indeed because they only have uncertain and indirect effects on trade. In fact, it conceded that the national legislation at issue in the *Keck* case may have restricted the volume of sales of products from other Member States.[63] The Court held that rules relating to selling arrangements fall outside the scope of the free movement provisions because their application to the sale of products from other Member States 'is not by nature such as to prevent their access to the market or to impede access any more than it impedes the access of domestic products'.[64] Under the *Keck* test, the focus is not on whether market access has merely been 'affected', but rather on whether market access has been 'prevented'. If access has not been prevented, the national rule will only be vulnerable where there has been discrimination, in law or in fact, against imports.

It is worth reflecting a little on the distinction between affecting and preventing market access. Where the national rule in question is a rule relating to the characteristics of goods, the distinction is immaterial. For example, in the famous *Cassis de Dijon* case,[65] the rule at issue was a German rule which prescribed a minimum alcohol requirement of 25 per cent for all fruit liqueurs marketed in Germany. This rule not only affected the market access of French Cassis de Dijon, but also prevented its access into the German market. The distinction is, however, important in other areas. One such area is rules relating to selling arrangements. But, there is also a range of other rules, including environmental and labour law rules, in the context not so much of the free movement of goods but rather of the free movement of persons, free establishment, and the free provision of services, in relation to which the distinction between affecting and preventing may be of decisive importance. The following are examples of this. Rules which prohibit resale at a loss, rules which prevent shops from opening on a Sunday, and rules which prohibit cold calling in the financial services sector are all capable of affecting—but not

---

[61] Cases C-267 and 268/91 *Keck and Mithouard* [1993] ECR I-6097 [16]. For Weatherill, 'the ruling was flawed by the absence of an adequate articulation of just why it was possible to conclude that no sufficient impact on trade between States was shown'; Weatherill (n 60 above) 887, 894.

[62] K Armstrong, 'Regulating the Free Movement of Goods: Institutions and Institutional Change' in Shaw and More (n 36 above) 165, 182; and N Reich, 'The November Revolution of the European Court of Justice: *Keck, Meng* and *Audi* Revisited' (1994) 31 CML Rev 459.

[63] *Keck* (n 61 above) [13].   [64] ibid [17].

[65] Case 120/78 *Rewe-Zentral v Bundesmonopolverwaltung für Branntwein* [1979] ECR 649 (*Cassis de Dijon*).

preventing—market access.[66] Similarly, as will be seen in chapter 4 below, most labour law rules are capable of affecting—but not preventing—market access. Rules which insist that out-of-State service providers must comply with the labour law rules of the host State when providing services in that State, clearly affect, but equally clearly do not prevent, the market access of service providers to the host State.[67] The *Keck* test holds that such rules do not amount to barriers to free movement, subject to the condition that they do not have discriminatory effects; ie subject to the condition that they do not affect or impede the market access of imports any more than they affect the market access of domestic factors.

Thus, the Court of Justice's case law under the free movement provisions of the Treaty offers two possible definitions of the barrier to free movement. The dominant strand of the case law, which starts with the *Dassonville* formula, takes the view that all rules which are liable to hinder trade, or, to put this in terms of market access, all rules which are liable to affect access to markets, are caught by the free movement provisions. The consequence is that all such rules have to be justified according to EU law criteria. Under *Dassonville*, almost any disparity between national labour law rules is problematic, and almost all national labour law rules are vulnerable to challenge. If a *de minimis* test were to be read into the *Dassonville* test, some labour law rules would escape the reach of the free movement provisions. If, on the other hand, the scope of the free movement provisions were to be extended so as to catch the actions of private, as well as State, bodies, almost all regulation of the employment relationship at the collective and even individual level would be vulnerable.

The *Keck* case introduced a very different test. If the reasoning in *Keck* were to be embraced by the Court in labour law cases, this would have profound implications for our understanding of this limb of the integrationist rationale. Under the *Keck* test most national labour law rules escape the scrutiny of the Court. There are many rules which can be said to affect market access (and which would therefore, under *Dassonville*, be caught by the free movement provisions), but which do not prevent such access and which, at least arguably, do not discriminate against imported factors of production (and which would therefore, under *Keck*, not be caught). The labour law cases will be examined in chapter 4 below, where the implications of these two very different conceptions of this limb of the integrationist rationale will be examined closely.

The exercise of competence under Article 95 EC

The case law of the Court relating to the competence of the political institutions to pursue a positive integration programme allows us to consider the definition of the barrier to free movement from a different perspective. Recent cases, which shed some light on the definition of the barrier to free movement, have concerned the limits of the competence to intervene under Article 95 EC.

---

[66]   *Keck* (n 61 above); Case C-332/94 *Semarano Casa Uno* [1996] ECR I-2975; and *Alpine Investments* (n 57 above).   [67]   See eg Case C-113/89 *Rush Portuguesa* [1990] ECR I-1417.

The limits of Article 95 EC were scrutinized closely in *Germany v Parliament and Council* (*Tobacco Advertising*).[68] The facts were these. The European Parliament and Council enacted Directive 98/43/EC prohibiting all consumer-oriented advertising of tobacco products away from the point of sale. Germany challenged the choice of Articles 95, 47, and 55 EC as the legal bases for the Directive. The Court's analysis was centred on Article 95 EC. The Court made it clear that Article 95 EC does not vest in the legislature a general power to regulate the internal market.[69] A measure adopted under Article 95 'must genuinely have as its object the improvement of the conditions for the establishment and functioning of the internal market'.[70] The Court's focus was on the elimination of barriers to free movement and distortions of competition. As regards the former, it stated that 'recourse to Article [95] is possible if the aim is to prevent the emergence of future obstacles to trade resulting from the multifarious development of national laws. However, the emergence of such obstacles must be likely and the measure in question must be designed to prevent them'.[71]

The Court went on to examine the capacity of the Directive to eliminate obstacles to the free movement of goods and the freedom to provide services. It observed that 'it is clear that, as a result of disparities between national laws on the advertising of tobacco products, obstacles to the free movement of goods or the freedom to provide services exist or may well arise',[72] and held that 'in principle, therefore, a Directive prohibiting the advertising of tobacco products in periodicals, magazines and newspapers could be adopted on the basis of Article 95 EC'.[73] Notwithstanding this, the Court held that the legislature could not rely on the need to eliminate barriers to free movement in order to adopt the Directive in question. This was for two reasons.[74] First, the Directive was overly broad. The Court held that certain of the prohibitions in the Directive (for example those relating to advertising on posters, parasols, and ashtrays) 'in no way help to facilitate trade in the products concerned'.[75] The existence of disparities between national laws relating to these products did not have an effect on trade. Second, the Directive was not fit for the purpose of eliminating barriers to free movement, quite simply because it did 'not ensure free movement of products which are in

---

[68] Case C-376/98 *Germany v Parliament and Council* [2000] ECR I-8419 (*Tobacco Advertising*). See Editorial Comments, 'Taking (the limits of) competences seriously' (2000) 37 CML Rev 1301, and P Syrpis, 'Smoke without Fire: The Social Policy Agenda and the Internal Market' (2001) 30 ILJ 271.

[69] *Tobacco Advertising* (n 68 above) [83].   [70] ibid [84].

[71] ibid [86]. See also Case C-350/92 *Spain v Council* [1995] ECR I-1985 [35].

[72] *Tobacco Advertising* (n 68 above) [96].

[73] ibid [97]. See further Joined Cases C-154/04 and C-155/04 *Alliance for Natural Health* [2005] ECR I-6451. The Court, at [33], makes it clear that Art 95 EC authorizes the Community legislature to intervene by eg 'requiring all the Member States to authorise the marketing of the product or products concerned, subjecting such an obligation of authorisation to certain conditions, or even provisionally or definitively prohibiting the marketing of a product or products'.

[74] See M Kumm, 'Constitutionalising Subsidiarity in Integrated Markets: The Case of Tobacco Regulation in the European Union' (2006) European Law Journal 503, 507, arguing that the Directive was both 'straightforwardly unsuitable and insufficiently narrowly tailored'.

[75] *Tobacco Advertising* (n 68 above) [99].

conformity with its provisions'.[76] In other words, it did nothing to prevent States from imposing stricter requirements than those in the Directive and preventing the free movement of products which, while in conformity with the provisions of the Directive, did not meet the higher national standard.

Although the judgment of the Court was interesting in constitutional terms, it has, as later cases appear to make clear, done little to frustrate the ambitions of the legislature.[77] At any rate, for present purposes it is the discussion of barriers to free movement which is most pertinent. The judgment makes it clear that the competence to act under Article 95 EC will be triggered where differences between the laws of the Member States create barriers to trade. But, how does the Court define the barrier to free movement?

Frustratingly, the Court is not explicit on this point. Nevertheless, two aspects of the judgment are worthy of comment. First, the focus of the Court's judgment, which in this regard mirrors the Preamble to the Directive, is not cigarettes or other tobacco products but rather the products which serve as the media for tobacco advertising, such as magazines, newspapers, parasols, ashtrays, and the like. While the multifarious development of national laws on tobacco advertising would only affect, rather than prevent, the market access of imported cigarettes,[78] it might well prevent the market access of products which serve as the media for tobacco advertising. Second, various parts of the judgment make it clear that there is a *de minimis* test, that is that the EU will not have the competence to act under Article 95 EC in response to uncertain and indirect effects on trade.[79] While potential and indirect effects on trade have been held, in almost all cases, to be sufficient to bring national rules within the scope of Article 28 EC and the other free movement

---

[76] *Tobacco Advertising* (n 68 above) [101].

[77] In the aftermath of the tobacco advertising case, the Community legislature adopted Directive 2001/37/EC of 5 June 2001 on the approximation of the laws, regulations and administrative provisions of the Member States concerning the manufacture, presentation and sale of tobacco products [2001] OJ L194/26. This Directive, also based on Art 95 EC, was upheld by the Court of Justice in Case C-491/01 *BAT (Investments) Ltd* [2002] ECR I-11453 (*Tobacco Labelling*); Case C-434/02 *Arnold André* [2004] ECR I-11825; and *Swedish Match* (n 42 above). See also Case C-377/98 *Netherlands v Parliament and Council* [2001] ECR I-7079 (*Biotechnology Patents*); and *Alliance for Natural Health* (n 73 above).

[78] One would anticipate that the demand for cigarettes—both domestically produced and imported—would be affected as a result of a stringent tobacco advertising ban in any given State.

[79] See *Tobacco Advertising* (n 68 above) [84], in which the Court held that 'if a mere finding of disparities between national rules and of the abstract risk of obstacles to the exercise of fundamental freedoms or of distortions of competition liable to result therefrom were sufficient to justify the choice of Article [95] as a legal basis, judicial review of compliance with the proper legal basis might be rendered nugatory'. See also ibid [86], in which the Court held that 'recourse to Article [95] is possible if the aim is to prevent the emergence of future obstacles to trade resulting from the multifarious development of national laws. However, the emergence of such obstacles must be likely'; and ibid [99] where the Court held that certain of the prohibitions in the Directive (eg those relating to advertising on posters, parasols, and ashtrays) 'in no way help to facilitate trade in the products concerned'. See also D Wyatt, 'Constitutional Significance of the Tobacco Advertising Judgment of the European Court of Justice', in University of Cambridge Centre for European Legal Studies, *The ECJ's Tobacco Advertising Judgment* (CELS Occasional Paper No 5, Cambridge 2001) 29.

provisions,[80] they are, it seems, insufficient to trigger the exercise of competence under Article 95 EC.[81]

Conclusions

The Court's case law is, as stated at the outset, neither consistent nor convincing. There is continuing uncertainty surrounding both the horizontal scope of the free movement provisions and the existence or otherwise of a *de minimis* test. Even more significant, is the existence of two different tests to determine the existence of barriers to free movement.

Under the *Dassonville* test, Member States' freedom to set their own regulatory standards is restricted. EU law rules operate so as to protect the market access of mobile factors of production. Where national rules affect market access, there is an onus on the State to justify the application of its national standards. Where the legitimacy of protection at national level is accepted, and where, as a consequence, barriers to free movement persist, a positive integration strategy is employed in order to facilitate free movement. This strategy involves intervention of a specific type. While harmonization measures may, according to this analysis, be successful in eliminating barriers to trade, more flexible measures, for example those which lay down minimum standards and which authorize Member States to apply higher standards to both domestic and imported factors, may very well be held by the Court not to be fit for purpose.

Under the alternative *Keck* test, there is no great need for EU action—based on either a negative or a positive integration strategy—in order to eliminate barriers to free movement. This is because under the logic of *Keck*, differences between national laws are not, without more, held to create barriers to free movement. The *Keck* approach provides much greater scope for States to set their own regulatory standards. EU intervention is called for only in relation to national laws and practices, which either prevent access to national markets, or discriminate in law or in fact against mobile factors of production.

As will become clear in the course of this book, I lean towards an interpretation of the integrationist rationale which endorses the *Keck* test for barriers to free movement.[82] The approach in *Dassonville*, under which almost all national regulation is subjected to scrutiny by the courts, and under which almost all disparities between national law rules are seen as problematic, is readily explicable in historical

---

[80] Contrast *Peralta* (n 60 above) [24]; and *Comune di Bassano* (n 60 above) [29], discussed above; and Case C-190/98 *Graf* [2000] ECR I-493 [25], discussed in ch 4.

[81] See also *Swedish Match* (n 42 above) [33]: 'where there are obstacles to trade or it is likely that such obstacles will emerge in future because the Member States have taken or are about to take divergent measures with respect to a product or a class of products such as to ensure different levels of protection and thereby prevent the product or products concerned from moving freely within the Community, Article 95 EC authorises the Community legislature to intervene by adopting appropriate measures'.

[82] See also J Weiler, 'The Constitution of the Common Market Place: Text and Context in the Evolution of the Free Movement of Goods' in P Craig and G De Búrca (eds), *The Evolution of EU Law* (OUP, Oxford 1999) 349, 372.

and political terms. As Weiler has argued, 'when establishing a common market you may want to lean on the side of rigour'.[83] By contrast, the approach in *Keck* is much more tolerant of regulatory diversity within the European market. My contention is that the *Keck* approach is better suited to the specific market-building endeavour within today's EU. The *Keck* test enables the EU and the Member States to pursue their economic and social goals and suits a Union whose normative orientation is agnostic as between integration and diversity.[84] Nevertheless, it is important to acknowledge that the implications of a wholesale shift towards the *Keck* approach are stark. Much of the free movement case law, in particular in relation to the free movement of persons, the freedom of establishment, and the freedom to provide services, would fall to be reconsidered. The focus would no longer be on whether particular national rules 'affect' access to markets, but rather on whether they 'prevent' access to markets or are discriminatory. The implications for domestic labour law are discussed in detail in chapter 4 below.

Intervention to eliminate distortions of competition

It will be recalled that the removal of barriers to free movement represents only one aspect of the integrationist rationale. It is entirely uncontroversial that the existence of distortions of competition also affects the establishment and functioning of the market. EU intervention in the labour law field can be said to be based on the integrationist rationale where it can be shown to remove such distortions.

One of the activities of the Community under the Treaty of Rome was to institute 'a system ensuring that competition in the common market is not distorted'.[85] Article 3(1)(g) EC now refers to 'a system ensuring that competition in the internal market is not distorted'. It is accepted by the institutions that the maintenance of undistorted conditions of competition is essential for the establishment and functioning of the market. Competition may be distorted by acts of the Member States,[86] by the activities of private sector bodies,[87] and by the political institutions.[88]

---

[83] Weiler (n 82 above) 362–3.

[84] According to Bermann, the *Keck* ruling 'demonstrates the Court's willingness to leave Member States the kind of regulatory scope that the principle of subsidiarity requires of the Community's political branches'; G Bermann, 'Taking Subsidiarity Seriously: Federalism in the European Community and the United States' (1994) 94 Columbia Law Review 331, 402. See further ch 3 below.

[85] Art 3(f) EEC, now amended.

[86] Acts of the Member States may be caught by Arts 81 and 82 EC, as well as by Arts 86 and 87 EC. In interpreting 'the second paragraph of Article 5 [now 10] and Article 85 [now 81] of the Treaty it should be noted that Article 85 [now 81], read in isolation, relates only to the conduct of undertakings and does not cover measures adopted by Member States by legislation or regulations. However, the Court has consistently held that Article 85 [now 81], read in conjunction with Article 5 [now 10] of the Treaty, requires the Member States not to introduce or maintain in force measures, even of a legislative or regulatory nature, which may render ineffective the competition rules applicable to undertakings'; Case C-2/91 *Meng* [1993] ECR I-5751 [14], and Case C-67/96 *Albany International* [1999] ECR I-5751 [65] and Opinion of AG Jacobs [301]. See more broadly, Baquero Cruz (n 51 above) ch 8.

[87] Arts 81 and 82 EC.

[88] There are fears that many Articles of the Treaty introduced by the TEU, eg Art 157 EC, 'offer a considerable number of opportunities for the EC authorities to [pursue] discretionary policies

However, the definition of the distortion of competition has, just like the definition of the barrier to free movement, proven to be extremely controversial. The result is that 'the Community's position is a highly uncertain one when it proposes taking regulatory action in the social policy field in order to remedy a distortion of competition'.[89] There is no definition of the distortion of competition in the Treaty, thus no obvious yardstick for distinguishing between differences in competitive conditions that are acceptable and those that amount to distortions.[90] This section on distorted conditions of competition builds on two 'ideologies' identified by Francis Snyder in the context of the common organization of the market in sheepmeat and goatmeat. According to Snyder, 'the distortion of competition' has 'at least two sharply contrasting connotations';[91] each of which might provide the necessary yardstick.

One perspective, the free trade perspective, holds that ' "the distortion of competition" is defined as the restriction of free trade'.[92] Adherents of this view speak in terms of 'free' rather than 'fair' competition,[93] and tend to rely on a neo-classical understanding of the workings of markets based on the formal equality of individuals. They often characterize national-level regulation as a means by which artificial and inefficient pockets of comparative advantage are created. The second perspective, termed the market structure and structural policy perspective, is more fearful of the consequences of free trade, and lacks confidence in the workings of the 'unadulterated' free market: 'Free trade ... would amount to unfair competition: It would "distort" the conditions of competition by leading to non-negotiated changes in production and marketing structures.'[94] Adherents of this perspective seek to ensure that certain outcomes are realized through the workings of the market, thus assuming both that the economic system lends itself to 'effective end-dependent rule-setting', and that 'sufficient steering-knowledge is available to achieve ends related to what is considered as social justice'.[95]

incompatible with the principle of undistorted competition'; M Streit and W Mussler, 'The Economic Constitution of the European Community—"From Rome to Maastricht" ' (1995) 1 European Law Journal 5, 22.

[89] Simitis and Lyon-Caen (n 43 above) 5.

[90] ibid 9. Art 81 EC prohibits agreements which have as their object or effect the 'prevention, restriction or distortion of competition'. Jones and Sufrin state that 'anyone who could define exactly what amounts to a restriction of competition would have achieved the competition law equivalent of finding the Holy Grail': A Jones and B Sufrin, *EC Competition Law: Text, Cases and Materials* (OUP, Oxford 2001) 149.

[91] F Snyder, *New Directions in European Community Law* (Weidenfeld and Nicolson, London 1990) 63.   [92] ibid 75.

[93] Both 'free' and 'fair' competition are referred to in the EC Treaties. For example, the Preamble to the Treaty of Rome called for 'concerted action in order to guarantee steady expansion, balanced trade and fair competition'; while Art 4(1) EC, introduced in the TEU, calls for the activities of the Member States and the Community to be 'conducted in accordance with the principle of an open market economy with free competition'. Both terms are controversial; see further R Howse and M Trebilcock, 'The Fair Trade/Free Trade Debate: Trade, Labor, and the Environment' (1996) 16 International Review of Law and Economics 61.   [94] Snyder (n 91 above) 77.

[95] Streit and Mussler (n 88 above) 11. See more generally F Hayek, *Law, Legislation and Liberty, Volume Two 'The Mirage of Social Justice'* (Routledge and Kegan Paul, London 1982).

As Snyder illustrates in relation to agricultural policy, and as I hope to demonstrate in relation to labour law, both perspectives are important. The institutions have, in the labour law context, at different times adopted one or other perspective, but they have failed to make the reasons for their changing choice of ideology explicit. In this section I identify no fewer than five conceptions of the distortion of competition, the first three based on the free trade perspective,[96] and the last two based on the structural policy perspective, all of which appear to have had some influence on the institutions.

  (I) all differences between the laws of the Member States are capable of distorting competition;
 (II) only those differences between the laws of the Member States which do not reflect differences in productivity are capable of distorting competition;
(III) mere differences between the laws of the Member States are not capable of distorting competition;
(IV) distortions of competition occur where standards are unacceptably low;
 (V) the collective quest for competitive advantage is capable of leading to distortions of competition.

The free trade perspective

Conception I: All differences between the laws of the Member States are capable of distorting competition

According to the first conception, 'conditions of competition are distorted by differences in national legislation and other national measures which result in businesses in different Member States operating under different economic and commercial regimes'.[97] Under this conception, the creation of a single market is said to demand a level playing field, on which undertakings can compete on equal terms.

This argument, which has persisted since the early days of the Community, has a certain instinctive appeal: 'Obviously, a true common market requires that enterprises should compete within it on equal terms. Equally obviously, most social costs fall directly or indirectly on enterprises, so that differences in social systems might be regarded, strictly speaking, as distortions of competition.'[98]

If differences between the laws of the Member States are adjudged capable of distorting competition, the Community institutions can intervene to remedy distortions wherever there are differences between the laws of the Member

[96] My analysis of the distortion of competition differs from Snyder's mainly because I believe that it is possible to identify three, mutually exclusive, versions of the free trade approach.
[97] P Collins and M Hutchings, 'Articles 101 and 102 of the EEC Treaty: Completing the Internal Market' (1986) 11 ELR 191, 194.
[98] M Shanks, 'The Social Policy of the European Communities' (1977) 14 CML Rev 375, 376. See also W Sengenberger, 'International Labour Standards in a globalized economy: The issues' in W Sengenberger and D Campbell (eds), *International Labour Standards and Economic Interdependence* (International Institute for Labour Studies, Geneva 1994) 3, 4: 'The argument that for social progress all competitors have to obey the same rule has a long history.'

States.[99] However, the action must be of a specific kind. The action must result in the elimination of the differences between the laws of the Member States which were such as to create the distortion.

Many of the Directives which have been adopted under Articles 94 and 95 EC, for example in the consumer protection,[100] and environmental law fields, rely on this conception of the distortion of competition. The belief of many Member State governments, who 'consider that differences in social costs are an extremely important determinant of their competitive position',[101] has been supported by the Commission, the European Parliament, and the Court of Justice.

In *Commission v Italy*, for example, in the context of Italian non-implementation of Directive 75/716/EEC,[102] the Court held that 'it is by no means ruled out that provisions on the environment may be based upon Article [94] of the Treaty. Provisions which are made necessary by considerations relating to the environment and health may be a burden upon the undertakings to which they apply and if there is no harmonization of national provisions on the matter, competition may be appreciably distorted'.[103]

The *Tobacco Advertising* case, discussed in the section above on the definition of the barrier to free movement, provides another example of this approach. The Court stated that 'national laws often differ regarding the conditions under which the activities they regulate may be carried on', and went on to hold that 'this impacts directly or indirectly on the conditions of competition for the undertakings concerned'.[104] But, in keeping with the relatively strict approach it adopted to the competence of the institutions, the Court held that the legislature may not rely on Article 95 EC 'with a view to eliminating the smallest distortions of competition'.[105] Instead, the Court must 'verify whether the Directive actually contributes to eliminating appreciable distortions of competition'.[106] It is apparent from this that the Court accepts that differences between national laws are liable

---

[99] A McGee and S Weatherill, 'The Evolution of the Single Market—Harmonisation or Liberalisation' (1990) 53 MLR 578, 594.

[100] See the Preamble to Council Directive 88/378/EEC of 3 May 1988 on the approximation of the laws of the Member States concerning the safety of toys [1988] OJ L187/1: 'Whereas the laws, regulations and administrative provisions in force in the various Member States relating to the safety characteristics of toys differ in scope and content; whereas such disparities are liable to create barriers to trade and unequal conditions of competition within the internal market . . .' 'Whereas these obstacles to the attainment of an internal market in which only sufficiently safe products would be sold should be removed; whereas for this purpose, the marketing and free movement of toys should be made subject to uniform rules . . .'.

[101] E Whiteford, 'W(h)ither Social Policy?' in J Shaw and G More (eds), *New Legal Dynamics of European Union* (Clarendon, Oxford 1995) 111, 118.

[102] The Preamble to Council Directive 75/716/EEC of 24 November 1975 on the approximation of the laws of the Member States relating to the sulphur content of certain liquid fuels [1975] OJ L307/22 focuses on the obstacle to free movement rather than on the distortion of competition: 'Whereas the differences in these laws . . . constitute a barrier to trade in these products, thereby directly influencing the establishment and functioning of the common market.'

[103] Case 92/79 *Commission v Italy* [1980] ECR 1115 [8].

[104] *Tobacco Advertising* (n 68 above) [107].   [105] ibid.   [106] ibid [108].

to create distortions, but that it decided that the competence to act under Article 95 will only be triggered where the distortions are appreciable. It held that where differences between national laws create competitive advantages that are 'remote and indirect', the resulting distortions cannot be described as appreciable.[107]

If a State's autonomous policy choices are to be condemned on the basis of the integrationist rationale, it seems to me that there must be good reasons. It is far from obvious why mere differences between the laws of the Member States must be held to create distorted conditions of competition. Some go so far as to claim that the arguments in support of a level playing field are economically incoherent.[108] Although there can be no doubt that differences between the laws of the Member States result in competition between legal regimes, there is no reason to assume that this competition will be distorted.[109] The Commission has stated that 'each state has the sovereign right to choose what labour laws it will enact and the choice made will reflect both the country's level of economic development and its political and social priorities'.[110] Howse and Trebilcock put the point in the following way: 'Assuming there is nothing wrongful with another country's environmental or labor policies ... then why should a cost advantage attributable to these divergent policies not be treated like any other cost advantage, i.e. as part and parcel of comparative advantage?'[111]

Conception II: Only those differences between the laws of the Member States which do not reflect differences in productivity are capable of distorting competition

The Spaak and Ohlin Reports of 1956 formed the basis for the social provisions of the Treaty of Rome.[112] The Ohlin Report rejects the view that all differences between the laws of the Member States are capable of distorting competition. It states that as 'differences in the general level of wages and social charges between different countries broadly reflect differences in productivity',[113] 'the notion that

---

[107] *Tobacco Advertising* (n 68 above) [109].

[108] B Langille, 'Eight Ways to think about International Labour Standards' (1997) 31(4) Journal of World Trade 27, 37–8; and S Deakin, 'Labour Law as Market Regulation: the Economic Foundations of European Social Policy' in P Davies *et al* (eds), *European Community Labour Law: Principles and Perspectives; Liber Amicorum Lord Wedderburn* (Clarendon, Oxford 1996) 63, 77.

[109] N Bernard, 'The Future of European Economic Law in the light of the Principle of Subsidiarity' (1996) 33 CML Rev 633, 642–7.

[110] Commission Communication, 'The Trading System and Internationally Recognized Labour Standards' COM(96)402, 24 July 1996, 6.   [111] Howse and Trebilcock (n 93 above) 74.

[112] See Spaak Report, Political and Economic Planning (1956) Planning No 405; and for the Ohlin Report, International Labour Office, 'Social Aspects of European Economic Cooperation' (1956) 74 International Labour Review 99. See also P Davies, 'The Emergence of European Labour Law' in Lord McCarthy (ed), *Legal Intervention in Industrial Relations: Gains and Losses* (Blackwell, Oxford 1992) 313; and S Giubboni, *Social Rights and Market Freedom in the European Constitution— A Labour Law Perspective* (CUP, Cambridge 2006).

[113] Ohlin Report (n 112 above) 102. See also G Fels, 'An Economic View of the Social Charter' in W Däubler (ed), *Market and Social Justice in the EC—the Other Side of the Internal Market* (Bertelsmann Foundation, Gutersloh 1991) 166. He argues, following the Ohlin Report, that 'the less developed

a general harmonization of social policy is justified by reference to "distortions of competition" brought about by differences between the labour law regimes of Member States is a delusion'.[114] According to Spaak, only where there are 'specific distortions which favour or handicap certain branches of economic activity',[115] is there a need for harmonization of laws to assist in the establishment and functioning of the market.

Thus, under this conception of the distortion of competition, it is only where a specific sector or group of enterprises in a Member State has, as a result of the way in which it is affected by national law rules, an advantage over other sectors or groups in that same Member State which is not attributable to differences in productivity, that EU action is warranted in order to eliminate a distortion of competition. The distortion operates vis-à-vis undertakings operating in the same sector in other Member States, which do not have a comparable advantage over other industries in their States. On these grounds the Ohlin Report did, exceptionally,[116] argue for action in relation to equal pay:

A certain distortion of competition arises from differences in the extent to which the principle of equal pay for men and women applies in different countries. Countries in which there are large wage differentials by sex will pay relatively low wages in industries employing a large proportion of female labour and these industries will enjoy what might be considered a special advantage over their competitors abroad where differentials according to sex are smaller or non-existent.[117]

This approach was the basis for the inclusion of Article 141 [formerly 119] EC in the Treaty at the behest of the French. It was also the basis for part of the reasoning of the Court of Justice in the *Defrenne II* case. The Court held that one of the objectives of what is now Article 141 EC is 'to avoid a situation in which undertakings established in States which have actually implemented the principle of equal pay suffer a competitive disadvantage in intra-Community competition as compared with undertakings established in States which have not yet eliminated discrimination against women workers as regards pay'.[118]

Where differences between national law rules affect industry in general, conditions of competition, under this approach, cannot be said to be distorted, as national law rules will reflect productivity levels. According to Ohlin, adjustments in, for example, the exchange rate, can accurately reflect changes in relative productivity among countries,[119] and this renders harmonization unnecessary. This, however, relies on two, at best questionable, assumptions. First, it assumes that there is a mechanical relationship between labour standards, productivity levels, and the

members are only competitive vis-à-vis the highly industrialized states of the Community and the world as long as their costs and standards in terms of social policy correspond to their productivity level'.

[114] Deakin (n 108 above) 92.   [115] Spaak Report (n 112 above) 233–4.

[116] The difficulty in identifying distortions ruled out attempts at harmonization as regards social security contributions and employment taxation; Ohlin Report (n 112 above) 108.

[117] ibid 107.   [118] Case 43/75 *Defrenne II* [1976] ECR 455 [9].

[119] Davies (n 112 above) 321.

exchange rate; an assumption which no longer holds true, given the importance of speculative markets for financial assets to the determination of the exchange rate. Second, it assumes that Member States have the freedom to set their own exchange and interest rates. As we will see below, economic and monetary union threatens 'the very freedom of action at the level of the nation State which the Ohlin Report considered essential if economic integration was to lead to improved living and working conditions':[120] 'Particularly after the establishment of fixed exchange rates the common market will become more susceptible to serious distortions of competition ... the presuppositions on the basis of which the Spaak Report excluded the necessity for Community action to combat general (or global) distortions are no longer valid.'[121] Thus, the Ohlin and Spaak Reports' suggestion that 'specific' differences between national laws can create distortions, whereas 'general' differences cannot, at least arguably no longer holds true, as active economic policy at the level of the nation state is no longer capable of providing the 'essential mechanism of adjustment'.[122]

In 1990 the Commission made a different distinction, based on the view that differences in direct wage costs reflect differences in productivity and thus do not amount to distortions of competition, whereas differences in indirect wage costs do not reflect differences in productivity and thus constitute 'veritable' distortions of competition.[123] This distinction is much criticized by commentators,[124] and is economically unsound in as much as changes in productivity levels tend to be reflected not only in changes in direct wage costs but also in changes in indirect costs. The Ohlin Report, for example, did not distinguish between direct and indirect costs, stating that 'differences in the general level of wages and social charges between different countries broadly reflect differences in productivity'.[125]

In fact, there are fundamental reasons to be suspicious of the approach adopted in both the Ohlin Report and the 1990 Memorandum. In much the same way as it may be doubted that the harmonization of nominal costs is necessary for the establishment and functioning of a market, it can also be doubted that equivalence of unit costs across the EU is necessary. This is the view adopted by adherents of the third version of the free trade approach.

Conception III: Mere differences between the laws of the Member States are not capable of distorting competition

This conception of the free trade approach is the one which reflects the greatest confidence in the workings of markets. The two conceptions discussed above

---

[120] Deakin (n 108 above) 82–3.

[121] L Gormley, P Kapteyn, and P VerLoren van Themaat, *Introduction to the Law of the European Communities* (2nd edn, Kluwer, Deventer 1989) 487.   [122] Deakin (n 108 above) 67.

[123] Commission, 'Explanatory Memorandum on the Proposals for Directives concerning certain employment relationships' COM(90)228, 13 August 1990 [25].

[124] See Lord Wedderburn, 'Workers' Rights: Fact or Fake?' (1991) 13 Dublin University Law Journal 1, 22; and S Deakin and F Wilkinson, 'Rights vs. Efficiency? The Economic Case for Transnational Labour Standards' (1994) 23 ILJ 289, 302.   [125] Ohlin Report (n 112 above) 102.

assume that competition between enterprises will produce beneficial results; but argue that such competition will only be undistorted if enterprises compete on equal terms within a market. They differ in how they define competition on equal terms. The first insists that enterprises must operate under the same legal regime in order for competition to be undistorted, whereas the second holds that competition will be undistorted if costs per unit of output are equal.

Conception III does not argue that competitive conditions within the European market need to be equal in order for competition within the market to be undistorted. According to this conception, so long as—and this is an important condition—free movement between Member States is guaranteed, competition between legal regimes is not incompatible with the establishment of the common or internal market. In fact, harmonization might 'negate the competitive process which it was the very purpose of the principle of free movement ... to stimulate'.[126] Indeed, 'it is one of the fundamental features of the Common Market, which is to be attained inter alia by the freedom to provide services, that when providing services in another Member State any employer may in principle make use of the cost advantages existing in his country'.[127] The key question, over which adherents of the three free trade conceptions of the distortion of competition differ, is whether cost advantages derived from differences in legal regime should be included.

Conception III relies on regulatory competition:[128] 'Regulatory competition is the alteration of national regulation in response to the actual or expected impact of internationally mobile goods, services, or factors on national economic activity.'[129] It is predicated on the assumption that mere differences in national laws do not constitute distortions of competition. Differences in regulatory standards across the EU encourage mobile factors of production to locate in their jurisdiction of choice, and States compete to attract investment by adapting national legislation to the perceived needs of mobile investors. The regulatory choices made by each Member State remain mutually exposed to the discipline of market forces.[130] It is claimed that regulatory competition provides 'a market-driven way

---

[126] M Freedland 'Employment Policy' in Davies *et al* (n 108 above) 296.

[127] Cases 62 and 63/81 *Seco* [1982] ECR 223, Opinion of AG VerLoren van Themaat, 244. See also Council Resolution of 6 December 1994 on certain aspects for a European Union social policy: a contribution to economic and social convergence in the Union [1994] OJ C368/6, 9: The Council 'considers unification of national systems in general by means of rigorous approximation of laws an unsuitable direction to follow as it would also reduce the chances of the disadvantaged regions in the competition for location'.

[128] See D Esty and D Geradin (eds), *Regulatory Competition and Economic Integration: Comparative Perspectives* (OUP, Oxford 2001).

[129] J Sun and J Pelkmans, 'Regulatory Competition in the Single Market' (1995) 33 JCMS 67, 68–9. See also C Joerges, 'Product Safety in the European Community: Market Integration, Social Regulation and Legal Structures' (1992) 39 Journal of Behavioural Sciences 132, 144: Regulatory competition is 'none other than the adjustment of economic and social regulation by a competitive regime'.

[130] M Dougan, 'Vive la Différence? Exploring the Legal Framework for Reflexive Harmonization within the Single European Market' in R Miller and P Zumbansen (eds), *Annual of German and European Law Volume I (2003)* (Beghahn, New York 2004) 116–7.

to "discover" which regulations offer "protection" that is demanded by the residents and firms of a given jurisdiction, and which are deemed superfluous'.[131] According to this view, the results of the process of regulatory competition are unimportant. Regulatory competition may 'bring about a "market-driven" regulatory convergence',[132] or alternatively, under the effect of the uneven but lively opportunism of individual Member States, regulatory competition might even accentuate existing disparities.[133]

The key claim is that competition will not be distorted by mere differences between national law rules—provided that free movement is guaranteed. This brings us back to the debate on the definition of the barrier to free movement. If all differences between the laws of the Member States are regarded as barriers to free movement (and this is where an acceptance of the *Dassonville* test leads) there will be little or no space for regulatory competition and much of the argument advanced in this section becomes meaningless.

Deakin argues that 'as long as undertakings have equal access to the domestic market of the State in question, in the sense of freedom to supply both goods and services, there is no reason to assume that differences in labour standards of themselves give rise to a distortion of competition'.[134] The notion of equal access comprises two elements. First, access must be possible. The institutions should intervene to ensure that market access for all factors of production is not barred or prevented. Second, imported factors of production should not suffer discrimination. There should not be a greater impediment to the market access of imported, as compared with domestic, factors of production. The parallel with the *Keck* test is exact.[135]

An important part of the argument in this book is that it is important to be alert to the ways in which various dimensions of each of the three rationales for EU intervention in domestic labour law fit together. It is, as a further step, also important to be aware of the way in which the three rationales fit together. When one is, for example, examining the definition of the distortion of competition, it is important to be aware of the other dimensions of the integrationist rationale, including the definition of the barrier to free movement and the impact of economic and monetary union. It is also important, and especially so given that integration is pursued not as an end in itself but as a means towards the realization of economic and social ends, to be alert to the economic and social implications of particular choices.

For example, if it is accepted that all differences between the laws of the Member States amount to distortions of competition, then it must make sense to

---

[131] Sun and Pelkmans (n 129 above) 83; and Kumm (n 74 above) 509.

[132] Sun and Pelkmans (n 129 above) 70. See also Art 117 EC; and S Deakin, 'Legal Diversity and Regulatory Competition: Which Model for Europe?' (2006) 12 European Law Journal 440, 451, 453, arguing that models of regulatory competition based on a US pattern of 'competitive federalism' tend to give rise to a race to converge (either to the top or the bottom).

[133] S Simitis and A Lyon-Caen, 'Community Labour Law: A Critical Introduction to its History' in Davies *et al* (n 108 above) 7.   [134] Deakin (n 108 above) 74–5.

[135] Cases C-267 and 268/91 *Keck and Mithouard* [1993] ECR I-6097 [17].

accept the *Dassonville* test for barriers to free movement. Differences between national laws would be liable to be condemned as either barriers or distortions, and it would be clear that the integrationist rationale was, in a variety of ways, seeking to eliminate differences between the laws of the Member States. On the other hand, if it is accepted that mere differences between the laws of the Member States do not amount to distortions of competition, then it must make sense for the free movement case law to allow some scope for regulatory competition. The test in *Keck* is better suited to that task than the test in *Dassonville*. Under this second approach, it would be clear that the integrationist rationale was not calling for uniformity, but rather that, subject to conditions, it was tolerant of regulatory diversity within the EU.

My view is that either one or the other approach could be adopted. Both are consistent with the objective of creating a market within Europe. But clearly, the two approaches would lead to the building of different sorts of markets, with different economic and social ramifications. One's preference will ultimately be determined by one's views on the specific nature of the market-making endeavour in today's EU, and one's views concerning the relationship between the integrationist, economic, and social rationales. As mentioned above, for reasons which will become clear in the course of this book, I lean towards an interpretation of the integrationist rationale which endorses the *Keck* test for barriers to free movement and conception III of the distortion of competition. Under such an approach, the Member States are given the space to pursue their economic and social goals, free in the knowledge that their interventions are not seen as problematic from an integrationist perspective. This suits a Union whose normative orientation is agnostic as between integration and diversity, and is, as we will see in chapter 3 below, in accord with the dictates of the principles of subsidiarity and proportionality.

The market structure and structural policy perspective

Opportunities for EU intervention in domestic labour law under the integrationist rationale—not aimed towards the elimination of disparities between national rules—emerge if it is accepted that the definition of the distortion of competition may be amended so as to take account of the economic and social concerns which may be overlooked by regulatory competition.

The market structure and structural policy ideology identified by Snyder builds on conception III in that it again rejects the view that the harmonization of (nominal or unit) cost levels is required for the establishment and functioning of the common market and again relies on regulatory competition. However, it distinguishes between various types of competition.[136] Those that produce what are termed 'positive outcomes' are welcomed. Those that do not are condemned as distortions. The distinctions are made, at least in part, because 'implicit in the

---

[136] See Deakin (n 132 above).

concept of regulatory competition is the subjugation of "externalities" contained within the goal of regulation—distributive justice or other socio-political interests— to market forces'.[137] This approach, which recognizes that markets are not always the best institutional form for economic coordination,[138] is designed precisely to ensure that those socio-political interests which may be overlooked by the market are given due prominence. Adherents of this ideology make a distinction between productive and destructive, fair and unfair, or legitimate and illegitimate competition, and they do so according to economic and social criteria. Some economists, however, object to such an approach. They argue that competition is the 'process which deals best with our endemic lack of knowledge'. To seek to identify certain rules as distortions of competition on the basis of their economic and social effects is to illustrate 'the fundamental misunderstanding inherent to constructivist views of the market process'.[139] In what has been termed the neo-liberal competitive federalism constitutional model, 'the supranational legal order does not deliberately—and should not—carry out corrective or redistributive functions aimed at compensating, at the more general level, the (predetermined) reduction of autonomous powers of intervention arising from regulatory competition'.[140] If this approach is accepted, conceptions IV and V of the distortion of competition will be rejected out of hand, and the competence of the institutions to intervene under this limb of the integrationist rationale will be restricted accordingly.

I identify two rather different situations in which the institutions may have the competence to act in response to what can, given an acceptance of the market structure and structural policy approach, be said to be distortions of competition. First, the institutions may, in creating the European market, set the baseline rule of economic ordering within it. Second, they may intervene to prevent the collective quest for competitive advantage leading to sub-optimal levels of regulation throughout the European market, and thereby distorting competition.[141]

In both cases, the rationale for EU intervention may be integrationist. EU intervention is premised on the need to eliminate distortions of competition which interfere with the establishment and functioning of the market. However, the distortion of competition is defined with economic and social objectives in

---

[137] Joerges (n 129 above) 142. See more generally, J Gray, *False Dawn: The Delusions of Global Capitalism* (Granta, London 1998) ch 4.

[138] See D Ashiagbor, *The European Employment Strategy: Labour Market Regulation and New Governance* (OUP, Oxford 2006) 22; Ch 1 is an excellent account of the legacy of Coase, and the debate between 'Chicago-school' and 'new institutional' economists.

[139] Streit and Mussler (n 88 above) 25. Thus, with a free-market ideology in place, labour standards are condemned as 'no more than a distorting mechanism which will facilitate the achievement of results which are actually antithetical to those which their well-meaning but misguided proponents seek to achieve'; P Alston, 'Post-post-modernism and international labour standards: The quest for a new complexity' in Sengenberger and Campbell (n 98 above) 95, 98.

[140] Giubboni (n 112 above), 257.

[141] See B Langille, 'Labour standards in the globalized economy and the free trade/fair trade debate' in Sengenberger and Campbell (n 98 above) 329, 334–7.

mind. Accordingly, as we shall see below, it may be difficult to maintain a clear distinction between the integrationist and the economic and/or social rationales for intervention.

Conception IV: Distortions of competition occur where standards are unacceptably low

Contrary to the assumption of many free trade theorists, the baseline rule of economic ordering need not be the operation of the unregulated free market.[142] An alternative perspective holds that 'markets are social constructs, constituted by law and social norms'.[143] Regulation is not something which is extrinsic to markets, but rather something which is essential for the very existence of markets. According to this latter perspective, the EU may, in the course of its market-building endeavour, insist on certain market rules, for example that labour standards are not unacceptably low.

Where a Member State seeks to compete on the basis of unacceptably low standards, the competition may be judged unfair, with the result that a distortion of competition can be said to have occurred. The Commission has attempted to define social dumping as 'the gaining of unfair competitive advantage within the Community through unacceptably low social standards'.[144] Standards can be said to be unacceptably low, either because of their adverse social effects, for example because of their impact on workers' rights, or, though this is less likely, because of their adverse economic effects.[145] We can return to the quotation from Howse and Trebilcock: 'Assuming there is nothing wrongful with another country's environmental or labor policies ... then why should a cost advantage attributable to these divergent policies not be treated like any other cost advantage, i.e. as part and parcel of comparative advantage?'[146]

Where social standards are unacceptably low, the necessary element of wrongfulness is introduced, and a distortion of competition can be said to have occurred. It is, of course, difficult to determine when a social standard is 'unacceptably low', or, to put this another way, where the boundary between fair and unfair competition should be located.[147] If conception IV of the distortion of competition is adopted, minimum standard setting, not harmonization, is the appropriate policy response.

---

[142] Langille (n 108 above) 41. This assumption of free trade theorists is seldom articulated.

[143] Ashiagbor (n 138 above) 30.

[144] Commission Green Paper on European Social Policy: Options for the Union, COM(93)551, 17 November 1993, 7.

[145] See Lord Wedderburn, *Labour Law and Freedom: Further Essays in Labour Law* (Lawrence and Wishart, London 1995) 253.   [146] Howse and Trebilcock (n 93 above) 74.

[147] M Kumm, 'Constitutionalising Subsidiarity in Integrated Markets: The Case of Tobacco Regulation in the European Union' (2006) 12 European Law Journal 503, 509, argues that at least in the EU context, 'there are reasons to think that arguments concerning minimal moral standards are more often than not merely a cover for rent-seeking'. His suspicion is that 'established industries and their employees in high-cost jurisdictions are enlisting the cooperation of self-aggrandising European institutions to engage in anti-competitive rent-seeking, thus precluding competitors and workers in low-cost jurisdictions from reaping the rewards of a legitimate comparative advantage'.

In chapter 5 below, interventions based on this limb of the integrationist rationale are discussed; as is the relationship between this limb of the integrationist rationale and the social rationale.

Conception V: The collective quest for competitive advantage is capable of leading to distortions of competition

Distortions of competition can also occur without the need for a demonstration that standards in any State are 'unacceptably low'. Conception V provides for EU intervention in rather different circumstances. In many ways, it provides the most formidable challenge for EU labour law.

Langille describes the way in which the collective quest for competitive advantage might distort competition.

> In a world of unemployment in which investment is sought, it might well be in the interest of any one island jurisdiction to lower its optimal standards in an effort to attract the benefits of further jobs brought by investment. And it might be logical for that single jurisdiction to calculate that the loss of optimality in its labour policy would be more than compensated for by the gains in additional investment. The problem is that every other jurisdiction will see the same thing and engage in a process of lowering their labour standards as well ...[148]

It is certainly possible that competition between legal regimes might be destructive in this manner, that the competitive process might result in a so-called 'race to the bottom', and that social standards may, as a result, become sub-optimal in much of Europe.[149] In order for the EU to be able to intervene in relation to a distortion of competition on these grounds, one must show that Member States do attempt to attract investment through changes in their labour law regime and that their resulting policy is sub-optimal;[150] or at least that there is a likelihood that States will lower standards to sub-optimal levels in an attempt to gain a competitive advantage.[151] Many Member States have, as a result of economic and monetary union, lost the ability to regulate interest and exchange rates. As Barnard explains, they only retain their independence 'in respect of the regulation—or

---

[148] Langille (n 108 above) 42.

[149] See eg Deakin (n 108 above) 83; Dougan (n 130 above) 118–22. Langille argues that the core disagreement between 'free traders' and 'fair traders' 'is whether it is possible rationally to perceive what is socially optimal in any other way than that defined by the market'; Langille (n 141 above) 336.

[150] Contrary to popular opinion, there is little evidence to suggest that deregulation of the labour market attracts inward investment. See OECD, *Trade, Employment and Labour Standards: A Study of Core Workers' Rights and International Trade* (OECD, Paris 1996) 9. See also Langille (n 108 above) 43, and C Barnard, 'Social Dumping and Race to the Bottom: Some Lessons for the EU from Delaware?' (2000) 25 ELR 57. The much publicized Hoover affair represents an isolated exception. In 1993, Hoover decided to close its factory near Dijon and transfer production to the UK, leading to accusations of social dumping; see Editorial Comments, 'Are European Values Being Hoovered Away?' (1993) 30 CML Rev 445.

[151] In line with the approach adopted by the Court in Case C-376/98 *Germany v Parliament and Council* [2002] ECR I-8419 (*Tobacco Advertising*), the 'abstract risk' of a distortion of competition should not be sufficient to trigger European intervention.

rather deregulation—of labour standards and wages'.[152] Race to the bottom problems are likely to be aggravated as the number of dimensions along which competition occurs is reduced.[153]

There is a widespread belief that 'sovereign states are waging a war of competitive deregulation, forced on them by the global free market'.[154] Ryan states that 'the most basic rationale for Community intervention in the field of social policy' is 'to forestall "competitive deregulation"—or, government attempts to attract trade and investment by lowering social and employment standards'.[155] Bell concludes that 'the market integration model now accepts the need for some basic labour law standards to combat destructive competition within the internal market'.[156] It is important, in this context, to grasp the powerful impact which (even potentially) mobile investors, encouraged to move by the elimination of barriers to free movement within the EU, have on government policy.[157] Kumm argues that locational competition creates incentives not to impose costs on mobile actors, shifting the burden and costs of regulation to those who lack a meaningful exit option, and resulting in a structural bias in Member States' democratic processes.[158] The fear of a legal flight of companies 'to evade not only unfavourable corporate and (maybe) fiscal legislation, but also a number of labour law provisions',[159] has a hold on Member States, and has also, as we shall see, influenced the development of EU policy.[160]

If conception V is accepted—and acceptance involves not only endorsing the market structure and structural policy perspective, but also finding evidence that States are at least likely to deregulate their labour standards to sub-optimal levels—the challenge lies in articulating the policy response.[161] European standards must prevent government attempts to attract trade and investment by lowering social and employment standards to sub-optimal levels. The European-wide harmonization of social obligations at a high level is not likely to be the appropriate response. Indeed, it will only be the correct response if each State's optimal level of social regulation is identical. Instead, attention has turned towards what Simon Deakin has termed 'reflexive harmonization'.[162] Under a regime of reflexive harmonization, the role for EU authorities properly consists in setting certain basic parameters for

[152] C Barnard, 'EC "Social" Policy' in P Craig and G De Búrca (eds), *The Evolution of EU Law* (OUP, Oxford 1999) 479, 507.   [153] Kumm (n 147 above), 512.

[154] Gray (n 137 above) 78.

[155] B Ryan, 'Pay, Trade Union Rights and European Community Law' (1997) 13 International Journal of Comparative Labour Law and Industrial Relations 305, 317.

[156] M Bell, *Anti-Discrimination Law and the European Union* (OUP, Oxford 2002) 29.

[157] See C Pierson, A Forster, and E Jones, 'The politics of Europe: (un)employment ambivalence', in B Towers and M Terry (eds), *Industrial Relations Journal European Annual Review 1997* (Blackwell, Oxford 1998) 16–21.   [158] Kumm (n 147 above) 513.

[159] Däubler (n 113 above) 69–71.

[160] 'It may only take a few searchers and movers to cause powerful responses by competing governments'; F Easterbrook, 'Antitrust and the Economics of Federalism' (1993) 26 Journal of Law and Economics 23, 44.   [161] See Kumm (n 147 above) 510–15.

[162] See S Deakin, 'Two Types of Regulatory Competition: Competitive Federalism versus Reflexive Harmonization. A Law and Economics Perspective on *Centros*' (1999) 2 Cambridge Yearbook of European Legal Studies 231.

Member State action, but otherwise respecting the autonomy and diversity of national legal orders.

Other action to assist the market-building process

It is not only action which eliminates barriers to free movement and distortions of competition which can properly be based on the integrationist rationale. Any other action which can be shown to assist in the market-building process can also be based on the integrationist rationale. It is, inevitably, difficult to list the interventions which may fit within this category. One example, which is not considered in any depth here, is any intervention which, though it does not contribute directly towards the elimination of barriers to free movement or distortions of competition, makes it easier for persons or enterprises to exploit the potential of the single market.[163] The provision of information relating to employment or investment opportunities throughout the EU would, for example, fit into this category. These interventions are likely to be on the periphery of the integrationist rationale, and it may, as we shall see, be difficult to determine whether such interventions should be classified as integrationist, rather than as economic or social.

In this section, interventions associated with the establishment of Economic and Monetary Union (EMU) are discussed. The first attempts to realize EMU date back to the 1960s, and the long and tortuous history of the EMU project need not detain us here.[164] The EMU project represents a significant moment for Europe,[165] and is a major development as regards the integrationist rationale. The existence of a single currency leads to significant transaction cost savings and removes risks associated with currency fluctuations.[166] It is, therefore, uncontroversial to state that EMU contributes towards the establishment and functioning of a single market within Europe. Exchange rate transaction costs amount to discriminatory barriers to trade. They increase the cost of marketing imports, while they have no impact on the sale of domestic products. Currency fluctuations can

---

[163] See also G Davies, 'Can Selling Arrangements be Harmonised?' (2005) 30 ELR 371. He states (at 378) that measures which 'genuinely contribute to creating and maintaining the single market'— he gives the example of 'common standards of consumer protection' which 'could provide an appreciable contribution to creating trust, and increasing cross-border shopping'—may be based on Art 95 EC. He also argues (at 380) that competence under Art 95 extends, and should extend, to non-trade measures, 'for which the need arises as a result of other trade measures, or as a result of cross-border trade, and whose aims cannot be met by Member States acting alone'.

[164] For an excellent summary, see F Snyder, 'EMU Revisited: Are We Making a Constitution? What Constitution are We Making?' in Craig and De Búrca (n 152 above) 417, 421–35.

[165] It is described as 'the third major phase in the construction of the European Community, following the original Treaty of Rome and the completion of the single market with the Single European Act'; D Chalmers *et al*, *European Union Law* (CUP, Cambridge 2006) 507.

[166] See Commission, 'One market, one money: an evaluation of the potential benefits and costs of forming an economic and monetary union' (European Economy No 44, October 1990) ch 3; and Commission Communication, 'The Impact of Currency Fluctuations on the Internal Market' COM(95)503, 31 October 1995. The predictions of the Commission need not, of course, be taken at face value. See further P De Grauwe, *Economics of Monetary Union* (6th edn, OUP, Oxford 2005).

be seen as distortions of competition, in particular if conception V of the distortion of competition is accepted. States may, for example, choose to devalue their currency to a sub-optimal level in order to improve the competitive position of domestic traders. For this reason, I choose to classify interventions directly associated with EMU as integrationist.

But, it is also clear that the EMU project is concerned with more than market integration, and that it has more far-reaching implications. Snyder convincingly argues that it 'was created mainly for political rather than economic reasons'.[167] It is also clear, as we shall see, that political opportunism rather than integrationist logic was responsible for the way in which various elements of EMU were designed, or have come to operate. This section describes the current state of play as regards EMU. It moves on to consider the Treaty provisions relating first to the transition to EMU, and then to EMU itself.

EMU has now been a reality for a number of years. The European Central Bank (ECB) came into existence in 1998, the currencies of eleven of the Member States were locked together in 1999,[168] and euro banknotes and coins were placed into circulation, in what has come to be known as the eurozone, in 2002. One of the most significant features of EMU, at least from the integrationist perspective, is that fourteen Member States do not (yet) participate in the single currency. The UK and Denmark negotiated opt-outs;[169] as for the remaining Member States, their participation depends on the Council's assessment of the convergence criteria. The States which have not adopted the euro are referred to as 'Member States with a derogation', with the result that many of the provisions relating to monetary union, and a small minority of the provisions relating to economic policy coordination, do not apply to them.[170] EMU is the most significant example of what has been termed 'differentiated integration'.[171] A large number of Member States do not participate in what is a key phase in the development of the EU; either as a result of their own political choice, or because the Council has not ruled that they are ready to participate. The result is that the most obvious integrationist benefits of the EMU project—transaction cost savings and the removal of the risks of currency fluctuations—do not apply to all Member States, and that there is closer integration within the eurozone than there is in the EU as a whole.

The transition to EMU was approached in stages.[172] The Treaty on European Union (TEU) includes a number of provisions which set the timetable for EMU

---

[167] Snyder (n 164 above) 419.
[168] Greece joined monetary union in 2001; Slovenia in 2007. The eurozone now includes 13 Member States.
[169] See Protocols 25 and 26 attached to the TEU.   [170] Art 122 EC.
[171] See F Tuytschaever, 'EMU and the Catch-22 of EU Constitution-Making', in G De Búrca and J Scott (eds), *Constitutional Change in the EU: From Uniformity to Flexibility?* (Hart, Oxford 2000) 173, 175. In the social field, the best example is the UK's opt-out from the social provisions of the Treaty.
[172] The TEU follows the approach laid down in the Delors Report (Commission Committee for the study of economic and monetary union, *Report on economic and monetary union in the European Community*, 12 April 1989). See further K Dyson and K Featherstone, *The Road to Maastricht: Negotiating Economic and Monetary Union* (OUP, Oxford 1999).

and detail the conditions which Member States have to meet before being able to participate in EMU.[173] The most important of the conditions relate to the independence of the central bank, and the achievement of what is described in Article 121(1) EC as 'a high degree of sustainable convergence'. The perceived need for convergence in the context of EMU is said to be 'interesting in being so very much at odds with the "comparative advantage" approach, which had dominated the Treaty of Rome, tolerating the absence of a "level playing field" in labour costs between Member States'.[174] The approach adopted in the TEU (and before the Treaty, in the Delors Report) adopts economists' coronation theory of monetary union. The argument, and it is one on which economists differ, is that the permanent convergence of national economies and the creation of a stable macroeconomic environment throughout the EU is necessary to 'provide the backdrop for the successful operation of the single currency'.[175] In so far as it is accepted that the convergence and subsequent coordination of Member States' economic policies is indeed necessary for the success of EMU, EU intervention directed towards those objectives should be classified as integrationist.

The famous 'convergence criteria', which were only agreed at the Maastricht Intergovernmental Conference (IGC), relate to price stability, sustainable government finance, exchange rate stability, and long-term interest rate levels.[176] The criteria have, unsurprisingly, generated a great deal of debate. They are criticized from a number of perspectives. First, in the interpretation of the criteria there is, as Snyder illustrates, significant room for discretion.[177] This means that the decision on whether or not to allow States to adopt the single currency, taken by the Council, meeting in the composition of the Heads of State or Government on the basis of reports submitted by the Commission and the European Monetary Institute (EMI),[178] is best characterized as political rather than economic. Second, the criteria appear to relate to a country's nominal monetary conditions and state of public finances, and not the situation of its real economy. This is perhaps explicable on the basis that it is 'almost impossible to capture real convergence in binding and effective legal terms'.[179] Nevertheless, the fact that the decision whether to allow a State to progress to the single currency is based on a political assessment of indicators which may be unable to capture the situation in the real economy, creates significant concerns about the way in which the coronation theory has operated in the EMU context. Finally, and

[173] See Arts 116–124 EC.

[174] Ashiagbor (n 138 above) 102. As explained above, the Ohlin and Spaak Reports, upon which the social provisions of the Treaty of Rome were based, adopted conception II of the distortion of competition.

[175] Chalmers (n 165 above) 525. cf the Optimum Currency Area (OCA) approach, discussed in F Mongelli, 'What is European Economic and Monetary Union telling us about the Properties of Optimum Currency Areas?' (2005) 43 JCMS 607.

[176] See Art 121 EC and the accompanying Protocol on the Convergence Criteria.

[177] Snyder (n 164 above) 444–8.

[178] Art 117 EC. The EMI is the predecessor to the ECB; Art 123(2) EC.

[179] Chalmers (n 165 above) 526–7.

this is a point of particular relevance in the labour law context, concerns have been expressed about the absence of social, employment, or industrial policy indicators from the EMU convergence criteria.[180]

Article 2 EC makes it clear that establishing an economic and monetary union, just like establishing a common market, is a means through which the Community is to achieve its economic and social ends. Article 4(1) EC provides that 'the activities of the Member States and the Community' shall include the adoption of an economic policy 'based on the close coordination of Member States' economic policies' and 'conducted in accordance with the principle of an open market economy with free competition'. Article 4(2) EC provides for a single monetary and exchange rate policy, whose primary objective is said to be 'to maintain price stability and, without prejudice to this objective, to support the general economic policies in the Community'. Article 4(3) EC then states that 'these activities of the Member States and the Community shall entail compliance with the following guiding principles: stable prices, sound public finances and monetary conditions and a sustainable balance of payments'. Of particular note are the overriding nature of the commitment to price stability,[181] and the division between centralized monetary and coordinated economic policy.

The provisions on monetary policy are Articles 105 to 111 EC. Much of the academic attention has focused on the European System of Central Banks (ESCB— the European Central Bank and the national central banks),[182] and in particular on its independence, which is enshrined in Article 108 EC. The chosen system, modelled on the German Bundesbank, tends to be criticized in terms of its lack of democratic accountability,[183] but praised in terms of its credibility.[184] The ESCB has a mandate, which is enshrined, perhaps even constitutionalized in the Treaty, to

---

[180] See Ashiagbor (n 138 above) 103. Dyson and Featherstone make the point that the EMU negotiations were a 'core executive' activity. Sectoral interests, including employers' organizations and trade unions, were excluded from the EMU negotiations, both at national and EC level; Dyson and Featherstone (n 172 above) 13–15.

[181] It could be said that the EU has taken on 'an added functional specialization in providing macroeconomic stability'; K Dyson (ed), *European States and the Euro: Europeanization, Variation and Convergence* (OUP, Oxford 2002) 26. M Herdegen, 'Price Stability and Budgetary Restraints in the Economic and Monetary Union: Law as the Guardian of Economic Wisdom' (1998) 35 CML Rev 9, 21, refers to price stability as the new Grundnorm of the Community.

[182] Participation in the Governing Council and Executive Board of the ECB is restricted to eurozone countries.

[183] See F Amtenbrink, *The Democratic Accountability of Central Banks: A Comparative Study of the European Central Bank* (Hart, Oxford 1999); W Buiter, 'Alice in Euroland' (1999) 37 JCMS 181; and O Issing, 'The Eurosystem: Transparent and Accountable or "Willem in Euroland" ' (1999) 37 JCMS 503.

[184] See G Majone, 'The Credibility Crisis of Community Regulation' (2000) 38 JCMS 273. In relation to the ECB, see J De Haan, F Amtenbrink, and S Waller, 'The Transparency and Credibility of the European Central Bank' (2004) 42 JCMS 775; and J De Haan, S Eijffinger, and S Waller, *The European Central Bank: Credibility, Transparency and Centralization* (MIT Press, Cambridge, 2005) 80, arguing that the ECB has been 'quite successful' in its monetary policy. They add that it cannot be said to have been 'overly aggressive in pursuing its primary objective to the detriment of other considerations'.

'maintain price stability',[185] and without prejudice to that, to 'support the general economic policies in the Community with a view to contributing to the achievement of the objectives of the Community as laid down in Article 2'.[186]

The coordination of economic policy is dealt with in Articles 98 to 104 EC. Article 99(1) EC states that 'Member States shall regard their economic policies as a matter of common concern', and Article 99(2) EC authorizes the Council to adopt broad guidelines of the economic policies of the Member States and of the Community. It is in relation to the coordination of economic policy that the open method of coordination (or OMC), now a key weapon in the EU's armoury in the social arena, was first utilized.[187] Articles 101 to 103 EC impose constraints on certain forms of government financing, and Article 104 EC represents an attempt to limit government spending, aiming to ensure that Member States avoid 'excessive deficits'.[188] The Stability and Growth Pact, developed in 1997, is intended to ensure that the excessive deficit procedure outlined in Article 104 EC is applied strictly,[189] and that the fiscal irresponsibility of national governments does not threaten the stability of the single currency. Events have, however, made it clear that the operation of the Stability and Growth Pact, rather like the reading of the convergence criteria, is a matter of some political discretion: 'the existing rules [ie those in place until 2004] have proven to be largely incapable of avoiding the emergence of excessive deficits in times of ailing national economies'.[190] Opinion is divided on the 2005 reforms,[191] which introduce some stricter rules, but also embrace a more flexible approach towards excessive deficits.[192]

---

[185] This is rather vague. The ECB has set itself the objective of maintaining inflation in the eurozone at a level below, but close to, 2% in the medium term; ECB, *The Monetary Policy of the ECB* (January 2004).   [186] Art 105 EC.

[187] See D Hodson and I Maher, 'The Open Method as a New Mode of Governance: The Case of Soft Economic Policy Co-ordination' (2001) 39 JCMS 719.

[188] Neither Art 104(9) nor Art 104(11) applies to 'Member States with a derogation' (Art 122(3)). This in effect means that sanctions cannot be imposed on States which have not adopted the euro and which operate excessive deficits.

[189] See Resolution of the European Council on the Stability and Growth Pact, Amsterdam, 17 June 1997 [1997] OJ C236/1; Council Regulation (EC) 1466/97 of 7 July 1997 on the strengthening of the surveillance of budgetary positions and the surveillance and coordination of economic policies [1997] OJ L209/1; and Council Regulation (EC) 1467/97 of 7 July 1997 on speeding up and clarifying the implementation of the excessive deficit procedure [1997] OJ L209/6.

[190] F Amtenbrink and J De Haan, 'Reforming the Stability and Growth Pact' (2006) 31 ELR 402, 403. In 2004, the Commission brought an action against the Council, in the wake of the Council's refusal to take action against Germany and France; see Case C-27/04 *Commission v Council* [2004] ECR I-4829.

[191] See Council Regulation (EC) 1055/2005 of 27 June 2005 amending Regulation (EC) 1466/97 on the strengthening of the surveillance of budgetary positions and the surveillance and coordination of economic policies [2005] OJ L174/1; and Council Regulation 1056/2005 (EC) of 27 June 2005 amending Regulation (EC) 1467/97 on speeding up and clarifying the implementation of the excessive deficit procedure [2005] OJ L174/5. For the reasons underlying the amendments, see Brussels European Council, Presidency Conclusions, 22 and 23 March 2005, Annex II (Council Report to the European Council, 'Improving the Implementation of the Stability and Growth Pact').

[192] See Editorial Comments, 'Whither the Stability and Growth Pact' (2004) 41 CML Rev 1193; Amtenbrink and De Haan (n 190 above); and J-V Louis, 'The Review of the Stability and Growth Pact' (2006) 43 CML Rev 85.

The EMU project does not have a direct impact on domestic labour law, largely because labour law matters were (controversially) excluded from its scope. However, EMU has indirect effects on domestic labour law. There are two main factors at work. First, EMU has increased the interdependence of national economies. Second, EMU has constrained the freedom of action of the Member States. Eurozone Member States have lost the power to make adjustments in their exchange and interest rates, and all Member States have, at least to an extent, had their spending constrained by the provisions on the coordination of economic policy. The risks of competitive deregulation in the labour law field are, as we shall see in greater detail in chapter 5 below, exacerbated by the existence of EMU.

Conclusions

The integrationist rationale is concerned with the establishment and functioning of the market in Europe. At its core, it is concerned with the elimination of barriers to free movement and distortions of competition. At its periphery, it encompasses any other action which assists in the market-building process.

The above subsections serve to make clear that the scope of the integrationist rationale is contested. There is an unresolved tension between two extreme positions: one which suggests that it is disparities between national rules which create impediments to the establishment and functioning of the market (such disparities may, depending on the context, be seen as either barriers to free movement or distortions of competition), and a second which is tolerant of the existence of national regulatory diversity.

The main purpose of the analysis in this section has been to shed light on the different approaches which have, at various times in the EU's history, been adopted by key institutional actors. As we will see in more detail in later chapters, the institutions have been anything but consistent in their approach to the challenges of integration, adopting very different perspectives to the task of constructing a European market, reflecting very different ideological positions. The Court has a tendency to view disparities between national rules as problematic, and as a result imposes an obligation on States to justify their policy choices. The political institutions appear unconcerned by the existence of national diversity. This section has begun to examine the rationales for, and merits of, intervention strategies centred on mutual recognition, harmonization, minimum standard setting, regulatory competition, and more controlled systems of regulatory differentiation, such as coordination and reflexive harmonization. Chapters 4 and 5 take this analysis further in the labour law context.

The argument advanced here is that mere differences between the laws of the Member States need not be regarded as creating either barriers to free movement or distortions of competition. The *Keck* test for the barrier to free movement, and conceptions III, IV, and V of the distortion of competition, allow for the preservation of some degree of national autonomy. Nevertheless, the integrationist rationale operates to constrain the diversity between national systems in a number of different ways. My analysis of the barrier to free movement and the distortion of competition suggest that it is important for the integration of markets within Europe that mobile factors of production have equal access to all national markets and that the potential adverse consequences of regulatory competition are managed. My analysis of EMU suggests that the EU needs to take heed of the fact that a consequence of the centralization of monetary policy and the coordination of certain aspects of economic policy is that States may be constrained in their ability to spend or invest in the labour law arena. EU intervention may therefore be required in order to ease the pressure on States to deregulate in the labour law arena.

The Relationship Between the Integrationist Rationale and the Economic and Social Rationales

The relationship between the integrationist and the economic and social rationales is complicated. In this section, I explain the various ways in which the three rationales may intersect.

First, the market-building endeavour cannot be understood 'without recognizing that a market is not organized by itself, but always operates within a political and legal framework that provides the rules of the game'.[193] The market-building endeavour will, inevitably, involve the making of a number of choices which are political in nature,[194] each of which may have significant economic and social implications. My analysis of the various limbs of the integrationist rationale illustrates this point. The definitions of the barrier to free movement and the distortion of competition are, as we have seen, far from straightforward. Choices between the *Dassonville* and *Keck* tests for the barrier to free movement and between the two perspectives of the distortion of competition have significant economic and social ramifications. Economic and social concerns are openly brought into the fabric of the integration process, first to the extent that Member States are called upon to justify rules which fall within the scope of the free movement provisions of the Treaty, and second to the extent that the market structure and structural policy perspective on the definition of the distortion of competition are accepted.[195] But even, or perhaps especially, in situations in which economic and social concerns are not explicitly brought to the fore, it is important to be alert to the fact that they are an integral part of the integration process.[196]

---

[193] M Egan, *Constructing a European Market* (OUP, Oxford 2001) 2.

[194] See eg L Tsoukalis, 'The JCMS Lecture: Managing Diversity and Change in the European Union' (2006) 44 JCMS 1, 5, 8.

[195] The implications for domestic labour law are considered in chs 4 and 5 below.

[196] See eg M Maduro, 'Europe's Social Self: "The Sickness Unto Death" ' in J Shaw (ed), *Social Law and Policy in an Evolving European Union* (Hart, Oxford 2000) 325, 328.

Second, as stated above, the integrationist rationale is of a different order than the economic and social rationales. Article 2 EC makes it clear that integration is pursued not as an end in itself, but rather as a means through which other—essentially economic or social—ends are to be realized. What may be termed the meta-objective of intervention under the integrationist rationale is economic and/or social. Thus, the distinction made in this book between, on the one hand, the integrationist, and on the other, the economic and social rationales, is a rather subtle one. The distinction is between the achievement of economic and social objectives through the pursuit of European integration (such intervention is termed integrationist), and the achievement of the same objectives through other means (such intervention is termed economic and/or social).

Interestingly, under the Treaty establishing a Constitution for Europe (TeCE), it is more difficult to establish the nature of the relationship between integration and the values and objectives of the Union. The Union's 'values' are listed in Article I-2.[197] The Union's objectives are listed in Article I-3. Article I-3 is divided into five paragraphs. The first refers to the promotion of 'peace, its values and the well-being of its peoples'. The second states that 'the Union shall offer its citizens an area of freedom, security and justice without internal frontiers, and an internal market where competition is free and undistorted'. Integration is presented as an end in itself. There is no link between the second paragraph and the third, which lists economic and social objectives, and does so rather more fully than the existing Article 2 EC.[198] The fourth paragraph relates to the Union's relations with the wider world, while the fifth states that 'the Union shall pursue its objectives by appropriate means, depending on the extent to which the relevant competences are conferred upon it in the Constitution'. There has been some speculation concerning the way in which judges might interpret the Constitution, given that the old 'frame of reference' would be superseded.[199] It is certainly true that the Constitution no longer makes it clear that the integrationist project has economic and social meta-objectives. Perhaps this is assumed. However, it is also true, as discussed above, that the Preamble to the Treaty establishing a Constitution for Europe is rather less suggestive of the primacy of integration over diversity than

---

[197] Art I-2 TeCE reads as follows: 'The Union is founded on the values of respect for human dignity, liberty, democracy, equality, the rule of law and respect for human rights, including the rights of persons belonging to minorities. These values are common to the Member States in a society in which pluralism, non-discrimination, tolerance, justice, solidarity and equality between women and men prevail.'

[198] Art I-3(3) TeCE reads as follows: 'The Union shall work for sustainable development of Europe based on balanced economic growth and price stability, a highly competitive social market economy, aiming at full employment and social progress, and with a high level of protection and improvement of the quality of the environment. It shall promote scientific and technological advance. It shall combat social exclusion and discrimination, and shall promote social justice and protection, equality between women and men, solidarity between generations and protection of the rights of the child. It shall promote economic, social and territorial cohesion, and solidarity among Member States. The Union shall respect its rich cultural and linguistic diversity, and shall ensure that Europe's cultural heritage is safeguarded and enhanced.'

[199] T Koopmans, 'Guest Editorial: In Search of Purpose' (2005) 42 CML Rev 1241, 1243.

the existing Treaties. All in all, it is impossible to avoid the conclusion that the market building endeavour involves the making of political choices, and that, if Europe ever comes to operate under the new frame of reference provided by the Constitution, those political choices should be made with regard to the economic and social objectives outlined in the Constitution.

Third, it is in this context worth paying some attention to the distinction between 'the establishment' and 'the functioning' of the market in Europe. Action to establish a single market in Europe is integrationist. But as the market becomes progressively established, it becomes more difficult to maintain a clear distinction between integrationist measures designed to improve the functioning of the market, and economic measures designed to improve the EU's economic performance. My argument here is not, and I want to be explicit on this point, that the integrationist rationale will in the fullness of time run its course. The single market in Europe will never be complete. There will always be a role for interventions premised on the integrationist rationale to, for example, remove barriers to free movement and distortions of competition which may arise at any time as a result of the policy choices of Member States and perhaps also of individual enterprises. To the extent that institutions are intervening so as to make the market function more like a single, integrated unit, they are acting on the basis of the integrationist rationale; even if their interventions are concerned with 'market management' rather than 'market building'.[200] To the extent that they are intervening to improve economic performance but not by making the market function more like a single, integrated unit, for example by encouraging States to take a more active approach to the problem of unemployment, they are acting on the basis of the economic rationale. In practice, and in particular as the market becomes more integrated, it may be extremely difficult, if not impossible, to see the distinction.

The proximity between the integrationist and the economic and social rationales is also apparent in the discussion on EMU. The EMU project involves not only a centralized monetary policy, but also—and this can be attributed to the acceptance, by key actors at a key time, of the coronation theory of monetary union—the coordination of Member States' economic policies. As will be seen below in the sections on the economic and social rationales, once economic policies were coordinated at the European level, there were strong calls for the coordination of other aspects of States' policies, including their employment policies and various aspects of their social policies.[201] In fact, since 2005, the Broad Economic Policy and Employment Guidelines have been integrated, as part of the relaunch of the Lisbon Strategy.[202] But how is one to classify these interventions? My decision to classify EMU as integrationist was made because of the fact that the introduction

[200] cf B Fitzpatrick, 'Straining the Definition of Health and Safety' (1997) 26 ILJ 115, 116–19.
[201] This 'spill-over' is familiar from the neo-functionalist analysis of European integration; see eg E Haas, *Beyond the Nation State* (Stanford University Press, Stanford 1964).
[202] See Brussels European Council, Presidency Conclusions, 22 and 23 March 2005.

of a single currency makes the EU (or, at any rate, the eurozone) function more like a single, integrated market. It eliminates barriers to free movement and, at least according to some analyses, distortions of competition. I also treat the coordination of economic policies as integrationist, simply because the Treaty and the institutions have treated the coordination of economic policies as a necessary part of the EMU project. The coordination of employment and social policies is included within the economic and social rationales, rather than the integrationist rationale, for similar reasons; according to the Treaty, the coordination of employment and social policies is not part of the EMU project. This classification is, of course, controversial,[203] and I am aware that I may be accused of allowing the Treaty to have too much influence over my analytical framework. My response to such an accusation would be two-fold. First, the wording of the Treaties (and the practice of the institutions) is, to my mind, the natural starting-point for any attempt to classify the rationales for EU intervention. Second, and more important, my hope is that the detailed analysis of each of the rationales provokes thought about the scope and extent of EU intervention under each of the rationales. This book is successful if it makes readers think about the potential, and limitations, of each of the three rationales. It aims to provoke readers to think, for example, about whether EMU may or should be classified as integrationist or economic, and about the extent to which the coordination of economic, employment, social, and environmental policies may or should be treated as a necessary part of the EMU project.

In relation to the relationship between the three rationales, there are two issues which are of fundamental importance. The first is the debate over the nature and scope of the integrationist project. The second is the debate over the extent to which the EU is, and should be, doing something more than 'mere' market building. The first debate is internal to the integrationist rationale. It takes many forms. It may, for example, be about the extent to which the European single market does and should tolerate regulatory diversity, the measures which are and should be taken to ensure the proper functioning of the market, or the limits of the EMU project. The second, analytically distinct question, is about the extent to which the EU is, and should be, basing its policy decisions on the economic and social, rather than the integrationist, rationale. It is to that debate which I now turn.

The Economic Rationale

Where the institutions intervene under the economic rationale, they are intervening in order to improve the performance of the European economy, for example by encouraging growth, reducing unemployment, enhancing efficiency, investing

---

[203] See eg Tsoukalis (n 194 above) 6, arguing that monetary union 'needs a more effective coordination of fiscal policies that goes beyond restrictions on budget deficits and Broad Economic Policy Guidelines, usually too broad to have a real effect on national policies'.

in infrastructure, and improving Europe's international competitiveness. As stated in the above section, interventions directed towards the creation of a single market in Europe, which may well be directed towards similar ultimate objectives, are included not within economic, but instead within the integrationist rationale.

The competence of the EU to take action under the economic rationale is both restricted and disputed. Nevertheless, at least since the adoption of the Treaty on European Union in 1992, it has been clear that the EU has some competence to act to improve the performance of the European economy.[204] The objectives outlined in Article 2 EC are to be achieved not only 'by establishing a common market and an economic and monetary union', but also via the 'activities referred to in Articles 3 and 4'. Article 3 EC states that the activities of the Community shall include, among others, 'the promotion of coordination between employment policies of the Member States with a view to enhancing their effectiveness by developing a co-ordinated strategy for employment', 'the strengthening of the competitiveness of Community industry', and 'the promotion of research and technological development'.[205] These activities need not be associated with the establishment and functioning of the market within Europe. They may, therefore, be classified as economic rather than integrationist.

Given that I categorize the coordination of the economic policies of the Member States, together with other aspects of economic and monetary union, as integrationist, and Articles 136 to 145 EC as social,[206] the only economic legal bases under which the institutions have acted so as to produce significant effects on domestic labour law, are those in the Employment Title of the Treaty (Articles 125 to 130 EC). It is under these legal bases that the European Employment Strategy (EES) has operated since 1997.[207] It is obvious even from a cursory reading of these provisions that the competence to intervene is tightly constrained. The institutions are not afforded the competence to enact binding legislation. Instead, their role is to coordinate the employment policies of the Member States. The Employment Title makes it clear that the Member States and the Community should 'work towards developing a coordinated strategy for employment and particularly for

---

[204] The Commission endeavours to ensure that 'we do not rely on market forces to resolve the highly complex problems of achieving higher economic and employment performance'; Commission White Paper 'Growth, Competitiveness, Employment: The challenges and ways forward into the 21st century' COM(93)700, 5 December 1993, 16.

[205] Arts 3(i), (m), and (n) EC. Note that Art 3(i), on the coordination of employment policies, was added only at Amsterdam.

[206] Note that both 'the promotion of employment' and 'the need to maintain the competitiveness of the Community economy' are referred to as objectives of the Community and the Member States in Art 136 EC. It is therefore the case that, as we shall see, economic objectives may be pursued via interventions based on the Social Provisions of the Treaty as well as through interventions based on the Employment Title.

[207] The Employment Title was introduced by the Treaty of Amsterdam, which came into force in 1999. In December 1997, the European Council 'decided that the relevant provisions of the new Title on employment in the Treaty of Amsterdam are to be put into effect immediately'; ensuring that the EES would come into being before the ratification of the Treaty of Amsterdam. See Luxembourg European Council, Presidency Conclusions, 12 and 13 December 1997, [3].

promoting a skilled, trained and adaptable workforce and labour markets responsive to economic change'.[208] Member States are to contribute to these objectives 'in a way consistent with the broad guidelines of the economic policies of the Member States and of the Community adopted pursuant to Article 99(2)';[209] a clause thought to render employment policy logically subservient to economic policy.[210] They are also to regard 'promoting employment as a matter of common concern'.[211] For its part, the Community is to encourage cooperation between Member States, and to support, and if necessary complement, their action. All the while it is to respect the competences of the Member States.[212]

Article 128 EC describes a method of EU intervention which has, since the Lisbon summit in March 2000, come to be known as the open method of coordination (or OMC). The respective roles of the European Council, the Council, the Commission, the European Parliament, the Economic and Social Committee, the Committee of the Regions, the Employment Committee,[213] and the Member States in the OMC process in the employment field are outlined. Each year, on the basis of its annual consideration of the employment situation in the Community, the European Council is to draw up guidelines which the Member States 'shall take into account in their employment policies'.[214] Each Member State is, in turn, to provide the Council and Commission with 'an annual report on the principal measures taken to implement its employment policy in the light of the guidelines'.[215] In the course of its 'examination of the implementation of the employment policies of the Member States in the light of the guidelines for employment', the Council may 'make recommendations to Member States'.[216] Finally, the Council and Commission 'make a joint annual report to the European Council on the employment situation in the Community and on the implementation of the guidelines for employment'.[217]

The OMC applies to a range of different policy areas. The term OMC 'stems from the Lisbon European Council, but draws its inspiration from earlier Council

---

[208] Art 125 EC.   [209] Art 126(1) EC.

[210] See S Ball, 'The European Employment Strategy: The Will But Not The Way' (2001) 30 ILJ 353, 360.   [211] Art 126(2) EC.

[212] Art 127 EC. Article 129 EC authorizes the Council to 'adopt incentive measures designed to encourage cooperation between Member States and to support their action in the field of employment' in a variety of ways, not including the harmonization of the laws of the Member States.

[213] This advisory committee is to promote coordination between Member States on employment and labour market policies; see Art 130 EC. The Committee, which replaced the Employment and Labour Market Committee set up by Council Decision 97/16/EC of 20 December 1996 setting up an Employment and Labour Market Committee [1997] OJ L6/32, was established in January 2000; see Council Decision 2000/98/EC of 24 January 2000 establishing the Employment Committee [2000] OJ L29/21. It collaborates closely with the social partners, in particular with those represented in the Standing Committee on Employment. It has, however, been said that its members (each Member State and the Commission appoint two) 'do not have strong legitimacy to intervene and point out the defects of the procedures'; S Sciarra, 'Integration Through Coordination: The Employment Title in the Amsterdam Treaty' (2000) 6 Columbia Journal of European Law 209, 228.

[214] Art 128(2) EC.   [215] Art 128(3) EC.   [216] Art 128(4) EC.

[217] Art 128(5) EC.

meetings at Luxembourg, Cardiff and Cologne, where a series of supply-sided policy initiatives were set up'.[218] The OMC applies to the coordination of economic policies under Article 99 EC, the coordination of employment policies under Article 128 EC, and in a rather less well-developed form, to the coordination of policies relating to social inclusion, social protection, pensions, and health.[219] It is a method 'designed to help Member States to progressively develop their own policies'. It involves 'spreading best practice and achieving greater convergence towards the main EU goals'. It encompasses:

- fixing guidelines for the Union combined with specific timetables for achieving the goals which they set in the short, medium, and long term;

- establishing, where appropriate, quantitative and qualitative indicators and benchmarks against the best in the world and tailored to the needs of different Member States and sectors as a means of comparing best practice;[220]

- translating these European guidelines into national and regional policies by setting specific targets and adopting measures, taking into account national and regional differences; and

- periodic monitoring, evaluation, and peer review organized as mutual learning processes.[221]

As we shall see, the institutions have placed significant emphasis on the synergies between the various OMC processes and on the fact that they are mutually reinforcing. The intention is that the various coordination processes should work together, in order to help the Community and the Member States to realize their various objectives. As seen above, the coordination of economic policies was seen as a necessary part of the EMU project. It is certainly possible to make an argument to the effect that the coordination of employment and social policies is also necessary, or at least desirable, in that same integrationist context. However, the various coordination processes are better regarded as economic to the extent that they are directed more towards improving the performance of the European economy than towards any aspect of the market-building endeavour.

Articles 2 EC and 2 EU express Europe's economic objectives in only the most general terms. In order to develop a true sense of what the commitment to the economic rationale may or must entail, it is necessary to look beyond the Treaty, to the pronouncements of the institutions. The European Council, which brings together

---

[218] Hodson and Maher (n 187 above) 723.

[219] See P Syrpis, 'Legitimising European Governance: Taking Subsidiarity Seriously within the Open Method of Coordination' (EUI Working Paper Law No 2002/10, Florence 2002), and E Szyszczak, 'Experimental Governance: The Open Method of Coordination' (2006) 12 European Law Journal 486.

[220] Benchmarking methods are 'devised by the Commission, networking with different providers and users, namely the social partners, companies and NGOs'; Lisbon European Council, Presidency Conclusions, 23 and 24 March 2000.

[221] Lisbon European Council, Presidency Conclusions, 23 and 24 March 2000 [37].

the Heads of State and Government and the President of the Commission, and provides the Union 'with the necessary impetus for its development' and defines its 'general political guidelines',[222] has played a decisive role here; though the Commission, Council, European Parliament, and a range of other advisory committees have also contributed to the development of the economic rationale at the European level. In this section I give an overview of the approach which has been adopted, quoting at length from the European Council Presidency Conclusions in order to give a flavour of the rhetoric which has come to dominate this area of policy. The implications for domestic labour law are considered in chapter 5 below.

It is clear that 'following the ratification of the TEU, combating unemployment and encouraging non-inflationary growth became central aims of the newly formed European Union'.[223] There were, and are, two key questions. First, what is the appropriate policy prescription for employment, stability, and growth? Second, at what level, or rather at what levels, should that policy be formulated?

The Commission's White Paper 'Growth, Competitiveness, Employment: The challenges and ways forward into the 21st century',[224] was influential in shaping thinking. However, the more expansionary elements within it, which serve to distinguish it from the OECD's Jobs Study,[225] and which, at least arguably, call for Keynesian economic government at European level, failed to command the support of the Member States,[226] and as a result slipped from the agenda.[227]

The current approach can be traced back to 2000. At Lisbon, the European Council set a new strategic goal for the Union: 'to become the most competitive and dynamic knowledge-based economy in the world, capable of sustainable economic growth with more and better jobs and greater social cohesion'.[228] The implementation of what has come to be known as the Lisbon Strategy was left to the open method of coordination, Europe's experimental new governance strategy,[229] 'with a stronger guiding and coordinating role for the European Council to ensure more coherent strategic direction and effective monitoring of progress'.[230] It was not felt necessary to transfer new competences to the Union.

---

[222] Art 4 EU.

[223] D Ashiagbor, *The European Employment Strategy: Labour Market Regulation and New Governance* (OUP, Oxford 2006) 102.   [224] COM(93)700 (n 204 above).

[225] OECD, *The OECD Jobs Study* (OECD, Paris 1994).

[226] See Essen European Council, Presidency Conclusions, 9 and 10 December 1994.

[227] For an excellent summary, see Ashiagbor (n 223 above) chs 3 and 4. See also J Goetschy, 'The European Employment Strategy: Genesis and Development' (1999) 5 European Journal of Industrial Relations 117.

[228] Lisbon European Council, Presidency Conclusions, 23 and 24 March 2000, [5]. See also Commission Communication, 'The Commission's Work Programme for 2000' COM(2000)155, 9 February 2000, 5: 'The key objective of the new economic and social agenda will be to develop a long-term strategy to build a competitive, innovative and inclusive knowledge-based economy.' In relation to 'better' jobs, see Stockholm European Council, Presidency Conclusions, 23 and 24 March 2001, [26].

[229] Szyszczak (n 219 above).

[230] Lisbon European Council, Presidency Conclusions, 23 and 24 March 2000 [7].

At Lisbon, the European Council set out its analysis of the Union's strengths and weaknesses. Its analysis provides a useful indication of the context within which the Lisbon Strategy was born, and is quoted here in full:

The Union is experiencing its best macro-economic outlook for a generation. As a result of stability-oriented monetary policy supported by sound fiscal policies in a context of wage moderation, inflation and interest rates are low, public sector deficits have been reduced remarkably and the EU's balance of payments is healthy. The euro has been successfully introduced and is delivering the expected benefits for the European economy. The internal market is largely complete and is yielding tangible benefits for consumers and businesses alike. The forthcoming enlargement will create new opportunities for growth and employment. The Union possesses a generally well-educated workforce as well as social protection systems able to provide, beyond their intrinsic value, the stable framework required for managing the structural changes involved in moving towards a knowledge-based society. Growth and job creation have resumed.

These strengths should not distract our attention from a number of weaknesses. More than 15 million Europeans are still out of work. The employment rate is too low and is characterised by insufficient participation in the labour market by women and older workers. Long-term structural unemployment and marked regional unemployment imbalances remain endemic in parts of the Union. The services sector is underdeveloped, particularly in the areas of telecommunications and the Internet. There is a widening skills gap, especially in information technology where increasing numbers of jobs remain unfilled. With the current improved economic situation, the time is right to undertake both economic and social reforms as part of a positive strategy which combines competitiveness and social cohesion.[231]

The Lisbon Strategy is difficult to evaluate. There are doubts over both the policy prescription advanced by the institutions and the mechanisms through which policy is advanced. There are, it seems to me, obvious tensions, which the Commission and Council have consistently failed to acknowledge, between the fiscal conservatism demanded of Member States in the context of economic and monetary union and reflected in the Broad Economic Policy Guidelines (BEPGs), and the pursuit of a vigorous employment policy able to produce more, and better, jobs.[232]

It was felt necessary to relaunch the Lisbon Strategy in 2005. The European Council delivered a damning indictment on progress to date.[233] 'Five years after the launch of the Lisbon Strategy, the results are mixed. Alongside undeniable progress, there are shortcomings and obvious delays. Given the challenges to be met, there is a high price to pay for delayed and incomplete reforms, as is borne

[231] Lisbon European Council, Presidency Conclusions, 23 and 24 March 2000 [3] and [4].

[232] See eg S Deakin and H Reed, 'The Contested Meaning of Labour Market Flexibility: Economic Theory and the Discourse of European Integration', in Shaw (n 196 above) 71, 99: 'as long as the priorities of EMU remain as they are ... there is a danger that the potential of the employment strategy will remain unfulfilled'.

[233] See also Commission Communication to the Spring European Council, Working Together for Growth and Jobs: A New Start for the Lisbon Strategy, COM(2005)24, 2 February 2005.

out by the gulf between Europe's growth potential and that of its economic partners. Urgent action is therefore called for.'[234] The European Council went on to
state that it was essential to 're-focus priorities on growth and employment', and 'to
mobilise all appropriate national and Community resources—including the cohesion policy—in the strategy's three dimensions (economic, social and environmental) so as better to tap into their synergies in a general context of sustainable
development'.[235] Although the OMC was not 'singled out as one of the reasons for
the failure of the Lisbon process to deliver its goals',[236] a key feature of the relaunch
is a simplified arrangement to 'improve the governance of' the Lisbon strategy. Its
aim is said to be threefold: 'to facilitate the identification of priorities while maintaining the overall balance of the strategy and the synergy between its various com-
ponents; to improve the implementation of those priorities on the ground by
increasing the Member States' involvement; and to streamline the monitoring procedure so as to give a clearer picture of national implementation of the strategy'.[237]
As a result, as we will see in chapter 5 below, the Broad Economic Policy and Employment Guidelines have been integrated, and are now based on a three-year cycle.[238]
However, no new competences have been transferred to the EU.

In the 2006 Journal of Common Market Studies Lecture, Loukas Tsoukalis
argues that:

. . . neither the internal market nor EMU has so far succeeded in injecting much-needed
dynamism into many of our national economies. For some time there has been broad agreement among economists and international organizations that Europe needs economic
reform, mostly in the direction of supply-side measures, in order to generate more growth
and more jobs; and this is meant to go beyond the further implementation of the internal
market programme.[239]

The relaunch of the Lisbon strategy involves a reorientation of the EU's policy
along these lines. The pursuit of growth and jobs appears to take precedence over
the both the macro-economic stability which was considered essential in the context of EMU, and measures to complete the internal market. The European institutions recognize that there is a need for the EU and the Member States to act to
improve economic performance in Europe.

The 2006 Presidency Conclusions serve as an example of the new, economic,
orientation of policy. In Part I, the European Council identified the following as
'specific areas for priority action': first, 'investing more in knowledge and innovation', second, 'unlocking business potential, especially of SMEs [small and

---

[234] Brussels European Council, Presidency Conclusions, 22 and 23 March 2005, [4].

[235] ibid [5] and [6]. The environmental dimension can be traced back to the Göteborg European
Council, 15 and 16 June 2001.   [236] Szyszczak (n 219 above) 501.

[237] Brussels European Council, Presidency Conclusions, 22 and 23 March 2005, [38].

[238] See Council Decision 2005/600/EC of 12 July 2005 on Guidelines for the employment policies of the Member States [2005] OJ L205/21; and Council Recommendation 2005/601/EC of 12
July 2005 on the broad guidelines for the economic policies of the Member States and the Community
(2005 to 2008) [2005] OJ L205/28.   [239] Tsoukalis (n 194 above) 3.

medium-sized enterprises]', and third, 'increasing employment opportunities for priority categories'.[240] In Part II, it began the process of defining an energy policy for Europe, aiming at increasing the security of supply, ensuring competitiveness, and promoting environmental sustainability. Only in Part III of the Conclusions, titled 'maintaining momentum across the board', did it turn its attention to 'ensuring sound and sustainable public finances',[241] 'completing the internal market and promoting investment',[242] 'enhancing social cohesion' and 'environmentally sustainable growth'.

This section has demonstrated that the EU is able to act so as to improve the performance of the European economy. But the EU's competence under the economic rationale is both restricted and disputed. The restrictions come about as a result of the fact that, at least under the Employment Title of the Treaty, the political institutions only have the competence to coordinate the policies of the Member States via the open method of coordination. The EU acts 'as an external catalyst and facilitator rather than a law-maker'.[243] The disputes arise because it is often difficult to determine whether particular interventions are, or should be, classified as economic, integrationist, or indeed social. The relationship between the economic and integrationist rationales has already been discussed. The coordination of employment (or indeed social) policies may be classified as integrationist to the extent that one of the following propositions may be advanced successfully. If the convergence of employment or social policies is necessary for the success of the single currency, then, so long as the achievement of EMU is classified as integrationist, so too is the coordination of employment or social policies. Alternatively, if it is held that the coordination, but not convergence, of employment or social policies is necessary so as to ensure (a) fiscal discipline within the euro area and (b) that States have the flexibility to deal with asymmetric shocks, then, again so long as the achievement of EMU is classified as integrationist, so too is the coordination of employment or social policies. Finally, given the coordination of economic policies and the restrictions inherent in the Stability and Growth Pact, it may be that the coordination of employment or social policies is necessary to prevent an aggravated risk of regulatory competition leading to a

[240] Priority categories are the young, women, older workers, persons with disabilities, and legal migrants and minorities; Brussels European Council, Presidency Conclusions, 23 and 24 March 2006 [34].
[241] In this context, the European Council calls on Member States to use the evolving economic recovery to pursue fiscal consolidation in line with the Stability and Growth Pact [52]. It urges States to improve the sustainability of their welfare systems, and meet the economic and budgetary consequences of ageing [53]. It underlines the need to improve the efficiency and effectiveness of public spending and taxes [54]. It also identifies the need for effective policy coordination to ensure fiscal discipline and flexibility to deal with asymmetric shocks, in particular within the euro area [55].
[242] The European Council states that 'the extension and deepening of the internal market is a key element for achieving the aims of the renewed Strategy' [56]. Particular emphasis is placed on making the internal market for services 'fully operational, while preserving the European social model, by securing a broad agreement on the Services Directive' [57]. The proposed Services Directive is discussed in ch 5 below.   [243] Tsoukalis (n 194 above) 4.

'race to the bottom'. In this context, their coordination would again be regarded as integrationist. Of course, the flip-side of this is that in the absence of arguments linking the coordination of employment (or social) policies with the market-building endeavour, or in the event of the failure of such arguments to command institutional or academic support, employment policies are best regarded as being based on the economic (or the social) rationale.

The remainder of this chapter deals with the social rationale. The next section outlines the social rationale for EU intervention, concentrating on the uneven evolution of competence under the social provisions of the Treaty. The final section examines the relationship between the economic and social rationales. As we shall see, the economic and social rationales intersect in two important ways. First, there are debates about whether high social standards, traditionally seen as burdens on business, might instead contribute towards the competitiveness and dynamism of the economy (ie debates about the extent to which the social can contribute to the economic). Second, there are debates about whether the social provisions of the Treaty may, or should, be used to promote economic rather than social objectives (ie debates about the extent to which the social may have come to be subsumed by the economic).

The Social Rationale

Interventions based on the social rationale aim to improve the position of workers. While the economic rationale calls for measures which improve the performance of the European economy, the social rationale is concerned with the distribution of the benefits derived from improved economic performance. The existence of the social rationale reflects the perceived need to intervene for the benefit of workers. As Davies argues, there is an 'acceptance within the "European social model" that the worker is the weaker party to the employment relationship and that labour regulation performs a legitimate function in protecting that weaker party'.[244] In this section I discuss the evolution of the social provisions of the Treaty, and discuss the different ways in which the social rationale may be conceptualized.

The evolution of the Social Provisions of the EC Treaty

The competence of the institutions to act under the social rationale is disputed. Those advocating interventions based on the social rationale have had to challenge the assumption, which is embedded in the Treaty of Rome, that the establishment of a common market in Europe leads to the upward harmonization of

[244] P Davies, 'Posted Workers: Single Market or Protection of National Labour Law Systems?' (1997) 34 CML Rev 571, 597–8.

national social and labour law systems.[245] The Treaty of Rome did not give the institutions specific competence to act in the labour law field, other than in relation to the elimination of specific distortions of competition. The protection of workers was left, in the first instance, to the operation of the market, and then to the Member States, whose powers to intervene in the social field, it was (wrongly) assumed, would be untouched by the integration process.

The need for European level action in the social field was first acknowledged in the 1970s.[246] However, by the end of that decade, market orthodoxy had returned. Only in the mid to late 1980s did the tide turn decisively. In 1989, the European Parliament stated that 'market forces should not be allowed to determine the social framework conditions of the internal market'.[247] Also in 1989, the European Community's Charter of the Fundamental Social Rights of Workers was adopted. It represents the assertion 'that the completion of the internal market could not be achieved without fully recognising that the aspirations, the interests and thus the rights of Europe's citizens—especially the workers—needed to be guaranteed'.[248] Experience seems to have taught the institutions that the market mechanism may, of itself, be an insufficient guarantor of social progress.[249]

As a result of these changes in approach, successive amendments to the EC Treaties granted the institutions a secure, expanding, though still restricted, competence to

---

[245] See Art 117 EEC. It states that improved working conditions and an improved standard of living for workers will ensue, in part, from the functioning of the common market, which will favour the harmonization of social systems. Giubboni claims that the 'illuminist notion of a natural and progressive tendency towards the upward harmonisation of national systems quickly showed itself to be a fatal illusion'; S Giubboni, *Social Rights and Market Freedom in the European Constitution—A Labour Law Perspective* (CUP, Cambridge 2006) 56. Dougan's view is that 'blind faith in the philanthropic benefits of the liberal capitalist model soon passed'; M Dougan, 'Minimum Harmonization and the Internal Market' (2000) 37 CML Rev 853, 857.

[246] See B Hepple, 'The Crisis in EEC Labour Law' (1987) 16 ILJ 77, 79: 'the official turning point was the declaration of Heads of Governments in October 1972'.

[247] European Parliament Resolution on the social dimension of the internal market (A2-399/88), 15 March 1989 [1989] OJ C96/61, 64. Streeck argues that the 'social dimension' project relied 'on an assumed functional necessity for markets to be socially regulated'; W Streeck, 'Neo-Voluntarism: A New European Social Policy Regime?' (1995) 1 European Law Journal 31, 43.

[248] Vasso Papandreou, then Commissioner for Employment, Industrial Relations and Social Affairs, in Commission, *Social Europe 1/90* (OOPEC, Luxembourg 1990) 8. With the adoption of the European Community's Charter of the Fundamental Social Rights of Workers 'the member states (minus UK) explicitly accepted that the European Community should consist not only of institutions making free competition possible, but also of institutions regulating matters concerning industrial relations'; C Jensen, J Madsen, and J Due, 'Phases and dynamics in the development of EU industrial relations regulation' (1999) 30 Industrial Relations Journal 118, 125. Note, however, that the Preamble to the Charter states that 'the completion of the internal market is the most effective means of creating employment and ensuring maximum well-being in the Community'.

[249] Similarly, OECD, *Trade, Employment and Labour Standards: A Study of Core Workers' Rights and International Trade* (OECD, Paris 1996) starts 'from the premise that market forces alone cannot automatically improve observance of core labour standards'; Commission Report pursuant to Article 7(2) of Council Regulations 3281/94 and 1256/96 on the Scheme of Generalized Preferences: Summary of Work conducted within the OECD, ILO and WTO on the link between international trade and social standards, COM(97)260, 2 June 1997, 4.

intervene for the achievement of social objectives.[250] In this section, I discuss the uneven way in which this competence has developed, focusing on Articles 136 and 137 EC, Article 141 EC, and Article 13 EC.

The Single European Act 1986 introduced what was Article 118a—now incorporated within Article 137 EC—the first Article under which the institutions were given competence to legislate in the area of labour law.[251] It granted them a restricted competence in the health and safety field. The Agreement on Social Policy attached to the TEU increased the competence of the institutions. However, under the TEU, the UK was granted a controversial opt-out. For many academic commentators, the opt-out appeared 'to conflict with fundamental principles upon which the Community legal order is based'.[252] Its legality was questioned, as was the Community character of legislation adopted under the Agreement on Social Policy.[253] Although the Protocol and Agreement on Social Policy were expressed to be 'without prejudice to the provisions of this Treaty, particularly those which relate to social policy which constitute an integral part of the *acquis communautaire*',[254] commentators were alert to the fact that the opt-out might create both barriers to free movement and distortions of competition.[255] The opt-out certainly operated so as to undermine any attempt to ensure that standards throughout the EU conform to a particular baseline level,[256] or to prevent competitive deregulation by Member States; indeed, the British Government's position was explicitly inspired by the desire to steal a competitive march on the rest of Europe.[257] It also meant that for six years the institutions were not able to intervene under the Agreement on Social Policy so as to improve the performance of the British economy or improve the position of British workers. In view of the clear opposition of the British Government,

[250] These are also reflected in changes to Arts 2 and 3 EC, and Art 2 EU.

[251] 'The Community ... enjoys an internal legislative competence in the area of social policy'; Opinion 2/91 [1993] ECR I-1061 [17], discussing Art 118a EC.

[252] E Whiteford, 'Social Policy after Maastricht' (1993) 18 ELR 202, 220. See also B Bercusson, 'The dynamic of European labour law after Maastricht' (1994) 23 ILJ 1.

[253] See C Barnard, 'A Social Policy for Europe: Politicians 1:0 Lawyers' (1992) 8 International Journal of Comparative Labour Law and Industrial Relations 15.

[254] For more on the relationship between the Agreement on Social Policy and the *acquis communautaire* see D Curtin, 'The Constitutional Structure of the Union: A Europe of Bits and Pieces' (1993) 30 CML Rev 17, 52–61.

[255] See B Fitzpatrick, 'Community Social Law after Maastricht' (1992) 21 ILJ 199, 203; and U Everling, 'Reflections on the Structure of the European Union' (1992) 29 CML Rev 1053, 1066, arguing that the Agreement on Social Policy 'is a questionable breach of the unity of Community law, on which the Court of Justice has always put so much emphasis, and could lead to distortions of competition'.

[256] The DGB, a German trade union, 'warned that it would be prepared to challenge the exclusion of the United Kingdom from the Treaty's social provisions on the grounds of unfair competitive advantage'; M Rhodes, 'The Social Dimension after Maastricht: Setting a New Agenda for the Labour Market' (1993) 9 International Journal of Comparative Labour Law and Industrial Relations 297, 301. In this formulation, everything hinges on the definition of the 'unfair' competitive advantage.

[257] The UK Government stated in 1992 that it believed that the Agreement on Social Policy 'is unnecessary and counterproductive and could jeopardize jobs and employment throughout the Community by jeopardizing the competitive position of the Community in the global market'; see House of Lords Select Committee on the EC (1991–1992), 7th Report [130].

and with the agreement of the governments of the other Member States, EU labour law did not extend fully to the UK.[258]

The Treaty of Amsterdam incorporated the Agreement on Social Policy into the main body of the EC Treaty, thereby ending the UK labour law opt-out, and made some amendments to the Social Provisions of the Treaty. These were further amended by the Treaty of Nice. What are now Articles 136 and 137 EC draw on both the Agreement on Social Policy and the old Article 117 EEC. This makes their meaning, even in a grammatical sense, rather obscure,[259] and forms the basis for much of my criticism of the provisions.

Article 136 EC outlines the objectives of the Community and the Member States in the social field.[260] It provides that the Community and the Member States:

> . . . **having in mind fundamental social rights such as those set out in the European Social Charter signed at Turin on 18 October 1961** and in the 1989 Community Charter of the Fundamental Rights of Workers, shall have as their objectives the promotion of employment, improved living and working conditions, *so as to make possible their harmonisation while the improvement is being maintained*, proper social protection, dialogue between management and labour, the development of human resources with a view to lasting high employment and the combating of exclusion.

> To this end the Community and the Member States shall implement measures which take account of the diverse forms of national practices, in particular in the field of contractual relations, and the need to maintain the competitiveness of the Community economy.

> *They believe that such a development will ensue not only from the functioning of the common market, which will favour the harmonisation of social systems, but also from the procedures provided for in this Treaty and from the approximation of provisions laid down by law, regulation or administrative action.*[261]

In the sections which are based on the old Article 117 EEC, Article 136 EC refers to the harmonization of living and working conditions, even the harmonization of social systems. These references to harmonization were not included in the Agreement on Social Policy, and they do not appear to be consistent either with the requirement, also in Article 136 EC, that the Community and the Member States take account of the diverse forms of national practices, or with the statement that provisions adopted under Article 137 EC 'shall not prevent Member States from maintaining or introducing more stringent protective measures compatible with the Treaty'.[262] This unwelcome confusion between harmonization and minimum standard setting—and the text of Article 136 EC is an illustration of an all-too-common tendency—is discussed in chapter 5 below, in which attention is paid to both social and integrationist implications.

---

[258] In relation to flexible integration, see also Art 11 EC, and the safeguards therein.

[259] L Betten, 'The Democratic Deficit of Participatory Democracy in Community Social Policy' (1998) 23 ELR 20, 27.   [260] See also Art 2 and 3 EC, and Art 2 EU.

[261] The section in bold was introduced at Amsterdam. The sections in italics are from the old Art 117 EEC. The remaining sections are from the Agreement on Social Policy.   [262] Art 137(4) EC.

With a view to achieving the objectives of Article 136 EC, the Community is given specific competences in Article 137 EC. Article 137 EC describes the types of EU intervention which are permitted in particular policy areas, and lays down the accompanying policy-making procedures. Under Article 137(2) EC, the Council may act in one of two ways.

First, under Article 137(2)(a) EC, added only at Nice, it 'may adopt measures designed to encourage cooperation between Member States through initiatives aimed at improving knowledge, developing exchanges of information and best practices, promoting innovative approaches and evaluating experiences, excluding any harmonization of the laws and regulations of the Member States'. The competence to act in this way extends to all the fields mentioned in Article 137(1) EC. In relation to the combating of social exclusion and the modernization of social protection systems (Articles 137(1)(j) and (k) EC) the Community may only act in this way, as in these fields the power to adopt minimum requirements by means of directives is explicitly excluded.[263] This provision has paved the way for the development of OMC processes in the social field.[264]

Second, under Article 137(2)(b) EC, it may adopt 'by means of directives, minimum requirements for gradual implementation, having regard to the conditions and technical rules obtaining in each of the Member States'. With regard to improvement in particular of the working environment to protect workers' health and safety; working conditions; the information and consultation of workers; the integration of persons excluded from the labour market without prejudice to Article 150; and equality between men and women with regard to labour market opportunities and treatment at work,[265] the Council has the competence to act 'in accordance with the procedure referred to in Article 251 of the Treaty, after consulting the Economic and Social Committee and the Committee of the Regions'.[266] With regard to social security and social protection of workers; protection of workers where their employment contract is terminated; representation and collective defence of the interests of workers and employers, including co-determination, subject to paragraph 5; and conditions of employment for third-country nationals legally residing in Community territory, it is more difficult for the Council to act. In these fields, the Council can only act unanimously, after consulting the European Parliament and the relevant committees.[267]

---

[263] See Arts 137(1) and (2) EC.   [264] The OMC is analysed in detail in ch 5 below.

[265] Art 137(1) EC.

[266] Art 137(2) EC. Art 251 EC describes the complex 'codecision' procedure involving the Commission, the European Parliament, and the Council, under which unanimity in the Council is not required. The obligation to consult the Committee of the Regions (see Arts 263–265 EC) was introduced by the Treaty of Amsterdam.

[267] Note that amendments agreed at Nice mean that a unanimous Council may decide to render the 'codecision' procedure applicable to three of these four fields. The exception is in relation to social security and the social protection of workers, which will remain subject to the unanimity rule.

Articles 138 and 139 EC provide for an alternative way for the institutions to intervene in domestic labour law.[268] Management and labour—the so-called social partners—are consulted on the possible direction and content of any envisaged proposal advanced under Article 137 EC.[269] What is interesting and innovative is that the Treaty goes on to afford the social partners the opportunity to play a much more significant role. If the social partners inform the Commission of their wish to initiate the process provided for in Article 139 EC, the dialogue between them at Community level may lead to contractual relations, including agreements. 'Agreements concluded at Community level shall be implemented either in accordance with the procedures and practices specific to management and labour and the Member States or, in matters covered by Article 137, at the joint request of the signatory parties, by a Council decision on a proposal from the Commission.'[270]

The final paragraphs of Article 137 EC place some restrictions on the competence of the institutions. Article 137(4) EC states that provisions adopted pursuant to Article 137 'shall not affect the right of Member States to define the fundamental principles of their social security systems and must not significantly affect the financial equilibrium thereof',[271] and also, as mentioned above, that they 'shall not prevent Member States from maintaining or introducing more stringent protective measures compatible with the Treaty'. The most significant restriction—at least as far as the realization of social objectives is concerned—is imposed by Article 137(5) EC. It provides that 'the provisions of this Article shall not apply to pay, the right of association, the right to strike or the right to impose lock-outs'. The precise scope of the restriction has yet to be determined.[272]

Two further social legal bases are considered in this book. Article 141(3) EC is concerned with gender equality, and Article 13 EC with anti-discrimination law. Article 141(3) EC, introduced at Amsterdam, affords the Council the power to 'adopt measures to ensure the application of the principle of equal opportunities and equal treatment of men and women in matters of employment and occupation, including the principle of equal pay for equal work or work of equal value'.[273] It is located within the social provisions of the Treaty, but is beyond the

---

[268] See further A Lo Faro, *Regulating Social Europe: Reality and Myth of Collective Bargaining in the EC Legal Order* (Hart, Oxford 2000); and T Novitz and P Syrpis, 'Assessing Legitimate Structures for the Making of Transnational Labour Law: The Durability of Corporatism' (2006) 35 ILJ 367.

[269] Arts 138(2) and (3) EC.   [270] Art 139(2) EC.

[271] Art 137(4) EC as amended at Nice.

[272] The scope of the restriction is considered in B Ryan, 'Pay, Trade Union Rights and European Community Law' (1997) 13 International Journal of Comparative Labour Law and Industrial Relations 305, 310–16. He concludes that Art 137(5) EC limits the competence of the Community to legislate in relation to pay and trade union rights, not only under Art 137 EC but also under Art 94 EC.

[273] Amsterdam also introduced Art 3(2) EC, the so-called 'mainstreaming' clause, which provides that in all its activities, 'the Community shall aim to eliminate inequalities, and to promote equality, between men and women'.

legislative remit of the social partners.[274] Article 13 EC, also introduced at Amsterdam, reads as follows: 'Without prejudice to the other provisions of this Treaty and within the limits of the powers conferred by it upon the Community, the Council, acting unanimously on a proposal from the Commission and after consulting the European Parliament, may take appropriate action to combat discrimination based on sex, racial or ethnic origin, religion or belief, disability, age or sexual orientation.' Unlike the other social legal bases, it is located in Part One of the Treaty, alongside Article 12 EC which prohibits discrimination on grounds of nationality and Articles 17 to 22 EC on citizenship of the Union.[275] 'The impression generated is that Article 13 now forms a core component of the essential social objectives of the Union' and 'a key element of the rights of Union citizens'.[276] However, the reference in Article 13 EC to the limits of the powers conferred by the Treaty,[277] indicates that EU anti-discrimination law will retain, at least until the competence of the institutions is decisively extended beyond the world of work, a strong link with participation in the labour market.

Under the Treaty Establishing a Constitution for Europe, there are almost no changes to the social provisions of the Treaty.[278] In the Constitution-making process, Working Group XI, whose remit was Social Europe, argued that existing competences were 'adequate'. Its view was that 'that European action, which should support and supplement the activities of the Member States, should primarily concern areas of action closely linked to the functioning of the internal market, preventing distortions of competition, and/or areas with a considerable cross-border impact'.[279]

Conceptions of the social rationale

As stated above, the social rationale for EU intervention is underdeveloped. Articles 2 EC and 2 EU outline the social objectives of the EU in only the most general terms, and give no indication of the way in which the balance between the EU's economic and social objectives is to be struck. Article 136 EC is similarly vague. This lack of specificity is damaging. First and foremost, it affects the capacity and willingness of the institutions to act on the basis of the social rationale.

---

[274] Kenner argues that this is 'a tacit acknowledgement perhaps of the need to separate sex equality at work from the corporatist mode of social policy governance'; J Kenner, *EU Employment Law: From Rome to Amsterdam and beyond* (Hart, Oxford 2002) 387.

[275] Under the TeCE, Art III-124 TeCE, which is almost identical to Art 13 EC, is to be found in Title II 'Non-Discrimination and Citizenship' of Part III 'The Policies and Functioning of the Union' of the Treaty.

[276] See M Bell, *Anti-Discrimination Law and the European Union* (OUP, Oxford 2002) 121.

[277] In Art III-24 TeCE the relevant phrase is 'within the limits of the powers assigned to it by the Union'. [278] The social policy provisions are Arts III-209 to III-219 TeCE.

[279] Final Report of Working Group XI on Social Europe, CONV 516/1/03 REV 1, 4 February 2003, 17.

But it also affects the operation of the integrationist rationale. European integration is pursued not for its own sake, but in order to realize the objectives of the EU and its Member States. If those objectives are unclear, then the criteria which influence the ways in which the political choices inherent in any market-building exercise fall to be made, will also be unclear.[280]

There are a variety of conceptual lenses through which the social rationale might be analysed.[281] At its most basic, the social rationale is about the protection of workers.[282] Workers, it is said, need protection because of the imbalance of power inherent in the employment relationship.[283] Their interests may be protected either through the development of substantive standards which protect workers' interests, or alternatively through the development of procedures and systems through which workers can bargain or negotiate with employers on equal, or at least more equal, terms.

But the social rationale may also be conceptualized in other ways. It may, for example, be about the preservation of the values associated with the 'European social model'; a concept to which the European Council has made increasing reference in recent years, perhaps in part because of its malleability.[284] In this context, ideas such as solidarity,[285] cohesion, and distributive justice may come to the fore. The relationship between the economic and the social, discussed below, assumes great significance, as does the relationship between workers and other groups within society who may also make legitimate claims for the State's assistance. As Maduro has argued, 'debates on efficiency versus distributive justice never have been peaceful and are not likely to be in the context of a "contested" European political community whose degree of cohesion and solidarity can only be said to be weak'.[286] Alternatively, the social rationale, especially in so far as the

---

[280] eg Fredman argues that ever since 'the EU has come to recognise its own role in the protection and promotion of social rights' it has had 'the potential to act as a powerful engine buttressing social rights against the "race to the bottom" created by competitive forces'; S Fredman, 'Transformation or Dilution: Fundamental Rights in the EU Social Space' (2006) 12 European Law Journal 41, 41. See also M Maduro, 'Europe's Social Self: "The Sickness Unto Death"' in J Shaw (ed), *Social Law and Policy in an Evolving European Union* (Hart, Oxford 2000) 325.

[281] See eg B Hepple, 'Social Values and European Law' (1995) 48 Current Legal Problems 39.

[282] Hepple distinguishes between the broad 'fundamental rights' approach exemplified by Art 119 [now 141 EC], and the more limited 'employment protection' approach exemplified by the Collective Redundancies and Acquired Rights Directives; B Hepple, 'The Implementation of the Community Charter of Fundamental Social Rights' (1990) 53 MLR 643, 649.

[283] See P Davies and M Freedland, *Kahn-Freund's Labour and the Law* (3rd edn, Stevens, London 1983) 18.

[284] 'The European Social Model is based on good economic performance, a high level of social protection and education and social dialogue'; Barcelona European Council, Presidency Conclusions, 15 and 16 March 2002, [22]. See also C Crouch, *Industrial Relations and European State Traditions* (Clarendon, Oxford 1993); and F Scharpf, 'The European Social Model: Coping with the Challenges of Diversity' (2002) 40 JCMS 645.

[285] See eg T Hervey, 'Social Solidarity: A Buttress Against Internal Market Law', in Shaw (n 280 above) 31; and M Dougan and E Spaventa (eds), *Social Welfare and EU Law* (Hart, Oxford 2005).

[286] Maduro (n 280 above) 341.

participation of management and labour in the law-making process and the involvement of workers in the decision-making structures of enterprises are concerned, may be linked with democracy.[287] But most significant in the EU context, have been the various attempts to harness the powerful languages of 'rights' and of 'citizenship' to the social rationale.

The language of rights is increasingly important in the EU context.[288] As early as 1970, the Court of Justice recognized, under pressure from national constitutional courts, that 'respect for human rights forms an integral part of the general principles of Community law protected by the Court of Justice'.[289] Initially, the Court drew inspiration from the common constitutional traditions of the Member States and from international treaties for the protection of human rights on which Member States collaborated or of which they are signatories; notably the European Convention for the Protection of Human Rights and Fundamental Freedoms (ECHR), signed in Rome in 1950. The obligation to respect fundamental rights was given a Treaty basis by Article 6 EU (introduced at Maastricht and amended at Amsterdam). In December 2000, a Charter of Fundamental Rights for the EU was solemnly proclaimed.[290] It forms Part II of the Treaty establishing a Constitution for Europe.[291] Although the Charter is not legally binding—its fate is now very much entwined with that of the Constitutional Treaty—it has had some influence, in particular on the Opinions of Advocates General and decisions of the Court of First Instance and, more recently, on the Court of Justice.[292]

Of particular interest in the context of the development of the social rationale for EU intervention, is the extent to which the EU's commitment to human rights extends to social rights. One significant step forward was taken in 1989, when the

---

[287] See R Dahl, *A Preface to Economic Democracy* (Polity Press, Cambridge 1985). 'Democracy in industry means fair participation by those who work in the decisions vitally affecting their lives and livelihoods'; C Summers, 'Models of Employee Representational Participation' (1993–1994) 15 Comparative Labor Law Journal 1, quoting Senator Wagner, the architect of the US National Labour Relations Act (1935). See further S Smismans, *Law, Legitimacy, and European Governance: Functional Participation in Social Regulation* (OUP, Oxford 2004), and A Mitchell, 'Industrial Democracy: Reconciling Theories of the Firm and State' (1998) 14 International Journal of Comparative Labour Law and Industrial Relations 3.

[288] G De Búrca, 'The language of rights and European integration' in J Shaw and G More (eds), *New Legal Dynamics of European Union* (Clarendon, Oxford 1995) 29; and P Alston (ed), *The EU and Human Rights* (OUP, Oxford 1999).

[289] Case 11/70 *Internationale Handelsgesellschaft* [1970] ECR 1125.

[290] On the Convention process employed in the drafting of the Charter, see G De Búrca, 'The Drafting of the EU Charter of Fundamental Rights' (2001) 26 ELR 126. See also Fredman (n 280 above) 55, who argues that 'in deciding to initiate a process of establishing a Charter of Fundamental Rights, the EU as a collectivity was clearly signifying that its *raison d'être* extended beyond the original economic aims'.

[291] Art I-9 of the TeCE provides that the Union 'shall recognise the rights, freedoms and principles set out in the Charter of Fundamental Rights which constitutes Part II'.

[292] See, eg, Case C-173/99 *Ex p BECTU* [2001] ECR I-4881, Opinion of AG Tizzano; and Case C-540/03 *European Parliament v Council* [2006] ECR I-5769 [38]. Academic opinion on the Charter is divided: cf J Weiler, 'A Constitution for Europe: Some Hard Choices' (2002) 40 JCMS 563, 576, and M De La Torre, 'The Law Beneath Rights' Feet' (2002) 8 European Law Journal 513.

European Council, minus the UK,[293] solemnly declared the Community Charter of Fundamental Social Rights of Workers. The Community Charter, accompanied by a Commission Action Programme,[294] is said to have 'acted as a catalyst for wider and deeper integration' and 'helped to broaden the Community's social objectives beyond the narrow confines of Articles 117–122 EEC'.[295]

The distinction between, on the one hand, civil and political, and on the other, social, rights merits close attention.[296] The Council of Europe makes a sharp distinction between the two sets of rights. Civil and political rights are protected via the ECHR, social rights only via the Social Charter, which has an inferior enforcement mechanism.[297] The Council of Europe's distinction is reflected within the EU. While the ECHR is referred to in Article 6 TEU, the only reference to the European Social Charter is in Article 136 EC. More importantly, the fundamental rights which derive from the former, though not the latter, instrument are said to be 'general principles of Community law'. Advocate General Jacobs has stated that 'the mere fact that a right is included in the [European Social] Charter does not mean that it is generally recognised as a fundamental right. The structure of the Charter is such that the rights set out represent policy goals rather than enforceable rights, and the States parties to it are required only to select which of the rights specified they undertake to protect'.[298]

The Charter of Fundamental Rights may represent something of a breakthrough from this perspective.[299] The Preamble states that 'the Union is founded on the indivisible, universal values of human dignity, freedom, equality and solidarity', indicating that social rights are to be given the same status as civil and political rights. However, it remains difficult to evaluate the contribution of the Charter.[300] Leaving the concerns about its legal status to one side,[301] there are

---

[293] See B Hepple, 'Social Rights in the European Community: A British Perspective' (1990) 11 Comparative Labor Law Journal 425.

[294] Commission Communication concerning its Action Programme relating to the Implementation of the Community Charter of Basic Social Rights for Workers, COM(89)568, 29 November 1989.

[295] Kenner (n 274 above) 152.

[296] On the distinction, see TH Marshall, *Citizenship and Social Class* (CUP, Cambridge 1950) 10. On the use of rights rhetoric in the labour law context, see T Novitz, *International and European Protection of the Right to Strike* (OUP, Oxford 2003); P Alston (ed), *Labour Rights as Human Rights* (OUP, Oxford 2005); and Fredman (n 280 above).

[297] See T Novitz, 'Remedies for Violation of Social Rights within the Council of Europe: The Significant Absence of a Court', in C Kilpatrick, T Novitz, and P Skidmore (eds), *The Future of Remedies in Europe* (Hart, Oxford 2000) 231.

[298] Case C-67/96 *Albany International* [1999] ECR I-5751 Opinion of AG Jacobs, [146].

[299] See M Gijzen, 'The Charter: A Milestone for Social Protection in Europe?' (2001) 8 Maastricht Journal 33.

[300] See the range of views expressed in T Hervey and J Kenner (eds), *Economic and Social Rights under the EU Charter of Fundamental Rights* (Hart, Oxford 2003). See also D Ashiagbor, 'Economic and Social Rights in the European Charter of Fundamental Rights' (2004) 1 European Human Rights Law Review 62; and Fredman (n 280 above) 55–60.

[301] B De Witte, 'Legal Status of the Charter: Vital Question or Non-Issue' (2001) 8 Maastricht Journal 81.

significant questions relating to the way in which social rights are formulated,[302] and also difficult issues arising as a result of the general provisions of the Charter, Articles 51 to 54.[303]

Like 'rights', 'citizenship' also has potential in so far as the development of the social rationale is concerned.[304] The TEU contains provisions on 'citizenship of the Union',[305] making it clear that citizenship of the Union is to complement, rather than replace, national citizenship, and giving Union citizens a number of rights. Article 18(1) EC is perhaps the most important of the citizenship provisions. It provides that 'every citizen of the Union shall have the right to move and reside freely within the territory of the Member States, subject to the limitations and conditions laid down in this Treaty and by the measures adopted to give it effect'.[306] The limitations and conditions clause has been thought to limit the personal scope of citizenship rights to economically active citizens who are able to participate in the market. This limited form of citizenship has been characterized as 'market citizenship',[307] which is contrasted with a broader and more inclusive form of 'social citizenship',[308] which, as Bell acknowledges, 'remains more an aspiration than a reality'.[309]

The languages of rights and of citizenship are rich in potential.[310] They are employed by the institutions because they inspire trust and commitment. They are capable of contributing to the development of the social rationale, but also capable of creating gains in terms of 'public allegiance to the integration process'.[311] They may therefore contribute to the realization of integrationist, as well social, objectives.

The Relationship Between the Economic and the Social Rationales

The final section of this chapter considers the relationship between the economic and the social rationales. As mentioned above, Article 2 EC outlines the task of the Community. It makes reference to a whole host of economic and social objectives,

---

[302] See Lord Goldsmith, 'A Charter of Rights, Freedoms and Principles' (2001) 38 CML Rev 1201, emphasizing the differences between the way in which civil, political, and social rights are protected in the text of the Charter.

[303] See R García, 'The General Provisions of the Charter of Fundamental Rights of the European Union' (2002) 8 European Law Journal 492.

[304] See eg J Shaw, 'The Interpretation of Union Citizenship' (1998) 61 MLR 293; N Reich, 'Union Citizenship: Metaphor or Source of Rights' (2001) 7 European Law Journal 4; and D Chalmers *et al*, *European Union Law* (CUP, Cambridge 2006) ch 13.   [305] Arts 17–22 EC.

[306] See Directive 2004/38/EC of 29 April 2004 on the right of citizens of the Union and their family members to move and reside freely within the territory of the Member States [2004] OJ L158/77.

[307] See M Everson, 'The legacy of the market citizen' in Shaw and More (n 288 above) 73.

[308] See B Fitzpatrick, 'Straining the Definition of Health and Safety' (1997) 26 ILJ 115, 117.

[309] Bell (n 276 above) 15–16.

[310] For more cautious approaches, see J Weiler, *The Constitution of Europe* (CUP, Cambridge 1999); and C Barnard, 'EC "Social" Policy' in P Craig and G De Búrca (eds), *The Evolution of EU Law* (OUP, Oxford 1999) 479.   [311] Bell (n 276 above) 14.

but does not indicate how they are to be prioritized.[312] The impression one gets from reading the Treaties—and, as we shall see, this impression is reinforced by reading the recent policy documents of the European institutions—is that there is no conflict between the economic and social (or indeed environmental) goals.

This view of the relationship between the economic and the social is controversial.[313] In this section, I first examine the extent to which there is perceived to be a positive relationship between high social standards and improved economic performance.[314] Next, I move on to examine the extent to which policy-making in the social field has become dominated by an economic discourse, highlighting the dangers of such a trend.

The traditional (neo-classical) view is that high labour standards are, or may be, damaging to the economy. They create rigidities in the labour market, and are likely to an adverse impact on both employment and competitiveness. This view gained widespread political acceptance, in the UK at least, during the Thatcher years.[315] Deregulation and flexibility were called for in order to inject dynamism into the economy and to improve Europe's economic performance relative to that of its main competitor—the US. Against this background, advocates of EU labour law were forced to engage with economic arguments. Labour law initiatives were defended from the charge that they would create burdens on business and would therefore be more likely to harm than to protect the interests of workers. More than that, new institutional perspectives on regulation were used to suggest that an efficiency argument could be made for legal regulation of the labour market.[316] Under this approach, attention is directed towards the fact that private ordering may lead to sub-optimal outcomes,[317] that there may be a tendency towards

---

[312] Much the same point could be made about the Treaty establishing a Constitution for Europe. There is no indication that there may be tension between the various objectives expressed in Art I-3 TeCE.

[313] See also B Langille, 'Seeking Post-Seattle Clarity—and Inspiration' in J Conaghan, R Fischl, and K Klare (eds), *Labour Law in an Era of Globalization: Transformative Practices and Possibilities* (OUP, Oxford 2002) 137, 147–56. He argues that on a 'pragmatic and strategic' view, 'the normative foundations of the economic and the social are different, and indeed contradictory, and the problem of governance is one of strategically managing these fundamental contradictions'. On a 'deeper' view, 'there is an integration, not segregation of the economic and the social'. On this view 'our normative architecture does not rest on two foundations but one'.

[314] For fuller treatments of this debate, see D Ashiagbor, *The European Employment Strategy: Labour Market Regulation and New Governance* (OUP, Oxford 2006) ch 1; and S Deakin and F Wilkinson, 'Rights vs. Efficiency? The Economic Case for Transnational Labour Standards' (1994) 23 ILJ 289.

[315] See S Fredman, 'The New Rights: Labour Law and Ideology in the Thatcher Years' (1992) 12 OJLS 24.

[316] See R Coase, 'The problem of social cost' (1960) 3 Journal of Law and Economics 1; and R Coase, *The Firm, the Market and the Law* (University of Chicago Press, Chicago 1988). See also A Ogus, *Regulation—Legal Form and Economic Theory* (Clarendon, Oxford 1994) chs 2–4; and M Rhodes, 'The Social Dimension of the Single European Market: National versus Transnational Regulation' (1991) 19 European Journal of Political Research 245, 247–52.

[317] See G Majone, 'The European Community Between Social Policy and Social Regulation' (1993) 31 JCMS 153. See also K Gatsios and P Seabright, 'Regulation in the European Community' (1989) 5 Oxford Review of Economic Policy 37, 39, arguing that 'the diagnosis of market failure is

damaging short-termism in the unregulated decisions of enterprises,[318] and that labour market institutions may therefore be viewed as governance mechanisms designed to enhance efficiency.[319] Deakin and Wilkinson argue that labour standard setting can, in general, operate as a guarantor of economic development, and as an incentive for enterprises, for example, to seek to compete not on the basis of low wages, but on the basis of product innovation.[320] Sengenberger states that 'innovation and dynamism are not derived from making labour resources cheaper, but from making labour more effective, productive and innovative. While enlightened firms may follow this advice independently, commonly agreed standards are needed to diffuse the productive impact of good labour use on a wider scale'.[321] The result of this approach is that social rights are 'reconceptualised, not as burdens on business, but as essential contributors to economic efficiency'.[322]

By the mid-1990s, the political landscape had changed. A 1996 OECD Report gave a boost to those who argue that international competitiveness is not improved by the lowering of social standards.[323] The Report focussed on 'core' labour standards: freedom of association and collective bargaining, elimination of exploitative forms of child labour, prohibition of forced labour, and non-discrimination in employment. The analytical part of the study concluded that 'developing countries must not fear that core labour standards would negatively affect their economic performance or their international competitive position'.[324]

The institutions also shifted their thinking.[325] In the 1990s, the Commission began to argue that 'economic and social progress must go hand in hand',[326] and

never sufficient to establish a case for regulatory intervention. For there are regulatory failures too'. See further B Langille, 'Eight Ways to think about International Labour Standards' (1997) 31(4) Journal of World Trade 27.

[318] See W Hutton, *The State We're In* (Jonathan Cape, London 1995) ch 6.

[319] See Ashiagbor (n 314 above) 22–8.

[320] Deakin and Wilkinson's argument for regulation adopts the view that unregulated markets are characterized by high transaction costs which derive from limited information and the bounded rationality of economic agents. It builds on Coase's view that State regulation should not be ruled out *a priori*. See S Deakin and F Wilkinson, 'Labour Law and Economic Theory: A Reappraisal' in G De Geest, J Siegers, and R Van den Bergh (eds), *Law and Economics and the Labour Market* (Edward Elgar, Cheltenham 1999) 5–8.

[321] W Sengenberger, 'International Labour Standards in a globalized economy: The issues' in W Sengenberger and D Campbell (eds), International Labour Standards and Economic Interdependence (International Institute for Labour Studies, Geneva 1994) 3, 10.

[322] Fredman (n 280 above) 41.

[323] OECD, *Trade, Employment and Labour Standards: A Study of Core Workers' Rights and International Trade* (OECD, Paris 1996).

[324] Commission Communication, 'The Trading System and Internationally Recognized Labour Standards' COM(96)402, 24 July 1996, 9.

[325] In the 1970s, the relationship between the social and the economic was thought to be much more confrontational. The Commission, for example, argued that its proposal for the Collective Redundancies Directive had to find an acceptable 'compromise between the workers' legitimate interest in security of employment and the understandable interest that the employers have in safeguarding a certain liberty of action with regard to personnel questions'; (1973) 4 Institute for Labour Relations Bulletin, 173.

[326] Commission White Paper, 'European Social Policy—A Way Forward for the Union' COM(94)333, 27 July 1994, 2.

that 'social progress is possible only through economic success but equally high social standards are a vital part of building a competitive economy'.[327] It also claimed that 'social policy and economic performance are not contradictory but mutually reinforcing'.[328] In 1994, the European Parliament disputed the notion that 'a social policy carried out at European level must be halted because it may be a burden or cost on society, believing instead that it is an essential prerequisite for economic prosperity and the proper functioning of markets'.[329] In 1997, the European Council observed a positive relationship between 'job creation, employability and social cohesion'.[330]

Since the dawn of the new millennium, what may be termed Third Way ideology,[331] has dominated EU thinking. 'Captured in the concept of the "modernised European social model", the aim is a synthesis between economic and social policy, market and state'.[332] As we shall see in the course of this book, Third Way rhetoric is pervasive. In order to get behind the rhetoric, it is necessary to examine the policy choices made by various institutional actors in concrete situations.[333] For, despite the rhetoric, 'the challenge of restructuring the economy while preserving the "European social model" is a daunting one'.[334] Somewhere along the line, conflicts between the economic and the social, or to put this in another way, between the interests of capital and labour, are inevitable. Hard choices cannot be avoided. Lord Wedderburn puts it characteristically well: 'the social can of course contribute to competitiveness, but when it conflicts with the economic, whatever the rhetoric, it has few friends'.[335] The impact of the ideological synthesis between the economic and social in concrete situations is examined in chapter 5 below.

---

[327] Commission Green Paper on European Social Policy: Options for the Union, COM(93)551, 17 November 1993, 14.

[328] Commission Communication, 'Modernising and Improving Social Protection in the European Union' COM(97)102, 12 March 1997, 1. The Community is committed to the promotion of 'improved working conditions ... as a key element in the search for improved competitiveness'; Commission Medium Term Social Action Programme 1995–97, COM(95)134, 12 April 1995, 15.

[329] European Parliament Resolution on the Green Paper entitled: 'European Social Policy—Options for the Union' (A3-0270/94), 3 May 1994 [1994] OJ C205/80.

[330] Amsterdam European Council, Presidency Conclusions, 16 June 1997.

[331] See A Giddens, *The Third Way* (Polity Press, Cambridge 1998); and J Kenner, 'The EC Employment Title and the "Third Way": Making Soft Law Work?' (1999) 15 International Journal of Comparative Labour Law and Industrial Relations 33.

[332] Fredman (n 280 above) 44. See in particular Commission Communication, 'Social Policy Agenda' COM(2000)379, 28 June 2000; Commission Communication on the Social Agenda, COM(2005)33, 9 February 2005; and the Lisbon European Council, Presidency Conclusions, 23 and 24 March 2000.

[333] See W Däubler (ed), *Market and Social Justice in the EC—the Other Side of the Internal Market* (Bertelsmann Foundation, Gutersloh 1991) 45: 'It is striking that the less decision-making powers an institution has, the stronger its social policy commitment is reflected in its declarations and drafts'.

[334] D Trubek and L Trubek, 'Hard and Soft Law in the Construction of Social Europe: the Role of the Open Method of Co-ordination' (2005) 11 European Law Journal 343, 345.

[335] Lord Wedderburn, *Labour Law and Freedom: Further Essays in Labour Law* (Lawrence and Wishart, London 1995) 391.

It is possible either that this linkage between the economic and the social will occur in the context of an activist social policy, or that it will mask the sacrifice of social objectives on the altar of economic efficiency. Most labour lawyers see few grounds for optimism. Barnard argues that 'the development of the Community's "social" policy is constrained—perhaps fatally—by the need to operate within both an economic and a social framework'.[336] Fredman's view is that 'the power of the market will always subordinate social rights where there is a conflict with efficiency, unless there is a bedrock of fundamental rights that owe their genesis to fairness and justice for its own sake, rather than as a means to efficiency ends'.[337]

I strongly endorse the view that it is important to pursue social objectives for their own sake, and not just as a means to economic ends.[338] There are, as has been explained in the course of this chapter, many regulatory choices which have to be made in the construction of the new Europe. Unless labour lawyers offer their critical, normative perspective—based on a conception of the social rationale—labour law as a discipline 'may dissolve into simply another economistic exercise of evaluation of the efficiency of market regulation'.[339]

---

[336] Barnard (n 310 above) 501.   [337] Fredman (n 280 above) 46.

[338] See also Deakin and Wilkinson (n 314 above) 310: 'The case for fundamental employment rights must rest, in the final analysis, on factors which lie beyond any purely economic calculus'.

[339] H Collins, 'Labour law as a Vocation' (1989) 105 LQR 468, 482. See also Ashiagbor (n 314 above) 50–1, 91–2.

3

Competence Questions

Introduction

In chapter 2 above, I laid out the parameters of three broad rationales for intervention in domestic labour law and examined where a commitment to each of the three rationales might lead. This chapter is concerned with the necessity, propriety, and desirability of EU level intervention in order to achieve integrationist, economic, and social objectives. The discussion might be thought to be dry and legalistic. If something is worth doing, and is able to realize particular policy objectives, does it matter whether it is done at the national or the European level?

I contend that it does. The EU is a multi-layered (or rather, in that it is less suggestive of a hierarchical relationship between different levels of governance, multi-centred) democracy, experimenting with various federal governance patterns.[1] It is suffering from what might be termed a legitimacy crisis.[2] It has, for a number of years now, been trying to engage more closely with its citizens.[3] The rejection of the Treaty establishing a Constitution for Europe in the French and Dutch referenda is of course difficult to interpret, but it is clear that 'the existence of a permissive consensus underpinning the essentials of the European project can no longer be taken for granted'.[4] The EU—an international unit of governance trying to establish a role for itself on the world stage and, as such, more sensitive to legitimacy concerns than are well-established nation states—must, as a matter of urgency, respond to the legitimacy crisis.

There are in my view two dimensions to the challenge encountered by the EU. These may be termed horizontal and vertical. The horizontal dimension directs attention towards the legitimacy of each level, or centre, of governance. In the EU context it calls specifically for 'better' decision-making at the EU level. Of course, it is not easy to establish the criteria according to which the quality of decision-making should be assessed. One criterion relates to what Neil Walker has termed

---

[1] See K Nicolaidis and R Howse (eds), *The Federal Vision: Legitimacy and Levels of Governance in the United States and the European Union* (OUP, Oxford 2001); and N Bernard, *Multilevel Governance in the European Union* (Kluwer, The Hague 2002).

[2] P Syrpis, 'Legitimising European Governance: Taking Subsidiarity Seriously within the Open Method of Coordination' (EUI Working Paper Law No 2002/10, Florence 2002) 1–11.

[3] See in particular, Laeken European Council, Presidency Conclusions, 14 and 15 December 2001, Annex I.   [4] See G De Búrca, 'After the Referenda' (2006) 12 European Law Journal 6, 7.

performance legitimacy. It involves an enquiry into the effectiveness of intervention and the ability to deliver policy goals. Both the choice of policy priorities and their realization are important. A second criterion relates to what Walker terms 'regime legitimacy', and involves a consideration of the pattern of political organization and the representative quality of the governing institutions.[5] Democratic arguments, of various types, dominate here. Performance and regime legitimacy are said to combine to generate polity legitimacy, which is more abstract and intangible. It is an 'umbrella term' which relates to the extent to which entities meet 'certain minimal conditions of political community'. 'A polity enjoys legitimacy qua polity to the extent that its putative members treat it as a significant point of reference within their political identity'.[6] The horizontal dimension is addressed in chapter 5 below. Attention is devoted not only to the way in which the integrationist, economic, and social rationales have been conceptualized and to the relationships between them; but also to the policy-making processes and governance strategies employed at European level.

This chapter is concerned with the vertical dimension of the legitimacy challenge. It examines which powers are, and should be, allocated to and exercised by each level or centre of governance. The focus is on the relationship between the EU and the Member States—though of course the relationship between national and sub-national levels,[7] and between the EU and global organizations such as the WTO and ILO,[8] is also of great significance. The powers of the EU are limited. The EU only has the power to act in so far as it is granted that power in the Treaties, by its constituent Member States.[9] According to Article 5(1) EC, the Community 'shall act within the limits of the powers conferred upon it by this Treaty and of the objectives assigned to it therein'. Articles 5(2) and (3) EC insist Community action must also be in conformity with the principles of subsidiarity and proportionality. These principles are intended to guide the institutions in relation to the exercise of the competence they have been granted in the Treaties, inviting them to consider whether their interventions are necessary and appropriate, and whether they might be overly intrusive. My contention is that respect for subsidiarity and proportionality may contribute in significant ways to the elimination of the legitimacy deficit in the European Union.

Debates about the vertical dimension of the EU's legitimacy challenge are complicated because of the fact that it is, in many instances, not possible or indeed desirable to draw clear lines between the respective spheres of influence of the European institutions and the Member States, especially in the context of the new

---

[5] N Walker, 'The White Paper in Constitutional Context' in C Joerges, Y Meny, and J Weiler (eds), *Mountain or Molehill? A Critical Appraisal of the Commission White Paper on Governance* (RSC Jean Monnet Working Paper No 6/01, Florence 2001) 33, 33.   [6] ibid, 36–7.

[7] S Tierney, *Constitutional Law and National Pluralism* (OUP, Oxford 2004).

[8] G De Búrca and J Scott (eds), *The EU and the WTO: Legal and Constitutional Issues* (Hart, Oxford 2001); and T Novitz, 'The European Union and International Labour Standards: The Dynamics of Dialogue Between the EU and the ILO' in P Alston (ed), *Labour Rights as Human Rights* (OUP, Oxford 2005) 214.   [9] A Dashwood, 'The Limits of EC Powers' (1996) 21 ELR 113, 114.

approaches to governance discussed in chapter 5 below. Action at different levels is able to combine in a variety of mutually beneficial ways. 'The imposition of an inflexible division between Union and state competences is likely to harm the EU's capacity to fulfil its mission by denying it an adaptable and efficiently-functioning system of governance that properly implicates several levels'.[10] As the Commission has stated, 'the real challenge is establishing clear rules for how competence is shared—not separated'.[11] Principles for the sharing of competence may not yield the clarity at least superficially associated with principles relating to its division—but in this case, the best solution is not the clearest. Actors at various levels are, and should be, involved in the planning, making, execution, and implementation of all decisions. Nevertheless, the fact that competence is shared does not mean that subsidiarity and proportionality become redundant. Far from it. They may be used as guiding principles in order to help fashion what will inevitably be a complex relationship between actors at various levels and to delineate their respective roles within an essentially cooperative process.

This chapter is structured in the following way. The first section examines the arguments for and against centralization in the particular context of today's EU. The aim is to show that a strong case can be made for the maintenance of a certain degree of autonomy at the level of the Member States. The next three sections examine the principles of conferral, subsidiarity, and proportionality. Although subsidiarity and proportionality have, to date, had 'little visible purchase in braking an EC institutional culture loaded in favour of legislative centralisation',[12] the argument advanced in the final section of the chapter is that a vigorous application of both principles has the potential to contribute to the enhanced legitimacy of EU intervention in domestic labour law.

Arguments For and Against Centralization in Today's EU

Ultimately, however, all such efforts to generate an ideal allocation of competences end up plagued by radical indeterminacy. Whether in the case of social welfare, economic development, or culture, there are good arguments that can be made for centralization, and good ones for decentralization too.[13]

Nicolaides and Howse go on to argue that there is a 'need to situate the debates about decentralization, devolution and subsidiarity in a broader theoretical context', and suggest that such a context may be 'provided through the optic of legitimacy'.[14]

In this section, the concept of legitimacy is used to shed light on the strength of the arguments for and against centralization in today's EU. In addition, attention is directed towards the implications which the commitments inherent in the

---

[10] S Weatherill, 'Better Competence Monitoring' (2005) 30 ELR 23, 30.
[11] Commission, 'European Governance: A White Paper' COM(2001)428, 25 July 2001, 35.
[12] Weatherill (n 10 above) 26.   [13] Nicolaidis and Howse (n 1 above) 3.   [14] ibid.

European project have for the debate on the proper allocation and exercise of competence. The aim of the chapter is relatively modest. Using some arguments which apply to federal systems in general and others which are specific to today's EU, I aim to show that the case for Member State autonomy is strong enough to warrant that the principles of subsidiarity and proportionality should play a full role in debates about the allocation and exercise of competence in today's EU.

The first stage of this enquiry involves an analysis of whether action at Member State or European level (or indeed some combination of the two) is more likely to score highly in performance, regime, and ultimately polity legitimacy terms.

First, performance legitimacy. The question here relates to the level at which policy goals are more likely to be delivered effectively, or to put this in another way, the level at which the preferences of the people are more likely to be satisfied. All other things being equal, it is easier to identify the preferences of the people in a small community. Thus, again with the proviso that all other things are equal, it should be easier to satisfy the preferences of a small population. Moreover, distance from specific practical situations may reduce the capacity to make wise regulatory decisions.[15] Any emergent presumption in favour of the performance legitimacy of smaller units of governance becomes stronger if it can be shown that the preferences of the people are more homogenous within the smaller community. The European context is, of course, relevant here. There are a whole host of historical, institutional, cultural, geographical, linguistic, social, and economic considerations which make preferences more homogenous within each Member State than they are within Europe as a whole.[16] Differences between the Member States will, in the short term at least, be exacerbated by the Eastern enlargement of the EU. To the extent that Member States are able to satisfy the (relatively homogenous) preferences of their populations, they score highly in performance legitimacy terms.

However, there are arguments which suggest that interventions at EU level may boost performance legitimacy. First, it is not just the Member States but also Europe itself which has 'a strong sense of regional and, very broadly, cultural identity'.[17] Second, reasonable pluralism, so clearly a feature of European life,[18] does not disappear at the boundaries of individual Member States. Conflict between rich and poor and left and right occurs, with refreshing regularity, even within Member States. Third, as a result of the internal market project and EMU—and,

---

[15] S Simitis and A Lyon-Caen, 'Community Labour Law: A Critical Introduction to its History' in P Davies *et al* (eds), *European Community Labour Law: Principles and Perspectives; Liber Amicorum Lord Wedderburn* (Clarendon, Oxford 1996) 1, 10.

[16] G Bermann, 'Taking Subsidiarity Seriously: Federalism in the European Community and the United States' (1994) 94 Columbia Law Review 331, 335, 449.

[17] G Bermann, 'Editorial: The European Union as a Constitutional Experiment' (2004) 10 European Law Journal 363, 364. The preservation (and modernization) of the 'European social model' is one example of particular relevance in the social field: F Scharpf, 'The European Social Model: Coping with the Challenges of Diversity' (2002) 40 JCMS 645.

[18] M Everson, 'Adjudicating the Market' (2002) 8 European Law Journal 152.

more broadly, the pressures of globalization—the capacity of States to satisfy the preferences of their populations is reduced. In chapter 2 above, I examined the budgetary and fiscal constraints under which national policy is now conducted and explained the existence of pressure on States to deregulate the labour market.[19] And fourth, EU intervention may lead to policies which are better able to meet the preferences of the people. States may lack the experience, expertise, know-how, or capacity necessary to deal with particular challenges and to implement the resulting policies. Certain fundamental problems may best be solved within a supranational framework, detached from 'immediate national constraints and political contingencies'.[20] Within the European context, it may, for example, be that dialogue, learning, and cooperation, not only between States, but also between States, European institutions, and a variety of other actors at global, regional, and local levels (such as, in relation to social matters, the International Labour Organization, the representatives of the social partners, and civil society) may, in various ways, lead to enhanced performance legitimacy. The EU may, for example, enable or, in one of a number of ways, facilitate Member States' achievement of particular objectives. Alternatively, it may act as a forum in which relevant actors are better able to identify, or align, their policy priorities. Where, for whatever reason, States acting alone are unable to satisfy the preferences of their populations, their performance legitimacy will progressively be undermined and arguments for European intervention will be strengthened.

Second, regime legitimacy. The questions here relate to representation, participation, and accountability; ie to the democratic credentials of the Member States and the EU.[21] The starting presumption is the same here as it is in relation to performance legitimacy. Other things being equal, individuals are more likely to be better represented, to have greater opportunities for participation, and to be better able to hold policy-makers to account in small political communities.[22] The

[19] Roger Van den Bergh, writing from a law and economics perspective, seeks to answer questions relating to the ways in which competence should be shared between decision-makers at various levels by employing criteria of economic efficiency. He concludes that 'the best choice is a mixed system, which leaves competences at the Member State level if the benefits of diversity [between legal regimes] outweigh the costs of externalities and opportunistic manipulation'; R Van den Bergh, 'The Subsidiarity Principle in European Community Law: Some Insights from Law and Economics' (1994) 1 Maastricht Journal 337, 354.

[20] J Goetschy, 'The European Employment Strategy: Genesis and Development' (1999) 5 European Journal of Industrial Relations 117, 132. Similar arguments are advanced in relation to the independence and credibility of the ECB; see J De Haan, F Amtenbrink, and S Waller, 'The Transparency and Credibility of the European Central Bank' (2004) 42 JCMS 775.

[21] See G Fox and B Roth (eds), *Democratic Governance and International Law* (CUP, Cambridge 2000); and D Held, *Democracy and the Global Order: From the Modern State to Cosmopolitan Governance* (Polity Press, Cambridge 1995).

[22] Stein argues that in relation to all international organizations seeking 'to meet the democracy-legitimacy requirement . . . dispersion of the organization's central power should be sought through reliance on regional and local authorities, and the principle of subsidiarity should be honored'; E Stein, 'International Integration and Democracy: No Love at First Sight' (2001) 95 American Journal of International Law 489, 532–3.

presumption in favour of smaller units of governance becomes stronger if it can be shown that the Member States are better placed than the EU in regime legitimacy terms. Mattias Kumm argues as follows:

The federalism stakes are higher in Europe than in the USA. The United States is a well established democratic nation with strong federal democratic institutions, a well established public sphere, and a strong collective identity. There is generally no comparatively strong identity shared by the inhabitants of the several states in the USA. In the European Union the situation is the inverse. Whereas there are strong identities connected to most Member States, many of whom are old European nations, European democratic institutions, as well as the sociological underpinnings that make democracy meaningful—a European public sphere and a European identity—are largely underdeveloped. More is lost when decision-making is ratcheted upwards from the Member States to the European level.[23]

But once again, there are arguments in favour of EU intervention. Member States have a number of democratic limitations which may be attributed to growing economic and social interdependence. National polities no longer control all the decision-making procedures which impact upon the lives of those on their territory. Similarly, they can no longer make provision for the participation and representation of all those who are affected by their decisions.[24] Locational competition may even create a 'structural bias of the democratic process' leading to incentives not to impose costs on mobile factors, and creating a shift of the burdens and costs of regulation to those parts of the population who do not have a meaningful exit option.[25] In this context it is also necessary to be aware of democratic innovations at European level. Attention should be paid to the identity of the parties involved and the nature of the policy-making processes. New approaches to governance are of particular relevance.[26]

Finally, polity legitimacy. In polity legitimacy terms, the Member States retain an enduring appeal. Europe has no *volk*, no *demos*, no polity, and no straightforward way of inspiring the commitment of its citizens. Europe is a Union of 'distinct peoples, distinct political identities, distinct political communities'.[27] We are at the stage of the integration process where the *demoi* (peoples) continue to think in terms of 'us and them'. The process through which old *demoi* start to think simply in terms of 'us'—in other words, to think of the federal community as their polity—takes time.[28] We may be waiting a long time for social borders to be

---

[23] M Kumm, 'Constitutionalising Subsidiarity in Integrated Markets: The Case of Tobacco Regulation in the European Union' (2006) 12 European Law Journal 503, 526–7.
[24] See M Maduro, 'Europe and the Constitution: What if this is as Good as it Gets?' (Con WEB No 5/2000) <http://les1.man.ac.uk/conweb>, 9.   [25] Kumm (n 23 above) 513.
[26] J Scott and D Trubek, 'Mind the Gap: Law and New Approaches to Governance in the European Union' (2002) 8 European Law Journal 1.
[27] J Weiler, 'Federalism Without Constitutionalism: Europe's *Sonderweg*' in Nicolaidis and Howse (n 1 above) 54, 67.
[28] A Estella, *The EU Principle of Subsidiarity and its Critique* (OUP, Oxford 2002) 47–53.

reconfigured and for there to be a transfer of loyalties to the supranational plane.[29] Nevertheless, the fact that the identity claims of the Union do not (yet) resonate in the political consciousness of its citizens,[30] is not necessarily damaging to the European project. There is, for example, 'no reason to presume that civic solidarity will find its limits at the borders of the Nation State'.[31] The absence of a European *demos* should encourage the EU to find innovative ways of engaging with the people, and not to rely on the bonds of nationality and ethnicity.[32]

Thus, arguments from legitimacy do not point clearly towards either the States or the Union. In general, smaller units of governance have legitimacy advantages over larger units. In the particular context of today's EU, the legitimacy advantages of the Member States are accentuated because of the comparative homogeneity of each State, their well-established democratic credentials, and the commitment which each State is able to inspire from its citizens. However, there are countervailing arguments. In particular, the increasing interdependence of States adversely affects both their performance and regime legitimacy, and is capable of leading to calls for EU intervention.

This section moves on to consider the implications which the commitments inherent in 'the European project' have for the debate on the proper allocation and exercise of competence. Scharpf's 'federal comity' model is of assistance here. Scharpf argues that European level policy-makers:

... must respect the need for autonomous solutions at the national level that reflect idiosyncratic preferences, perceptions, policy traditions and institutions. At the same time, however, national actors must respect the fact that they are members of a community of nation states that must take each others' interests and the commitment to a common venture into account when arriving at their autonomous solutions.[33]

---

[29] Lessons from the history of American federalism suggest that 'federal systems can smooth over— or cut through—quite profound cultural and political differences over the course of a couple of centuries'; E Young, 'Protecting Member State Autonomy in the European Union: Some Cautionary Tales from American Federalism' (2002) 77 New York University Law Review 1612, 1728.

[30] Walker (n 5 above) 39.

[31] J Habermas, 'So, Why Does Europe Need a Constitution?' (RSC, Florence 2001) 18. See further J Weiler, 'Does Europe Need a Constitution? Demos, Telos and the German Maastricht Decision' (1995) 1 European Law Journal 219; and P Craig, 'Constitutions, Constitutionalism, and the European Union' (2001) 7 European Law Journal 125, 136–9.

[32] See also I Ward, 'Beyond Constitutionalism: The Search for a European Political Imagination' (2001) 7 European Law Journal 24. One consequence of the lack of a *demos*, is that the case for European level decision-making which fosters the incorporation of all interests at stake and which relies on argumentation and conviction rather than the force of votes, becomes stronger. See also Estella (n 28 above) 47–53.

[33] F Scharpf, 'Balancing Positive and Negative Integration: The Regulatory Options for Europe' (RSC Policy Papers 97/4, Florence 1997) 13. Chalmers and Lodge argue that the Member States should adhere to the value of 'compatibility', which requires 'national policies not to have negative effects for the other Member States or the achievement of the objectives of the Union'; D Chalmers and M Lodge, 'The Open Method of Co-ordination and the European Welfare State' (ESRC Centre for Analysis of Risk and Regulation, Discussion Paper No 11, LSE June 2003) 3.

This approach acknowledges that both the EU institutions and the Member States have responsibilities. The EU should respect the need for autonomy at the national level; the States should respect each other and the commitment to a common venture.

The EU institutions appear to recognize the value of both autonomy and diversity, in part for their own sakes and in part also for instrumental reasons. At Laeken, the European Council referred to Europe as the continent of 'liberty, solidarity and above all diversity, meaning respect for others' languages, cultures and traditions'.[34] Article I-8 of the Treaty establishing a Constitution for Europe states that the motto of the Union shall be 'united in diversity'. Europe (much more than, for example, the US) aspires towards—even demands—a strong principle of federalism which 'maintains the states as culturally and politically autonomous units'.[35] The instrumental reason for the continuing appeal of autonomy and diversity can be linked to the three dimensions of the legitimacy challenge discussed above. Of particular relevance is the argument, based on performance legitimacy, that 'divergent legal rules are better able to satisfy heterogeneous preferences of a large population and may thus contribute to increased welfare in the European internal market'.[36] Affording States a measure of autonomy leaves the way clear for the process of regulatory competition to offer the best regulatory solutions.[37]

For their part, the Member States have a responsibility to consider more than their own particular interest.[38] Scharpf's 'federal comity' approach is reflected in one of the guidelines in Provision 5 of the Protocol on the Application of the Principles of Subsidiarity and Proportionality, added by the Treaty of Amsterdam. Community action is said to be justified where 'actions by Member States alone or lack of Community action would conflict with the requirements of the Treaty (such as the need to correct distortions of competition or avoid disguised restrictions on trade or strengthen economic and social cohesion) or would otherwise significantly damage Member States' interests'.

As part of 'the European project', Member States must take each others' interests into account. For Weiler, Europe is a process-oriented 'Community of Values,

---

[34] Laeken European Council, Presidency Conclusions, 14 and 15 December 2001, Annex I, Section I.

[35] Young (n 29 above) 1723. Young invites us to compare this with a more modest vision 'which would preserve some opportunity for cultural distinctiveness at the state level, while conceding that most citizens will think of themselves as citizens of the nation (or Union)'.

[36] R Van den Bergh, 'Subsidiarity as an Economic Demarcation Principle and the Emergence of European Private Law' (1998) 5 Maastricht Journal 129, 130.

[37] D Esty and D Geradin (eds), *Regulatory Competition and Economic Integration: Comparative Perspectives* (OUP, Oxford 2001); and S Deakin, 'Legal Diversity and Regulatory Competition: Which Model for Europe?' (2006) 12 European Law Journal 440. The potential negative effects of regulatory competition are considered in ch 2 above.

[38] The view that Europe's legitimacy falls to be judged solely on whether or not it serves the national interest 'is the hallmark of classical Euro-Scepticism'; see J Weiler, 'The Commission as Euro-Sceptic: A Task Oriented Commission for a Project-Based Union' in Joerges, Meny, and Weiler (n 5 above) 207, 209–10.

the principal one of which is a historical commitment to a different, more civil process of inter-statal intercourse'.[39] European intervention, either by the political institutions or the judiciary,[40] may be necessary so as to ensure that States take the interests of (nationals of) other States into account when making policy decisions.[41] Given that the extraterritorial effects of States' policies—intentional or otherwise—inevitably increase with economic and social interdependence,[42] the scope for EU intervention is increasing.

The extent to which EU intervention may be required in order to ensure that States respect the commitment to 'a common venture', or, to put this in the terms used in the Protocol on the Application of the Principles of Subsidiarity and Proportionality, 'the requirements of the Treaty', is difficult to determine.[43] The Treaty commits States to the pursuit of vague, economic, and social objectives, and strongly endorses the integrationist route towards their realization. The story of European integration can be presented as the story of the triumph of integrationist means over economic, social, political, and even human ends.[44] In the 1950s, agreement was reached on the creation of a common market, in the 1980s, on the completion of the internal market, and in the 1990s, thanks again in large part to the deliberate exclusion of matters 'political',[45] on economic and monetary union. As was seen in chapter 2 above, the integration project, in a variety of ways, imposes significant constraints on the freedom of action of the States. However, the Treaty fails to tell us, in anything other than the most general terms, what the ultimate ends or meta-objectives of the integration project are. The economic and social rationales are underdeveloped. 'The core of the problem is that there is no agreed narrative about what Europe is for and how it should get there'.[46] Thus, it must be doubted whether the commitment to a common venture can or should—at least given the current way in which the venture has been conceptualized—impose significant constraints on Member State autonomy.

Were the ultimate objectives of the European project to be spelled out more clearly it would of course become easier to argue that national autonomy should

[39] Weiler (n 38 above) 210.

[40] See eg Everson (n 18 above); O Gerstenberg, 'Expanding the Constitution Beyond the Court: The Case of Euro-Constitutionalism' (2002) 8 European Law Journal 172.

[41] It is possible to see this responsibility of States in terms of national self-interest; a reciprocal commitment to respect others brings mutual advantage. However, one need not rely on such a utilitarian calculation.   [42] Maduro (n 24 above).

[43] The obligation of the Member States to 'ensure fulfillment of the obligations arising out of this Treaty', to 'facilitate the achievement of the Community's tasks', and to 'abstain from any measure which could jeopardise the attainment of the objectives of this Treaty' are not in doubt—see Art 10 EC. It is the substantive content of this obligation which is questioned.

[44] The 'true nature of the European project' remains a 'vexed and vexing question'; N Lebessis and J Paterson, 'Developing new modes of governance' in O De Schutter, N Lebessis, and J Paterson (eds), *Governance in the European Union* (OOPEC, Luxembourg 2001) 259, 264–5. See also Ward (n 32 above).

[45] See K Dyson and K Featherstone, *The Road to Maastricht: Negotiating Economic and Monetary Union* (OUP, Oxford 1999).

[46] W Hutton, *The World We're In* (Little, Brown, London 2002) 303.

be constrained in the interests of the common venture. There are many who advocate such a course. Habermas argues that unless the European project is politicized, 'the hearts of an overwhelmingly negative, or, at the very least, cautious population' will not be won.[47] Weiler suggests that 'Europe would, however, be better served if the current debate about its future addressed not only means but ends too'.[48] However, while it may be that the objectives of the EU should be spelled out more clearly,[49] or as Maduro puts it, that the Union should acquire a soul,[50] it is, as the participants in the Convention on the Future of Europe discovered, not at all easy to reach agreement on the ends or objectives of the European project.[51]

This section has shown that neither an approach based on legitimacy, nor one based on an analysis of the commitments inherent in 'the European project' is able to settle the competence debate. There are some good arguments for centralization and some good arguments for decentralization. Any presumption against EU intervention is vulnerable not only to increasing interdependence, but also to the prospect that Europe will discover what it is for, and will, in pursuit of clear objectives, impose constraints on national autonomy. For now, it is clear that institutions at the European and national levels will have to find ways to cooperate and coexist. This may be no bad thing. It is at least arguable that the distinguishing feature of federalism lies precisely in not resolving the tensions which exist between the federal community and the States, or the One and the Many. The unstable equilibrium which is the hallmark of European federalism may be a force for good.[52]

The Principle of Conferral

The Community legal order is based on the principle of conferral (also designated the principle of attributed powers). As stated in Article 5(1) EC, 'the Community shall act within the limits of the powers conferred upon it by this Treaty and of the objectives assigned to it therein'.

All EU intervention must be founded on a particular legal basis which prescribes not only the procedure to be followed in the taking of action at European

---

[47] Habermas (n 31 above) 24.

[48] J Weiler, *The Constitution of Europe* (CUP, Cambridge 1999) 262.

[49] Note, however, the doubts expressed by Elazar, who argues that 'the EU is more likely to succeed because it has more limited ends'; D Elazar, 'The United States and the European Union: Models for Their Epochs' in Nicolaidis and Howse (n 1 above) 31, 49; and Bermann, who argues that the fact that the goals of the EU have not been spelled out clearly, is a factor which has propelled the EU forward; Bermann (n 17 above) 364.

[50] M Maduro, 'Europe's Social Self: "The Sickness Unto Death"' in J Shaw (ed), *Social Law and Policy in an Evolving European Union* (Hart, Oxford 2000) 325.

[51] For a careful analysis of the difficulties in the context of making a Constitution, see Craig, (n 31 above) 139–47.

[52] Weiler (n 27 above); and K Nicolaidis, 'Conclusion: The Federal Vision Beyond the Federal State' in Nicolaidis and Howse (n 1 above).

level, but also, and more importantly, the permissible objectives of any such action. As Dashwood explains, 'the principle of conferral has, as its corollary, the drafting technique that entails the specific and detailed attribution of competences to the Union, through provisions that constitute the legal basis authorizing action in a determined policy area or in pursuance of a determined objective'.[53] The legal bases under which the institutions have intervened in domestic labour law were considered in chapter 2 above. They were classified as either integrationist (Articles 40, 42, 44, 46, 47, and 55; 94 and 95; 98 to 124; and 308 EC), economic (Articles 125 to 130 EC), or social (Articles 13 and 136 to 145 EC). However, many of these legal bases are rather ambiguous with the result that it is often not possible to determine the permissible objectives of EU intervention with any clarity.

As has been repeated in many judgments of the Court of Justice, 'the choice of a legal basis for a measure must be based on objective factors which are amenable to judicial review'.[54] The Court is thus the ultimate arbiter of the legality of EU action and is able to annul measures either because they are based on the wrong legal basis, or, more fundamentally, because they are beyond the competence of the institutions. The Court's task is complicated by the ambiguities referred to above. Many question whether the Commission, Council, and Court take the limits on competence sufficiently seriously. 'What lies at the heart of the increasingly anxious debate about competence is the perception that the principle that the EC operates within the confines of attributed powers tends to be obscured by an open-handed reading of the matter in practice.'[55]

As a result of the way in which competences have been granted to the institutions, there is an almost bewildering array of different restrictions on the competence of the institutions. 'It is grindingly difficult to set out clearly an account of the nature of EC competence and its effect on state competence.'[56] Under some of the above legal bases, the EU is only able to take action if a Commission proposal secures the approval of a unanimous Council.[57] Under others, it has the power only to enact directives,[58] or only to coordinate the policies of the Member States.[59]

[53] A Dashwood, 'The Relationship between the Member States and the European Union/ European Community' (2004) 41 CML Rev 355, 357–8.

[54] See eg Case C-155/91 *Commission v Council* [1993] ECR I-939; Case C-269/97 *Commission and Parliament v Council* [2000] ECR I-2257 (*Beef Labelling*); and Case C-491/01 *BAT (Investments) Ltd* [2002] ECR I-11453 (*Tobacco Labelling*), [94]. See further K Bradley, 'The European Court and the Legal Basis of Community Legislation' (1988) 13 ELR 379; and R Barents, 'The Internal Market Unlimited: Some Observations on the Legal Basis for Community Legislation' (1993) 30 CML Rev 85.

[55] Weatherill (n 10 above) 23. See also Editorial Comments, 'Taking (the limits of) competences seriously' (2000) 37 CML Rev 1301; and M Pollack, 'Creeping Competence: The Expanding Agenda of the European Community' (1994) 14 Journal of European Public Policy 95.

[56] Weatherill (n 10 above) 24.   [57] Arts 13, 94, 137(1)(c), (d), (f), and (g), and 308 EC.

[58] Arts 44(2)(g), 94, and 137(2)(b) EC. Note that Article I-33 TeCE provides that 'directives' are to become 'European framework laws' (and that 'regulations' are to become 'European laws').

[59] Arts 99, 128, and 137(2)(a) EC.

The harmonization or approximation of the laws of the Member States may be required,[60] or alternatively excluded.[61] This complexity is damaging for the legitimacy of the EU. There is a link between 'simplification' and 'eliciting more popular support for the integration process'.[62] The popularity and legitimacy of the EU demand that the complex 'division of responsibilities between what falls within the competence of the Union and what belongs to the Member States' is 'explained relentlessly'.[63]

One of the aims of the Treaty establishing a Constitution for Europe was to clarify and simplify this aspect of the Treaties.[64] Title III of Part I of the Treaty sets out the competences of the Union. Article I-11 refers to the fundamental principles of conferral,[65] subsidiarity, and proportionality. Article I-12 defines various categories of competence. In some areas, for example 'monetary policy for the Member States whose currency is the euro', Union competence is exclusive (Article I-13). In some other areas, such as the protection of health, industry, culture, tourism, and education, youth, sport, and vocational training, the Union has the 'competence to carry out actions to support, coordinate or supplement the actions of the Member States' (Article I-17). In the remaining areas, Union competence is shared with the Member States (Article I-14). There are special provisions relating to common foreign and security policy (Article I-16), and the coordination of economic and employment policies (Article I-15); though interestingly, the open method of coordination (or OMC) is not mentioned by name.[66] Article I-15(1) provides that 'Member States shall coordinate their economic policies within the Union. To this end, the Council of Ministers shall adopt measures, in particular broad guidelines for these policies. Specific provisions shall apply to those Member States whose currency is the euro'. Article I-15(2) then provides that the Union shall 'take measures to ensure the coordination of the employment policies of the Member States, in particular by defining guidelines for these policies'; and Article I-15(3) that it may 'take initiatives to ensure coordination of Member States' social policies'.

---

[60] Arts 94 and 95 EC.   [61] Arts 13(2) and 137(4) EC.

[62] B De Witte, 'Simplification and Reorganization of the European Treaties' (2002) 39 CML Rev 1255.   [63] Editorial Comments, 'What now?' (2005) 42 CML Rev 905, 910.

[64] Laeken European Council, Presidency Conclusions, 14 and 15 December 2001, Annex I: 'Citizens often hold expectations of the European Union that are not always fulfilled. And vice versa—they sometimes have the impression that the Union takes on too much in areas where its involvement is not always essential. The most important thing is to clarify, simplify and adjust the division of competence between the Union and the Member States in the light of the new challenges facing the Union'. For analysis, see Dashwood (n 53 above).

[65] Art I-11(2) TeCE reads as follows: 'Under the principle of conferral, the Union shall act within the limits of the competences conferred upon it by the Member States in the Constitution to attain the objectives set out in the Constitution. Competences not conferred upon the Union in the Constitution remain with the Member States.'

[66] G De Búrca, 'The Constitutional Challenge of New Governance in the European Union' (2003) 28 ELR 814, 837–8.

The Principle of Subsidiarity

Subsidiarity is a principle which directs attention to the level, or levels, at which certain policy objectives can best be formulated and realized. It forms 'part of a language which attempts to articulate and mediate ... some of the fundamental questions of political authority, government and governance which arise in an increasingly interlocking and interdependent world'.[67] It imposes a burden on proponents of EU intervention to justify the need for action at that level. My claim is that given the current levels of legitimacy of the various levels of governance within the EU, the imposition of such a burden is warranted. The claim is not that the burden will never be, or even that it is only in extreme circumstances that it will be, displaced. 'So far as the concept of subsidiarity, not of sovereignty, is in use as the principle governing Community or Union, it presupposes the just and necessary interference from Brussels.'[68] However, it remains appropriate to insist that proponents of EU level action are able to explain the reasons for any shift of the locus of decision-making to the EU level and to demonstrate the advantages (in legitimacy terms) which EU level solutions provide.

At the outset, it is helpful to distinguish between the broad, basic meaning of subsidiarity and the more narrow formulation in the second paragraph of Article 5 of the Treaty.[69] According to the broad meaning, decisions should be taken 'as closely as possible to the citizen'.[70] The principle has roots in late nineteenth- and early twentieth-century social Catholicism and beyond that to Althusius, Aquinas, and Aristotle.[71] 'The ethos underlying subsidiarity is the protection of the autonomy of smaller entities (and in the last instance, the individual) against intervention by larger entities.'[72] The broad principle not only addresses the exercise of power in areas in which it is constitutionally shared; but is also able to influence the constitutional debate relating to the proper allocation of competences. It deals not only with whether action should be taken at one level or another, but also speaks to the identity of policy-makers at various levels, and the nature of their interventions. It thus has the capacity to appeal to the horizontal as well as the vertical dimension of the legitimacy challenge referred to in the introduction to this chapter.

[67] G De Búrca, 'Reappraising Subsidiarity's Significance After Amsterdam' (Harvard Jean Monnet Working Paper No 7/99) 3.

[68] K Endo, 'Subsidiarity and its Enemies: To what extent is Sovereignty Contested in the Mixed Commonwealth of Europe?' (EUI Working Paper RSC No 2001/24, Florence 2001) 25.

[69] Though only the narrow formulation, found in Art 5(2) EC is justiciable before the Court of Justice, both the broad and the narrow conceptions of the principle are influential at the political level.

[70] Art 1 TEU. At Laeken, the European Council identified 'the democratic challenge facing Europe'. As a first priority, 'within the Union, the European institutions must be brought closer to its citizens'; Laeken European Council, Presidency Conclusions, 14 and 15 December 2001, Annex I.

[71] Endo (n 68 above); and N Barber, 'The limited modesty of subsidiarity' (2005) 11 European Law Journal 308.

[72] A Estella, *The EU Principle of Subsidiarity and its Critique* (OUP, Oxford 2002) 80.

The narrower formulation in Article 5(2) EC specifically reflects the preference for decision-making at Member State rather than at Community level.[73] It reads as follows: 'In areas which do not fall within its exclusive competence, the Community shall take action, in accordance with the principle of subsidiarity, only if and in so far as the objectives of the proposed action cannot be sufficiently achieved by the Member States and can therefore, by reason of the scale or effects of the proposed action, be better achieved by the Community.'[74] Thus, subsidiarity asks 'whether the powers that do fall within the Community sphere should in fact be exercised ... It starts off precisely where the conventional tools of constitutional federalism leave off and where legislative politics is ordinarily thought to begin'.[75] The fact that the Community has the competence to act to further particular policy object-ives is no answer to the challenge of subsidiarity. The subsidiarity enquiry only begins once it is clear that the Community shares competence with the Member States.

A careful reading of Article 5(2) EC indicates that it contains two different, pos-sibly contradictory, tests—the 'sufficiency' test (ie can the Member States sufficiently achieve a given set of objectives?) and the 'value-added' test (ie can Community action better achieve these objectives?). Estella suggests the following reconciliation, which I endorse:

In principle, if Member States' proposed actions were sufficient to attain the objectives in question, Community action would be redundant, unless the Community's proposed action attains those objectives more completely, and added value is manifest. By contrast, in those cases in which the Member States' proposed actions are insufficient, the Community could not be presumed to have the freedom to act. Even in such cases, the Community would have to prove its proposal offers a substantial improvement over that of the Member States for the attainment of Community objectives.[76]

Bermann elaborates on the complexity of the subsidiarity calculus, rightly draw-ing attention to its hypothetical nature. In order to properly respect the principle, the Community institutions need to:

... forecast a whole range of actions or inactions which the Member States might engage in relation to a given Community goal, if the Community institutions allowed them to, and

---

[73] 'The thrust of the principle is perfectly clear: Community action should only be preferred to Member State action, if this will bring demonstrable advantages.' A Dashwood, 'The Limits of EC Powers' (1996) 21 ELR 113, 115.

[74] Art 5 EC. In Art I-11 TeCE the words 'either at central level or at regional and local level' are added after 'sufficiently achieved by the Member States'.

[75] G Bermann, 'Taking Subsidiarity Seriously: Federalism in the European Community and the United States' (1994) 94 Columbia Law Review 331, 366. This section owes much to Bermann's account of the subsidiarity principle.

[76] Estella (n 72 above) 94. Provision 5 of the Protocol on the Application of the Principles of Subsidiarity and Proportionality, added by the Treaty of Amsterdam, states that one of the guidelines to be used in examining whether Community action is justified, is that 'action at Community level would produce *clear benefits* by reason of its scale or effects compared with action at the level of the Member States' (my emphasis). This confirms Estella's position that the Community would have to prove its proposal offers a *substantial improvement* over that of the Member States.

make a utility assessment of each. Moreover, each Member State 'option' has to be dis-counted for the possibility that not all the Member States may take the action contemplated on a timely or adequate basis or indeed at all. It is only after some generalized assessment of Member State potential emerges from this enormously contingent and variable analysis that its overall 'adequacy' in achieving Community objectives can then be compared with that of the proposed Community measure, as the principle of subsidiarity demands.[77]

Thus, subsidiarity directs 'a genuine legislative inquiry into the consequences of the Community's refraining from taking a measure that it may legitimately take, in deference to the Member States' capacity to accomplish the same objectives'.[78] Unless there are clear benefits associated with European level intervention, sub-sidiarity asks that the Community refrains from taking action. The principle 'sys-tematically places the burden of proof on the proponents of Community action'.[79] Given the strength of the arguments for and against centralization in today's EU, I believe that it is right 'that those who wish to see power centralised' should 'bear the burden of the argument'.[80] Nevertheless, I make three important criticisms of the principle.

The first criticism is that the principle takes as its starting-point the objectives of the proposed action. It does not acknowledge that the Community and the Member States may have different objectives.[81] The result of this is that although the principle is able to operate well where there is a coincidence between the objectives of the Community and those of the Member States, it does not operate well where there may be a clash. The effect of this, as we shall see, is to reduce the value of the principle, in particular in relation to interventions based on the inte-grationist rationale. The second criticism is that under Article 5(2) EC, compara-tive efficiency—or performance legitimacy—is the criterion according to which the choice of Member State or Community intervention falls to be determined.[82] A formulation which made it clear that regime and polity legitimacy consider-ations were also relevant would, for the reasons given in the first section of this chapter, be preferable. The third criticism is that the principle envisages either action at the European level, or, if the case for EU intervention cannot be estab-lished, action at the level of the Member States.[83] I would argue for a formulation

---

[77] Bermann (n 75 above), 385.   [78] ibid 335.
[79] ibid 453. See also De Búrca (n 67 above) 8.   [80] Barber (n 71 above) 312–13.
[81] See G Davies, 'Subsidiarity: The Wrong Idea, in the Wrong Place, at the Wrong Time' (2006) 43 CML Rev 63, 67–8: 'Subsidiarity misses the point. Its central flaw is that instead of providing a method to balance between Member States and Community interests, which is what is needed, it assumes the Community goals, privileges their achievement absolutely, and simply asks who should be the one to do the implementing work'.
[82] Contrast Barber (n 71 above) 318, arguing that 'at least one of the objectives that can be fed into the European principle of subsidiarity's efficiency test is that of ensuring flourishing democratic government'.
[83] See I Cooper, 'The Watchdogs of Subsidiarity: National Parliaments and the logic of arguing in the EU' (2006) 44 JCMS 281, 301: 'The subsidiarity question is stark—is EU action warranted?—requiring a yes or no'. He goes on to make the point that 'the proportionality question is more nuanced: given the need for EU action, is the proposed measure the least burdensome legislative option?'

which openly invited an analysis of the ways in which action at various levels could be combined.

Notwithstanding these criticisms, the argument advanced in this book is that a vigorous application of the principle of subsidiarity, especially when combined with an even-handed and vigorous application of the principle of proportionality, is able to contribute to the legitimacy of EU intervention in domestic labour law. Subsidiarity, as we shall see in chapter 5 below, may limit the scope for EU intervention under the social rationale and may also influence the development of the open method of coordination.

The Principle of Proportionality

The principle of proportionality defines the permissible extent of Community action.[84] Article 5(3) EC states that 'any action by the Community shall not go beyond what is necessary to achieve the objectives of this Treaty'. There is some difficulty in establishing the meaning of 'beyond what is necessary'. It is very well established that in order to satisfy the principle of proportionality, action must be both suitable and necessary.[85] There must, in other words, be a relationship between the action and the objective pursued, and it must also be shown that without action of a particular intensity, the objective could not or would not be attained.[86] I argue that there is also a third dimension to any meaningful proportionality enquiry. Proportionality involves the weighing of different interests or objectives. Action which furthers particular objectives can only be described as proportionate (or disproportionate) with reference to other criteria. The principle of proportionality is well known in the human rights context. A Community measure which serves legitimate objectives will fail the proportionality test if it is held to have a disproportionate, or excessive, effect on an individual's rights.[87] The balancing test involves ascribing a value both to the objectives pursued by the Community measure in question and to the rights of the individual, and, with those values in mind, deciding whether or not the measure goes 'beyond what is necessary' (or is overly intrusive).

In the context of the relationship between the EU and the Member States, the principle of proportionality arises in two different contexts. First, national measures

[84] See further N Emiliou, *The Principle of Proportionality in European Law* (Kluwer, Deventer 1996); and E Ellis (ed), *The Principle of Proportionality in the Laws of Europe* (Hart, Oxford 1999).

[85] See eg Case C-359/92 *Germany v Council* [1994] ECR I-3681, [45] and [46].

[86] Provision 6 of the Protocol on the Application of the Principles of Subsidiarity and Proportionality, added by the Treaty of Amsterdam, provides that 'the form of Community action shall be as simple as possible, consistent with satisfactory achievement of the objective of the measure and the need for effective enforcement'. 'Other things being equal, directives should be preferred to regulations and framework directives to detailed measures'.

[87] See eg Case C-353/99 *Hautala v Council* [2001] ECR I-9565, and Joined Cases C-154/04 and C-155/04 *Alliance for Natural Health* [2005] ECR I-6451, [120]–[130].

which restrict free movement within the EU may, as we saw in chapter 2 above, under certain circumstances be justified. In order to justify a restrictive rule, Member States must show that the rule pursues legitimate objectives and that it is proportionate. In this proportionality enquiry, values are ascribed to the legitimate objective of the State and to the EU's interest in establishing a market in Europe. National measures go 'beyond what is necessary' unless they represent the least restrictive (of free movement) way to realize the State's legitimate objectives.[88] Second, the principle of proportionality may limit the exercise of the Community's competence. As seen above, the Community may go 'beyond what is necessary' to achieve the objectives of the Treaty through action which has an excessive effect on the rights of individuals. But, the Community may also go 'beyond what is necessary' through action which has an excessive effect on Member State autonomy. In this proportionality enquiry, values are ascribed both to the objectives of the Community and to the autonomy of the Member States, and with these values in mind, a decision is made as to whether or not the action of the Community goes 'beyond what is necessary'. In determining the need for and intensity of European intervention, it is necessary to take into account the potentially negative effects of European intervention on local standards and cultures.[89] The task for the Court is to determine the point at which intrusions into the autonomy of States are to be considered disproportionate.

There are, of course, important differences between the cases in which EU level action is said to have a disproportionate effect on an individual's rights, and those in which it is said to have had a disproportionate effect on Member State autonomy:

Courts are generally prepared to adjudicate on issues involving traditionally categorized individual rights, where interference with a discretionary policy decision can be explained not on the ground that it is not the most sensible or effective measure, but on the ground that it unjustifiably restricts an important legally recognized right, the protection of which is entrusted to the court ... They are more reluctant to adjudicate if the interest affected is seen as a collective or general public interest rather than an individual right, and if the interest of the State is a mixed and complex one.[90]

Nevertheless, the autonomy and diversity of the Member States are, as explained above, valued in the EU context, both in and of themselves and for instrumental reasons. The very inclusion of the principles of subsidiarity and proportionality in the Treaty is significant in this regard. Provision 7 of the Protocol on the Application of the Principles of Subsidiarity and Proportionality, added by the Treaty of Amsterdam, provides that 'Community measures should leave as much scope for national decision as possible, consistent with the aim of the measure and observing the requirements of the Treaty. While respecting Community law, care should

---

[88] See eg Case 104/75 *De Peijper* [1976] ECR 613.   [89] De Búrca (n 67 above) 27.

[90] G De Búrca, 'The Principle of Proportionality and its Application in EC Law' (1993) 13 Yearbook of European Law 105, 111–12.

be taken to respect well established national arrangements and the organisation and working of Member States' legal systems'.[91] Proportionality is said to require that 'the EU legislate with a light touch, choosing the instrument that imposes the least burden on, and most respects the autonomy of, the Member States'.[92] 'In cases where action by the Union is necessary, or is deemed appropriate, the proportionality principle requires the institutions to adopt means that will intrude as little as possible on the sovereignty of the Member States.'[93]

The next section examines the reasons for the Court's apparent reluctance or inability to use the principles of subsidiarity and proportionality to constrain the institutions. It then explores the potential which the principles have to contribute to the legitimacy of the EU, concentrating on the different ways in which they operate in relation to interventions based on the integrationist, economic, and social rationales.

The Potential of Subsidiarity and Proportionality

This section explores the ways in which the principles of subsidiarity and proportionality are able to contribute to the legitimacy of the EU, paying specific attention to each of the three rationales for EU intervention. First, however, I endeavour to explain why the Court of Justice has been reluctant to use the principles to annul actions of the institutions.[94]

One reason is said to be that the principles are 'devoid of clear legal content'.[95] Subsidiarity asks questions about the level at which particular objectives can best be, or can sufficiently be, realized. Proportionality asks that EU action does not go beyond what is necessary to achieve particular objectives. They are 'invitations to begin a debate festooned with awkward value judgments rather than helpfully precise benchmarks'.[96] Estella's view is that subsidiarity 'is difficult to handle from a legal perspective'.[97] He fears that the Court would be putting its legitimacy at risk if

---

[91] See also Art 5 of the Protocol on the Application of the Principles of Subsidiarity and Proportionality attached to the TeCE: 'Draft European legislative acts shall take account of the need for any burden, whether financial or administrative, falling upon the Union, national governments, regional or local authorities, economic operators and citizens, to be minimised and commensurate with the objective to be achieved.'

[92] Cooper (n 83 above) 300.

[93] Dashwood (n 53 above) 367. See also Dashwood (n 73 above) 115.

[94] There are many cases in which the Court has considered the principles. Case C-84/94 *UK v Council* [1996] ECR I-5755 (*Working Time*), the most important case in the labour law context, is considered in ch 5 below. Case C-376/98 *Germany v Parliament and Council* [2000] ECR I-8419 (*Tobacco Advertising*); and *Tobacco Labelling* (n 54 above) are also good illustrations of the way in which the Court treats the principles of subsidiarity and proportionality. Once it is established that competence exists, the Court seems unwilling to question the legitimacy of its exercise.

[95] Estella (n 72 above) 6.

[96] S Weatherill, 'Better Competence Monitoring' (2005) 30 ELR 23, 25.

[97] Estella (n 72 above) 166.

it decided to implement the principle.[98] He states that subsidiarity, at any rate in its material dimension, has 'an important degree of indeterminacy', that it constitutes 'a very elastic notion', and that it is 'diffuse and ambiguous, when not incoherent'.[99] His main point is that the 'transnational dimension' and 'market distortion' criteria, which he derives from Provision 5 of the Amsterdam Protocol, are 'incapable of offering a clear-cut answer to the question of whether the Community should or should not act'.[100] Davies' view is that proportionality review involves 'difficult political' decisions.[101] He states that 'Member States have had their chance to defend their interests in the Council',[102] the suggestion being that proportionality may be better protected via the operation of political, rather than legal, processes. These arguments lead one towards the conclusion that subsidiarity and proportionality are either unsuitable for judicial resolution[103] or, alternatively, that the Court should not apply the relevant tests with any vigour or intensity, and should only intervene where EU measures are manifestly inappropriate.[104]

However, while there can be no doubt that the difficulties facing the Court are real, they are not unusual. They are encountered in many contexts. It is, as the discussion in chapter two above demonstrates, far from easy for the Court to determine what constitutes a barrier to free movement and to identify the circumstances in which such a barrier may be justifiable. It is also difficult to establish what amounts to a distortion of competition within the market and determine the outer limits of Articles 94 and 95 EC. The Court's task in assessing compliance with subsidiarity and proportionality is no more difficult or politically sensitive than its task in determining the proper scope of the integrationist rationale.[105] In both contexts, the Court's decisions have a significant impact on the nature of the relationships between the EU and the Member States, and between integration and diversity.

The suggestion that the Court should not apply the principles vigorously because Member States are able to defend their interests in the Council should also be rejected. The argument is weak, not only because of the fact that qualified majority voting applies to Council decision-making under many legal bases,[106] but also, more fundamentally, because 'substantive policy commitments on particular

---

[98] See also M Kumm, 'Constitutionalising Subsidiarity in Integrated Markets: The Case of Tobacco Regulation in the European Union' (2006) 12 European Law Journal 503, 525, arguing that the subsidiarity and proportionality enquiry 'overstretches the institutional capacity of courts'.

[99] Estella (n 72 above) 80, 82, 96.   [100] ibid 132.   [101] Davies (n 81 above) 82.

[102] ibid.   [103] A Toth, 'Is Subsidiarity Justiciable?' (1994) 19 ELR 268.

[104] See eg *Tobacco Labelling* (n 54 above) [123], in which the Court holds that 'the Community legislature must be allowed a broad discretion in an area such as that involved in the present case, which entails political, economic and social choices on its part, and in which it is called upon to undertake complex assessments'; and Case C-210/03 *Swedish Match* [2004] ECR I-11893, [48]. For detailed comment on the proportionality enquiry in *Swedish Match*, see Kumm (n 98 above), 522–4.

[105] Estella's fear that that 'the debate on subsidiarity gives the impression that the *political* space for discussion should be sacrificed on the altar of technocracy', is also applicable to the debate on the scope of the integrationist rationale; Estella (n 72 above) 134. See also M Everson, 'Adjudicating the Market' (2002) 8 European Law Journal 152, who is acutely aware of the difficulties facing the Court in its role as 'a nexus of social and political debate'.   [106] See further Estella (n 72 above) 47–53.

issues often will overwhelm concerns about the institutional interests' of the government that the Minister represents. Member State representation within the Council is not a reliable safeguard against the gradual erosion of State autonomy.[107] If diversity and national autonomy are to be taken seriously as values—and my argument has been that the legitimacy of the European project demands that they are—it seems necessary that the Court of Justice pays close attention not only to the extent to which the integrationist rationale can and should constrain national autonomy, but also to the effective policing of the limits of Community compe-tence, via a vigorous application of the principles of conferral, subsidiarity, and proportionality.[108]

There is, however, said to be a second reason why the principles have not been well received by the Court. Subsidiarity is 'deemed by the Court to be counter to its own political agenda'.[109] Chalmers argues that the Court's commitment to integration explains its case law in relation to the principle of proportionality: 'Where national authorities obstruct the path of integration, the Court's instinct is to wield proportionality as a sword, but where a challenge is made to the suit-ability or necessity of a Community measure, its instinct is to use proportionality as a shield to protect the institutions.'[110]

The fact that the legitimacy and appropriateness of the Court's role are questioned[111] is hugely damaging for the EU: 'It is the proper function of the fed-eral constitution, umpired by a federal judiciary, to strike the appropriate balance between the federation and its component entities.'[112] If there is evidence that the federal judiciary is not fulfilling its task, and is not umpiring conflicts in an even-handed way, it seems inevitable that the legitimacy of the European project may be called into question. The Court cannot be seen to have a political agenda which entails a lack of respect for the proper application of the principles of subsidiarity and proportionality, and thereby the autonomy of the Member States.

But, given that the principles aim to protect the interests of Member States, it is rather strange, even counter-intuitive, that the institutions primarily responsible

---

[107] See E Young, 'Protecting Member State Autonomy in the European Union: Some Cautionary Tales from American Federalism' (2002) 77 New York University Law Review 1612, 1690–1.

[108] This is not, of course, to deny the role which the Treaty and the political institutions can and should also play.

[109] Estella (n 72 above) 7. At 170 he states that 'for the Court, subsidiarity threatened a hard-won achievement, since it could be used to stop the "natural" development of Community competences towards greater integration; it could even mean that Community competences would have to be returned to the Member States. From this perspective, subsidiarity was not only very difficult to deal with in strict legal terms, but also a real danger for the fulfilment of the Court's plans for integration'. See Opinion 1/91 [1991] ECR I-6079 (*Re EEA*) [17], in which the Court stated that 'the objective of all Community Treaties is to contribute together to making concrete progress towards European unity'.

[110] D Chalmers *et al*, *European Union Law* (CUP, Cambridge 2006) 452.

[111] See eg Davies (n 81 above). Contrast M Kumm, 'Who is the Final Arbiter of Constitutionality in Europe?' (1999) 36 CML Rev 346, who lays emphasis on the fact that national constitutional courts provide a check on the Court of Justice.

[112] K Lenaerts, 'Constitutionalism and the Many Faces of Federalism' (1990) 38 American Journal of Comparative Law 205.

for ensuring that subsidiarity and proportionality are adhered to, are supranational institutions; the Commission, which has the right of legislative initiative, and the Court. The Laeken Declaration paved the way for an interesting innovation, by asking whether national parliaments should 'focus on the division of competence between Union and Member States, for example through preliminary checking of compliance with the principle of subsidiarity'.[113] This idea was taken forward in the Treaty establishing a Constitution for Europe. Under the Protocol on the Application of the Principles of Subsidiarity and Proportionality attached to the Treaty, all draft legislation is to be sent to national parliaments for their consideration. Within a six-week period, a national parliament may send a reasoned opinion stating why it considers that the draft in question does not comply with the principle of subsidiarity. If at least one-third of national parliaments object, the Commission must review its draft, before deciding to maintain, amend, or withdraw the draft. Reasons must be given for this decision.[114] This seems a sensible approach. In any federal system, it is important to pay attention not only to 'substantive limits on central power', but also to process issues, ie to 'political and institutional checks that will make the federal balance as self-enforcing as possible'.[115] Acknowledging a role for national parliaments may allay public fears that the outer limits of the competence of the institutions will not be checked.

Nevertheless, I remain unconvinced by the arguments which have been advanced to explain the Court's reluctance to use the principles. While it is true that the principles are difficult to handle from a legal perspective and that they demand an acknowledgement of the value of autonomy and diversity alongside integration, it is a key function of the federal judiciary to operate in this awkward area. This section moves on to consider various ways in which the Court may be able to make better use of the principles of subsidiarity and proportionality, distinguishing between the operation of the integrationist, economic, and social rationales for intervention. In the context of the integrationist rationale, in which there are likely to be clashes between European and national interests, proportionality is likely to prove more significant. In the context of the economic and social rationales, in which the interests of the EU and the Member States are more likely to coincide, it is subsidiarity which is more likely to constrain the institutions. I begin with the integrationist rationale.

Where European institutions act on the basis of the integrationist rationale, they act with the aim of establishing, or improving the functioning of, the European market. As the long discussion in chapter 2 above demonstrates, it is not at all easy to determine what action is necessary to establish the market or to improve its functioning, for example in relation to the elimination of barriers to free movement and distortions of competition, or the achievement of EMU. Views about

---

[113] Laeken European Council, Presidency Conclusions, 14 and 15 December 2001, Annex I.

[114] See further Cooper (n 83 above); and Weatherill (n 96 above); both of whom welcome this innovation. Both make the point that proportionality should have been included alongside subsidiarity in Art 6 of the Protocol.   [115] Young (n 107 above) 1736.

the nature of markets and the nature of the market-making endeavour are relevant. So too are the economic and social meta-objectives of the integration process and, last but by no means least, understandings of the proper relationship between integration and national diversity.

Subsidiarity, at least in the narrow formulation in Article 5(2) EC, asks whether the integrationist objectives of proposed action can best be achieved at Member State or Community level. It, as Davies points out, 'assumes the primacy of the central goal, and allows no mechanism for questioning whether or not it is desirable, in the light of other interests, to fully pursue this'.[116] One's instinct is that if action is deemed necessary to promote the establishment and functioning of the market (for example to eliminate a barrier to free movement or to eliminate competition based on unacceptably low social standards), then such action must ordinarily be taken at European level, rather than by the Member States.[117] Member States acting alone are not able, for example, to identify the baseline rules of economic ordering for the European market or to prevent the collective quest for competitive advantage from creating distorted conditions of competition; European level intervention is required. Thus, subsidiarity, as defined in Article 5(2) EC, is only able to play a marginal role. It insists that Member States should take action to promote the Community's integrationist objectives in those cases in which they are sufficiently well placed and the Community is not better placed. To give just one, controversial, example from the labour law field, under Article 27 of the Community Charter of the Fundamental Social Rights of Workers, one of the particular responsibilities of the Member States was said to be 'to guarantee the fundamental social rights in this Charter and to implement the social measures indispensable to the smooth operation of the internal market as part of a strategy of economic and social cohesion'. If, however, the case can be made that social rights would be substantially better protected through action at European level, subsidiarity would not operate so as to block European level action in this field.

Proportionality is of much greater significance. It insists that the negative effects of European intervention on local standards and cultures are taken into account, opening the way for the Court to constrain the institutions where the integrationist objectives of the EU come into conflict with the legitimate objectives of the Member States.

But before considering the ways in which the Court might approach the task of balancing the interests of the EU with those of the Member States, I pause to consider the impact of the requirement that the EU should intervene 'only where necessary for the internal market to work effectively, and even then only to the extent

---

[116] Davies (n 81 above) 78.

[117] See also J Wouters, 'European Company Law: *Quo Vadis?*' (2000) 37 CML Rev 257, 290: 'developing the internal market and removing obstacles to the greatest possible freedom of movement for companies are objectives which, in the terms of Article 5(2) EC, "cannot be sufficiently achieved by the Member States and can therefore, by reason of the scale or effects of the proposed action, be better achieved by the Community"'.

necessary'.[118] Proportionality argues for the achievement of the EU's objectives in the least burdensome manner. This could be taken to mean that the EU should not embark on a positive integration strategy in those areas in which a negative integration strategy would achieve the EU's integrationist objectives;[119] or that when harmonizing national laws to the extent necessary for the establishment and proper functioning of the market, it should opt for harmonization at a low rather than a high level. Craig and De Búrca argue that 'no harmonization measures [are] required with respect to those national measures that would be condemned under the *Cassis* reasoning'.[120] Ehlermann goes further, suggesting that such rules 'cannot be harmonized'.[121] This, however, assumes that the EU's objectives are equally well served by negative and positive integration, and by harmonization at high and low levels. However, given that integration is a means to the realization of economic and social meta-objectives, it may be possible to counter these arguments from proportionality. In order to do so, one would need to establish that the broad economic and social meta-objectives of the EU are more likely to be achieved via positive rather than negative integration, or by harmonization at a higher level rather than a lower level. Chapters 4 and 5 below consider the ways in which such arguments may operate in the labour law field.

The focus here is on the way in which proportionality might be able to mediate clashes between the integrationist objectives of the EU and the legitimate interests of the States.[122] Gareth Davies considers two hypothetical legislative proposals; one for a common contract code, the other for a common high school curriculum.[123] Both measures, he argues, could be adopted under Articles 94 or 95 EC, as 'the existence of different national contract laws and high school systems both manifestly create obstacles to movement'.[124] Yet he argues that 'most people would consider that these measures go far too far'. The problem is that common

---

[118] Bermann (n 75 above) 383.

[119] Negative integration is 'politically attractive to the legislature since the burden of further enactment is removed ... It similarly proves advantageous to the process of market integration since barriers are thus set aside without the need for a prior harmonization of divergent regulatory concepts'; C Joerges, 'Product Safety in the European Community: Market Integration, Social Regulation and Legal Structures' (1992) 39 Journal of Behavioural Sciences 132, 142.

[120] P Craig and G De Búrca, *EU Law: Text, Cases and Materials* (3rd edn, Clarendon, Oxford 2003) 1190.

[121] C-D Ehlermann, 'The Internal Market following the Single European Act' (1987) 24 CML Rev 361, 400. Weiler is more circumspect. He argues that Community legislative competence (under Arts 94 and 95 EC) 'is triggered each time there is a finding of a *prima facie* transgression by a state measure of the *Dassonville* formula, even when, necessarily, the state measure in question is justified. This may not be the exclusive ground for using [the above Articles] but it is certainly a sufficient ground'; J Weiler, 'The Constitution of the Common Market Place: Text and Context in the Evolution of the Free Movement of Goods' in P Craig and G De Búrca (eds), *The Evolution of EU Law* (OUP, Oxford 1999) 349, 362.

[122] See also P Davies, 'Market Integration and Social Policy in the Court of Justice' (1995) 24 ILJ 49.

[123] Davies (n 81 above) 68–71. A hypothetical legislative proposal to establish a Community-wide minimum wage would fall to be analysed along similar lines (though, as noted in ch 2 above, Art 137(5) EC appears to rule out EU intervention in relation to wages).

[124] He is right under the prevailing *Dassonville* test. However, he may be wrong under the alternative *Keck* test which I advocate in ch 2 above, which focuses not on whether access to markets is

contract laws and educational systems would not only contribute to the EU's integrationist objectives, but 'also detract hugely from Member State autonomy, and impede national capacity to have and hold an independent educational and legal system'. 'The added value to the Community of the measures seems very small in comparison with the harm to the national interests.' His conclusion is that 'these objections can be summed up in a word—proportionality. The claim is that the Community measure would be disproportionate to its goals. While the legitimate Community goals would be advanced, the cost in Member State interests would be disproportionately large'.

As Gareth Davies acknowledges, it is, in many respects, entirely unsurprising that the Court has not been prepared to engage in this sort of proportionality review of acts of the Community institutions. It is difficult for the Court to know how to approach the task of weighing national socio-economic concerns against gains in the integration process. Nevertheless, the task is not one which is alien to the Court. There are a range of free movement cases in which the Court's task is to consider whether national rules constitute barriers to free movement and, if so, whether they are justifiable. These cases involve the Court in a delicate balancing exercise in which it has to weigh the European interest in integration against other legitimate objectives pursued at national, subnational, or enterprise level.[125] Also, in the *Tobacco Advertising* case, the Court showed some sensitivity to national autonomy when holding that the institutions may not rely on Article 95 EC 'with a view to eliminating the smallest distortions of competition'.[126]

Thus, although the narrow formulation of subsidiarity is only able to play a marginal role in relation to the operation of the integrationist rationale, the broad principle of subsidiarity, which asks that decisions are taken as closely as possible to the citizen, may, together with the principle of proportionality, be able to exert some influence on the way in which the integrationist rationale is conceptualized. A Europe which respects the principles of subsidiarity and proportionality, is a Europe which is tolerant of regulatory diversity between its constituent States.[127] It is a Europe in which there 'may be an unwillingness to accept that every marginal gain in market integration justifies deep intrusions into Member State autonomy'.[128] My analysis of the integrationist rationale in chapter 2 above suggests that the Court may re-examine the definitions of the barrier to free movement and the

---

merely affected by differences in legal regime, but instead on whether such access is prevented and on whether there is discrimination against imported factors.

[125] M Egan, *Constructing a European Market* (OUP, Oxford 2001) 89. Interestingly, Paul Davies notes that the free movement cases in which there is a low impact on inter-state trade, but highly sensitive national policies at stake, are, in the end, 'easy ones' for the Court; Davies (n 122 above) 68. For a full analysis of the approach of the Court in the labour law field, see ch 4 below.

[126] *Tobacco Advertising* (n 94 above) [107].

[127] See S Deakin, 'Legal Diversity and Regulatory Competition: Which Model for Europe?' (2006) 12 European Law Journal 440; M Dougan, 'Minimum Harmonization and the Internal Market' (2000) 37 CML Rev 853; and, more broadly, G De Búrca and J Scott (eds), *Constitutional Change in the EU: From Uniformity to Flexibility?* (Hart, Oxford 2000).   [128] Davies (n 122 above) 76.

distortion of competition, and come to a new understanding of the extent to which mere differences between the laws of the Member States are liable to compromise the establishment and functioning of the market in Europe. An approach which fully acknowledged the value of national autonomy alongside integration would also involve a more even-handed reading of the principle of proportionality. This would involve a balanced assessment, in the appropriate circumstances, not only of whether the legitimate objectives of the State could be achieved by means less restrictive of free movement, but also of whether integrationist objectives could be achieved by means less restrictive of national autonomy. Moreover, the Court can and should use the principles of subsidiarity and proportionality to inform its interpretations of the Treaty and the acts of the institutions, and the Commission can and should take heed of the principles before advancing proposals for legislation. The implications of such an approach for EU intervention in domestic labour law are spelled out in chapters 4 and 5 below.

In relation to measures based on the economic and social rationales, the impact of the principles of subsidiarity and proportionality is rather different. In large part because of the likely coincidence between the objectives of the EU and the Member States, it is the principle of subsidiarity which plays the more important role.

The first point to note is that the relevant provisions of the Treaty (Articles 13, 125 to 130, and 136 to 145 EC) restrict the competence of the Community. These restrictions serve to illustrate the sensitivities surrounding the maintenance of national autonomy in these areas, but can provide no answer to the challenge of subsidiarity and proportionality. Subsidiarity asks whether the Community institutions or the Member States are better placed to achieve economic or social objectives. Where the political institutions intervene in relation to 'matters that the States acting alone could have done a perfectly good job of regulating',[129] they will, regardless of the intensity of intervention, be infringing the principle of subsidiarity. Ryan, for example, considers an economic rationale for EU labour law, based on increasing competitiveness. But he finds that such a theory would be vulnerable to subsidiarity, in that it is not 'a convincing theory for regulation at the European level'.[130]

Under the principle of subsidiarity, the institutions must prove that they are better placed to realize particular objectives. It seems clear that they will be able to satisfy this burden in relation to policies of transnational scope which have significant cross-border effects.[131] It may be better, for a range of reasons associated with performance and regime legitimacy, for legislation to protect the interests of

---

[129] Bermann (n 75 above) 372.

[130] B Ryan, 'Pay, Trade Union Rights and European Community Law' (1997) 13 International Journal of Comparative Labour Law and Industrial Relations 305, 324.

[131] One of the guidelines in Provision 5 of the Protocol on the Application of the Principles of Subsidiarity and Proportionality, added by the Treaty of Amsterdam, provides that Community action is justified where 'the issue under consideration has transnational aspects which cannot be satisfactorily regulated by action by Member States'.

workers in transnational undertakings to be adopted at the European rather than the Member State level.

EU intervention may also be justified where there is reason to believe that the objectives of the proposed action could not be sufficiently achieved (or could not be achieved at all) by action at the level of the Member State. As we saw in chapter 2 above, as the internal market becomes progressively established, national governments become forced to conduct their policies 'in line with imperatives of international competitiveness, as gauged by their attraction for mobile investors'.[132] Their freedom to enact or maintain labour standards and their capacity to achieve given social objectives may therefore be diminished. If the institutions are able to demonstrate that, under these circumstances, social objectives can be better achieved by the Community than by the Member States, their competence to act on the basis of the economic and social rationales may survive the challenge of subsidiarity. Along these lines, Ryan argues that 'European action setting out minimum standards ... will be supported by those who believe that public policy ought to guarantee [such standards] and who believe that competitive pressures tend to undermine such regulation'.[133] In those areas in which competitive pressures are less intense it will be more difficult to make the case for EU intervention.

What of proportionality? Where the institutions take action under the economic or the social rationale, the extent of any action will be closely related to the way in which the objectives of the action are defined. The proportionality principle insists that intervention is necessary and operates so as to ensure that the means match the end. It may also have a role to play in those areas in which there is a clash between the economic and social interests of the EU and the Member States. Measures which serve the economic or social objectives of the EU, but which have an excessive effect on particular individuals, enterprises, or States might, as we shall see in chapter 5 below, be vulnerable to a vigorous application of proportionality.

Conclusions

An examination of the arguments for and against centralization in today's EU leads to the conclusion that although there may be a presumption against EU intervention and in favour of regulation at national level, this presumption is rebuttable. Where there is little or no evidence that EU intervention may lead to enhanced performance or regime legitimacy, the EU should respect the autonomy

---

[132] W Streeck, 'Neo-Voluntarism: A New European Social Policy Regime?' (1995) 1 European Law Journal 31, 55.

[133] Ryan (n 130 above) 320. Note, however, that minimum standard setting will be an insufficient response to competitive pressures. It is necessary to find ways to ensure that high- as well as low-standard States are prevented from cutting standards to sub-optimal levels in an attempt to attract inward investment. See further ch 5 below.

of the States. However, where there is evidence that the EU is able to 'add value', it can and should intervene. My contention is that a vigorous application of the principles of subsidiarity and proportionality may enable an appropriate balance to be struck between the federation and its component entities. Subsidiarity and proportionality are 'evidently statements of good governance in a multi-level system'.[134] The former insists that the EU should only intervene to the extent that it is substantially better able to realize particular objectives than are the States. The latter insists that the EU should seek to avoid action which has an excessive effect on national autonomy.

The objectives of EU intervention determine the way in which the principles operate. In relation to the integrationist rationale, it is the principle of proportionality which has the greater impact. It insists that the institutions have regard to national autonomy when acting under the integrationist rationale, and do not intrude further than is necessary on the legitimate objectives of the Member States. In relation to the economic and social rationales, subsidiarity is of greater significance. It is only where the institutions can demonstrate that their interventions can contribute to enhanced performance, or I would add regime legitimacy, that their competence should be exercised.

Chapters 4 and 5 below examine the case law of the Court and the various interventions of the political institutions in the labour law field. In the course of these chapters, close attention is paid to the way in which EU interventions contribute toward legitimacy and to the actual and potential impact of the principles of subsidiarity and proportionality.

---

[134] Weatherill (n 96 above) 25.

4

The Interventions of the Court of Justice

Introduction

Chapters 2 and 3 above provide the analytical framework for this book. In them, I explore three plausible rationales for EU intervention in domestic labour law and examine the extent to which the Treaties—in particular the principles of conferral, subsidiarity, and proportionality—constrain the ability of the EU to intervene. I argue that it is useful both for the institutions themselves, and for those endeavouring to discover what the proper role of the EU might be, to distinguish between the integrationist, economic, and social rationales for intervention, to reflect on where a commitment to each may or must lead, and to consider the relationship between the three rationales. It is also important for the legitimacy of the EU project for the institutions to respect the principles of subsidiarity and proportionality.

The most significant conclusions are that it is possible to conceptualize the integrationist rationale—which is, after all, only a means through which the EU aims to realize rather ill-defined economic and social meta-objectives—so that mere differences between the laws of the Member States are not, without more, regarded as problematic. Integration may be compatible with diversity. Nevertheless, the integration project imposes constraints on Member States and may call for intervention on the part of the institutions so as to ensure that, for example, national rules do not prevent access to markets, that they do not discriminate against mobile factors of production, that standards do not fall to unacceptably low levels, that regulatory competition does not lead to a 'race to the bottom', and that economic and monetary union operates successfully. In addition, the EU has the competence to intervene to pursue economic and social objectives, other than through integration. It should pay attention to the nature of the relationship between the economic and the social. When exercising its competence, it should pay close attention to the principles of subsidiarity and proportionality. It should, in other words, ensure that European level intervention is able to 'add value' in the context of the achievement of given integrationist, economic, and social objectives, and it should also ensure that EU intervention does not go beyond what is necessary, in terms of infringing the rights and interests of individual citizens and the autonomy of the Member States.

Chapters 4 and 5, the last substantive chapters of this book, examine the ways in which the institutions have intervened in the labour law field. The intention is not to provide an exhaustive account of European intervention in the labour law arena, but instead to explore the nature and extent of the commitments of the institutions to each of the rationales for EU intervention in domestic labour law and to the principles of subsidiarity and proportionality. In a relatively short book, it is necessary to be selective. I have elected to focus on those interventions which best illustrate the various approaches adopted by the Court of Justice and the political institutions. The aim is to expose some of the more profound areas of tension and to explore possible ways forward for European labour law.

This chapter analyses the negative integration case law of the Court, reflecting on the way in which the Court has attempted to protect the interests of workers in the course of its market-making endeavour. I am critical of the Court's approach. Chapter 2 above makes it clear that, in general, the Court is all too ready to hold that differences between the rules in force in the various Member States are problematic. This chapter shows the way in which this position has put a strain on the case law of the Court in the labour law field; an area of policy in which the Court is evidently receptive to the argument that the autonomy of the Member States should be respected.

The Negative Integration Case Law of the Court of Justice

In chapter 2 above, I discussed the integrationist rationale in great detail. I devoted considerable attention to the Court of Justice's approach to the definition of the barrier to free movement, and remarked that its approach was neither consistent nor convincing. I identified two tests used by the Court in its assessment of the barrier to free movement. The first is a broad test, which has its origins in the *Dassonville* case. It maintains that all rules which affect access to markets in other Member States are capable of amounting to barriers to free movement. The second is a much narrower test. It has its origins in the *Keck* case, and maintains that only rules which either prevent access to markets or discriminate against imported factors are capable of amounting to barriers.

This chapter explores the implications of the Court's negative integration case law for domestic labour law.[1] As we shall see, it appears that the Court is experimenting with various ways of stepping back from the logic of the extreme integrationist position it first adopted in the *Dassonville* case. My argument is that the best approach, given the economic and social meta-objectives of the integration project, and given the strength of the arguments for diversity and national autonomy within today's EU, involves a rejection of the *Dassonville* test, and an adoption instead of the *Keck* test in relation to the free movement of not only goods, but also workers, services, and establishment. I also consider the other route through which

---

[1] cf S Simitis, 'Dismantling or Strengthening Labour Law: The Case of the European Court of Justice' (1996) 2 European Law Journal 156.

the Court may be able to ensure that national autonomy in the labour law field is preserved. The Court may hold that national labour law rules infringe the free movement provisions of the Treaty, but that they are nevertheless justified. Although this route may preserve national autonomy in the labour law field, it institutionalizes a more profound tension between market integration and national labour law rules than that which would be held to exist were the Court to adopt the *Keck* test. The justification stage of the Court's negative integration case law was deliberately neglected in chapter 2 above. The objective of chapter 2 was to demonstrate the extent to which differences between the laws of the Member States are seen as problematic in integrationist terms, either as barriers to free movement, as distortions of competition, or as impediments to EMU. The justification stage is reached only after the Court has decided that a particular measure raises integrationist concerns. It provides a way in which it is possible to mediate the tension, or to find a balance, between the integrationist objectives of the EU and other legitimate objectives typically of the Member States. In my discussion of the justification stage, the potential significance of rights discourse is discussed, as is the Court's application of the principle of proportionality.

In the *Dassonville* case, the Court of Justice held that 'all trading rules enacted by Member States which are capable of hindering, directly or indirectly, actually or potentially, intra-Community trade' fall within the scope of Article 28 EC.[2] Under the *Dassonville* line of authority, which applies not only to the free movement of goods but also to the other freedoms,[3] the key question appears to be whether the trading rules in question affect access to markets in other Member States. A case at the 'outer limits of free movement jurisprudence' is *Centros*.[4] The Court held that the refusal of the Danish registrar of companies to register a branch of a company incorporated in the UK in Denmark, on the grounds that by incorporating in the UK and then seeking to operate only in Denmark the owners were trying to evade Danish rules on minimum capital requirements, was contrary to the free movement provisions of the Treaty:

The fact that a national of a Member State who wishes to set up a company chooses to form it in the Member State whose rules of company law seem to him the least restrictive and to set up branches in other Member States cannot, of itself, constitute an abuse of the right of establishment. The right to form a company in accordance with the law of a Member State and to set up branches in other Member States is inherent in the exercise, in a single market, of the freedom of establishment guaranteed by the Treaty.[5]

---

   [2] Case 8/74 *Dassonville* [1974] ECR 837 [5].
   [3] See eg Case C-55/94 *Gebhard* [1995] ECR I-4565 [37]; Case C-415/93 *Bosman* [1995] ECR I-4921 [103]; and Case C-384/93 *Alpine Investments* [1995] ECR I-1141 [38].
   [4] S Deakin, 'Legal Diversity and Regulatory Competition: Which Model for Europe?' (2006) 12 European Law Journal 440, 449.
   [5] Case C-212/97 *Centros* [1999] ECR I-1459 [27]. See also Case C-208/00 *Überseering* [2002] ECR I-9919; Case C-167/01 *Inspire Art* [2003] ECR I-10115; and Case C-411/03 *SEVIC Systems* [2005] ECR I-10805.

It can confidently be predicted that the *Centros* jurisprudence will herald an increase in regulatory competition in EU company law,[6] perhaps along the same lines as in the US.[7] There is a risk that States might be induced to lower their company law standards to sub-optimal levels in an attempt to attract inward investment.

If enterprises may elect not to move to Member States in which corporate and labour laws and practices may put an extra burden on their cost structures, or if workers may elect not to move to Member States in which their rights are not protected to the same extent or in the same way as in their home State—and note that under *Dassonville*, potential and indirect effects on trade suffice—the relevant national rules will, under *Dassonville*, be held to be capable of amounting to barriers to free movement. Given that both enterprises (in the context of the free establishment and the freedom to provide services) and workers (in the context of the free movement of workers) are able to challenge the legality of national labour law rules, it is not only States with low labour standards but also those with high labour standards which may find that their rules are challenged. Workers' and enterprises' access to markets is, at least potentially, affected by almost any difference in national labour law regimes. Of course, once they are classified as barriers to free movement, national labour law rules are vulnerable. There is an onus on Member States to justify the rules according to EU law criteria. The States must show that domestic rules serve legitimate objectives and that they satisfy a proportionality test (ie they must show that they do not impose any greater restriction on free movement than is necessary for the achievement of legitimate objectives). If national policies restrict free movement to a greater extent than necessary, they will be disapplied.[8]

---

[6] See J Armour, 'Who Should Make Corporate Law? EC Legislation versus Regulatory Competition' (2005) 58 Current Legal Problems 369.

[7] See W Cary, 'Federalism and Corporate Law: Reflections on Delaware' (1974) 83 Yale Law Journal 663.

[8] Paul Davies has argued that 'insistence on according to migrant workers and their families the full benefit of the labour and social systems of the host State has been one of the most dynamic areas of Community law'; P Davies, 'Posted Workers: Single Market or Protection of National Labour Law Systems?' (1997) 34 CML Rev 571, 588. He makes reference to Art 39(2) EC, Council Regulation 1612/68/EEC of 15 October 1968 on freedom of movement for workers within the Community [1968] OJ Spec Ed L257/2, and the case law of the Court interpreting Regulation 1612/68. One might also mention Art 12 EC, as interpreted in eg Case C-274/96 *Bickel and Franz* [1998] ECR I-7637; Directive 2004/38/EC of 29 April 2004 on the right of citizens of the Union and their family members to move and reside freely within the territory of the Member States [2004] OJ L158/77; and the case law of the Court relating to citizenship: Case C-85/96 *Martinez Sala* [1998] ECR I-2691, Case C-184/99 *Grzelczyk* [2001] ECR I-6193, Case C-413/99 *Baumbast* [2002] ECR I-7091, and Case C-209/03 *Bidar* [2005] ECR I-2119. Davies is right to argue that one way in which the free movement of persons has been promoted is through the insistence that migrant workers, and citizens, have full access to local protection. But a consequence of cases such as *Bosman* (n 3 above) and *Centros* (n 5 above), which make it clear that the broad *Dassonville* test applies beyond the free movement of goods, is that free movement is also to be protected by advancing a deregulatory threat to national labour law regimes. And of course, if any aspect of a national labour law regime fails to survive the scrutiny of the Court, it will not benefit migrant workers.

The broad reach of the free movement provisions—linked with the broad range of justificatory arguments available to the Member States and the existence of a proportionality test—is welcomed by some commentators. Gerstenberg, for example, considers that the Court's case law has democratic appeal. He argues that the Court's expansive interpretation of freedom of movement 'enhances the quality of democratic deliberation about the right balance between private autonomy and non-economic integrity-interests, and about the kinds and level of tolerable risks'.[9] Spaventa locates a normative foundation for what is said to be the Court's liberal aim of protecting the individual from unnecessary regulation, in the notion of Union citizenship.[10] She also argues that 'the move towards a non-discriminatory assessment of the rules imposed by the main (if not only) regulator adds a new dimension to the rights conferred upon the individuals by the Community'.[11]

I am more sceptical. The *Dassonville* test is so broad that it catches labour market regulation which does not, in any meaningful way, obstruct the establishment or functioning of the market. The free movement provisions are over-extended. As a direct result of the *Dassonville* line of authority the Court is in a position where it may have to assess the necessity of almost all regulation of the labour market. Moreover, if, in the aftermath of the *Bosman* and *Angonese* cases, it is held that the free movement provisions have horizontal scope and that individual employers as well as Member States are capable of infringing Articles 39, 43, and 49 EC, the limits will be pushed still further.[12] Also, the Court has no clear criteria to guide it in its assessments of the necessity of labour market regulation.[13] The broader the reach of the free movement provisions, the more such assessments the Court makes.

My sense is that the Court, in the labour law field, is experimenting with various ways of stepping back from the logic of the extreme integrationist position it first adopted in the *Dassonville* case. It seems to be searching for strategies which ensure that it reaches sensible outcomes which balance the need to eliminate obstacles to the establishment and functioning of the market and the legitimate interests served by labour market regulation at national (and even enterprise) level. It has, with varying success, experimented with a number of such strategies.

One strategy available to the Court is to hold that labour market regulation is caught by the free movement provisions of the Treaty, but then also to accept the

---

[9] See O Gerstenberg, 'Expanding the Constitution Beyond the Court: The Case of Euro-Constitutionalism' (2002) 8 European Law Journal 172, 181.

[10] See E Spaventa, 'From *Gebhard* to *Carpenter*: Towards a (Non-)Economic European Constitution' (2004) 41 CML Rev 743, 764–73. The Court discusses the extent of citizens' rights under Art 18 EC in *Martinez Sala, Grzelczyk, Baumbast* and *Bidar* (all n 8 above).

[11] Spaventa (n 10 above) 764. See further L Daniele, 'Non-Discriminatory Restrictions to the Free Movement of Persons' (1997) 22 ELR 191.

[12] See further ch 2 above, p 23. For discussion in the labour law context, see A Davies, 'The Right to Strike Versus Freedom of Establishment in EC Law: The Battle Commences' (2006) 35 ILJ 75, 76–8.

[13] P Davies, 'Market Integration and Social Policy in the Court of Justice' (1995) 24 ILJ 49.

arguments of the Member States at the justification stage without subjecting them to serious scrutiny. In the most important case dealing with the question of whether national labour law rules amount to barriers to free movement, *Rush Portuguesa*, the Court held that the host State, France, could not require that a Portuguese service provider obtain work permits for its Portuguese workers working temporarily in France, as that would amount to discrimination against it in relation to competitors established in France.[14] Yet 'the Court clearly felt the need to give some words of comfort to host States about labour standards as it proceeded to hold the work-permit rule contrary to Article [49]'.[15] In paragraph 18 of *Rush*, the Court baldly stated: 'Community law does not preclude Member States from extending their legislation, or collective labour agreements entered into by both sides of industry, to any person who is employed, even temporarily, within their territory, no matter in which country the employer is established ... '[16]

This holding makes it clear that 'a host Member State is entitled by Articles [43] and [50] to impose its own legislation upon nationals from other Member States who are operating in its territory, either by way of establishment or by providing services'.[17] However, it is not made clear how the Court reached this conclusion. Paragraph 18 of *Rush* can be reconciled with the approach in the *Dassonville* case if it is assumed that the Court reasoned in the following way. First, national labour law rules constitute barriers to free movement because they affect the access to markets of mobile factors of production, and therefore hinder trade. This step is entirely consistent with most of the free movement case law of the Court. Second, national labour law rules are always justified. It is this step which is unorthodox. The Court did not provide any reasons for its assertion in paragraph 18. While the lack of reasoning can be explained away given the facts of the case, the statement remains problematic. It is, as we shall see, extremely unusual for the Court to demand so little of Member States at the justification stage. Member States are usually asked to demonstrate that their national regime contributes to the realization of a legitimate objective, and that the legitimate objective in question could not be realized in any way less restrictive of free movement. In the *Rush* case there was no attempt to identify the (presumably social) objectives of national labour law and no attempt to assess whether those objectives could be achieved through measures less restrictive of free movement. Moreover, under this account, the Court's reasoning is, in normative terms, unconvincing. Having acknowledged the existence of a problem from the perspective of the integrationist rationale (ie the existence of disparities between national laws which operate in such a way as to impede the access to markets of mobile factors of production), why should the

---

[14] Case C-113/89 *Rush Portuguesa* [1990] ECR I-1417 [12].   [15] Davies (n 8 above) 589.

[16] *Rush Portuguesa* (n 14 above) [18].

[17] G Wolff, 'The Commission's Programme for Company Law Harmonisation: The Winding Road to a Uniform European Company Law?' in M Andenas and S Kenyon-Slade (eds), *EC Financial Market Regulation and Company Law* (Sweet and Maxwell, London 1993) 21.

Court then give wholesale preference to Member States' regulatory choices without subjecting them to meaningful scrutiny? While the result of this approach may be one which many labour lawyers would welcome, I agree with Paul Davies that 'the wholesale justification of national labour regulation, which *Rush* seems to accept' is 'vulnerable to attack and qualification at any time'.[18]

It is, however, also possible to seek to explain the *Rush* case in a different way. Rather than holding that national labour law rules amount to barriers to free movement but are justified, it may be that the Court adopted a different approach. It may be that the Court's statement in paragraph 18 can best be explained in the following way. The Court may have held that Community law does not preclude Member States from extending their labour legislation to all those employed in their territory, quite simply because the application of national labour law rules to mobile workers and enterprises does not amount to the creation of a barrier to free movement. Under this line of reasoning, it is the *Dassonville* test itself which is called into question. There are various ways in which the Court might plot a retreat from *Dassonville*.

One possibility is that labour law rules, or certain labour law rules, may simply be excluded from the ambit of the free movement and competition law provisions of the Treaty. One of Spaventa's conclusions is that 'in its erratic way of proceeding', the Court 'might well exclude some rules because of an a priori assessment of their legitimacy'.[19] This approach is evident in some of the Court's social security case law.[20] In the labour law context, it is most clearly evident in a competition law case, *Albany International*. In the *Albany* case the Court was faced with an argument that a collective agreement establishing a pension fund was, for the purposes of Article 81(1) EC, an 'agreement' between 'undertakings', which had as its 'object or effect' the 'prevention, restriction or distortion of competition'. The Court acknowledged that certain restrictions on competition were inherent in collective agreements, but went on to hold that 'the social policy objectives pursued by such agreements would be seriously undermined' if collective agreements were subject to Article 81(1) EC.[21] It concluded that 'it therefore follows from an interpretation of the provisions of the Treaty as a whole which is both effective and consistent that agreements concluded in the context of collective negotiations between management and labour in pursuit of [social policy] objectives must, by virtue

[18] Davies (n 8 above) 596. See also S Simitis and A Lyon-Caen, 'Community Labour Law: A Critical Introduction to its History' in P Davies *et al* (eds), *European Community Labour Law: Principles and Perspectives; Liber Amicorum Lord Wedderburn* (Clarendon, Oxford 1996) 1, 12.

[19] Spaventa (n 10 above) 764.

[20] See T Hervey, 'Social Solidarity: A Buttress Against Internal Market Law' in J Shaw (ed), *Social Law and Policy in an Evolving European Union* (Hart, Oxford 2000) 31. See also Joined Cases C-264/01, C-306/01, C-354/01, and C-355/01 *AOK Bundesverband* [2004] ECR I-2493. However, the Court's mantra, that 'Community law does not detract from the powers of the Member States to organise their social security systems', is, as Hervey explains, 'not strictly the case'.

[21] Case C-67/96 *Albany International* [1999] ECR I-5751 [59].

of their nature and purpose, be regarded as falling outside the scope of [Article 81(1)] of the Treaty'.[22]

This approach, under which certain sectors are in effect afforded immunity from the application of the EU free movement and competition law, is again unconvincing. As we have seen, so long as the *Dassonville* test prevails, it is clear that national labour law and social security rules affect market access (they are capable of affecting the locational decisions of employers and workers) and so should fall within the scope of the free movement provisions and require justification. The problem with an approach which excludes certain labour law rules from the ambit of the free movement and competition law provisions of the Treaty is that there is no explanation of why social security or labour law rules do not affect the establishment or functioning of the market, only an assertion that the rules in question fall outside the scope of the relevant Treaty provisions. While the result of this approach may well be one which labour lawyers welcome, the wholesale exclusion of national labour law rules is, rather like their wholesale justification, 'vulnerable to attack and qualification at any time',[23] as a result of the logic of the position which the Court has adopted under the *Dassonville* line of authority.

Of course, if the Court is prepared to question *Dassonville*, it may be able to explain why labour law rules might fall outside the scope of the free movement provisions of the Treaty. In the *Graf* case, the Court accepted that there may be a *de minimis* test. Consistent with the *Dassonville* case, the Court held that in order to be capable of constituting an obstacle to the free movement of workers, national provisions 'must affect access of workers to the labour market'.[24] But it went on to hold that the effect of the legislation at issue in the case, which related to entitlements to compensation on termination of employment, was 'too uncertain and indirect',[25] and was therefore able to conclude that Article 39 EC did not preclude the application of the national provisions in question. In this context, a *de minimis* test is helpful.[26] It enables the Court to give primacy to the legitimate interests of the State in all those cases in which there are only small negative effects on the integration project. It will, inevitably, be difficult to distinguish between impacts on the integration project which are *de minimis* and those which are not,[27] but it certainly seems right that the Court should decide not to interfere

[22] ibid [60]; and, on the scope of the exclusion, Joined Cases C-180/98 to C-184/98 *Pavlov* [2000] ECR I-6451, Opinion of AG Jacobs. See also, in the State aids context, Case C-189/91 *Kirsammer-Hack* [1993] ECR I-6185.   [23] Davies (n 8 above) 596.
[24] C-190/98 *Graf* [2000] ECR I-493 [23].   [25] ibid [25].
[26] As ch 2 above makes clear, a *de minimis* test was also deployed to good effect in Case C-376/98 *Germany v Parliament and Council* [2000] ECR I-8419 (*Tobacco Advertising*), in order to limit the competence of the Community under Art 95 EC. The Court, at [107], held that Community legislature may not rely on Art 95 EC 'with a view to eliminating the smallest distortions of competition'.
[27] One might, in fact, question whether the rule at issue in *Graf*, which removes the entitlement to compensation in all situations in which the employee is responsible for termination of employment, is only capable of having an uncertain and indirect effect on the free movement of workers. One might also question the extent to which it meets the social objectives of the State, or satisfies a proportionality test (see eg the argument at [11]); but of course, given that the Court held that the legislation

with national autonomy in the labour law field in circumstances in which the exercise of that autonomy has only marginal effects on integration.

A still better approach, in my view, would be to abandon the test in *Dassonville* and to adopt the test in *Keck*. In the *Keck* case, in the context of national provisions restricting or prohibiting certain selling arrangements, the Court held that national rules fall outside the scope of the free movement provisions because their application to the sale of products from other Member States 'is not by nature such as to prevent their access to the market or to impede access any more than it impedes the access of domestic products'.[28] Were the *Keck* test to be used to assess whether national labour law rules constitute barriers to free movement, the Court would have to determine whether they either (a) prevent access to markets, or (b) impede the access of imported factors of production in a discriminatory way. Although it is, of course, extremely unlikely that the Court, in paragraph 18 of *Rush*, was following the approach in *Keck*, a case still some two years away and concerned specifically with national provisions restricting or prohibiting certain selling arrangements, it may be possible to explain the statement in paragraph 18 of *Rush* in terms of the logic of the *Keck* case. The *Keck* test is capable of explaining why Community law might not preclude Member States from extending their labour law rules to all those employed, even temporarily, within their territory.

The first limb of the *Keck* test is straightforward in the labour law context. Differences between labour law regimes do not ordinarily prevent the market access of enterprises, service providers, or workers.[29] Enterprises are capable of providing services in, or relocating to, a range of States, regardless of the dictates of their labour law regimes. Similarly, workers are capable of working in States with unfamiliar, or unappealing, labour law regimes. This is not to deny that labour law rules may influence choice of location, but merely to make the point that access to markets remains possible notwithstanding differences in labour law regime.

The second limb of the *Keck* test is more complex. The crucial question is whether disparities between labour laws and practices in various Member States lead to discrimination against imported factors of production. The Court's case law on this point is not well developed. One of the virtues of the *Dassonville* line of authority, with its focus on hindrances to trade, is that the Court does not need to focus on the existence or otherwise of discrimination. In *Cassis de Dijon*, for example, the Court did not need to pay close attention to whether the German rule discriminated against French producers of Cassis. The rule was caught by Article 28 EC simply because it was an indistinctly applicable rule capable of hindering trade. However, post-*Keck*, the Court has had to address the question of discrimination

did not fall within the scope of Art 39 EC, there was no need for it to examine the State's objectives or to subject them to a proportionality test.

[28] Cases C-267 and 268/91 *Keck and Mithouard* [1993] ECR I-6097 [17].

[29] An example of a national rule which would be caught by the preventing market access test is the State monopoly considered by the Court of Justice in Case C-41/90 *Höfner v Macrotron* [1991] ECR I-1979.

in several selling arrangements cases.[30] In the *Burmanjer* case the Court stated that the information available to it did not enable it to establish whether the national rules in question (Belgian restrictions on itinerant sales) affected the marketing of imported products to any greater degree than the marketing of domestic products, and therefore left the final determination to the referring Court. The Court did, however, indicate that any discrimination against importers would have to satisfy a *de minimis* threshold.[31]

Simply because of the fact that the Court has not had reason to examine whether national labour law rules impede the access of imported factors of production in a discriminatory way, what follows is somewhat speculative. Discrimination exists where it is more difficult—perhaps, following the *Burmanjer* case, only where it is substantially more difficult—for certain imported factors of production to access a particular national market than it is for domestic factors. It exists if the imported factor of production faces a significant extra burden which the domestic factor does not encounter, and it may also be held to exist if it is more difficult for the imported factor to bear the same burden, for example because of the need to operate under a system of law with which it may be unfamiliar.[32] Discrimination may occur in the context of employment, establishment, or the provision of services; and it may potentially operate against migrant workers, non-national enterprises, and transnational enterprises.

I believe that it is difficult to argue that differences between national labour law regimes lead to discrimination against migrant workers; so long, of course, as the same legal rules apply to national and migrant workers. Migrant workers could only claim discrimination as regards market access if they successfully argued that a lack of familiarity with a particular Member State's labour law rules made it more difficult for them to find employment in that State. Any such relative disadvantage would probably be regarded as *de minimis*. Along very similar lines, it may be difficult to argue that differences between legal regimes discriminate against foreign enterprises of national scope seeking to establish themselves in a particular Member State (again, so long as the national and foreign enterprises are subject to the same legal regime). It is only to the extent that foreign enterprises are able to argue that a lack of familiarity with a particular State's rules makes it more difficult for them to access that market than it is for domestic enterprises, that discrimination could possibly be said to occur.

[30] See eg Case C-254/98 *Heimdienst* [2000] ECR I-151 [26]; Case C-405/98 *Gourmet* [2001] ECR I-1795 [21]; and Case C-71/02 *Karner* [2004] ECR I-3025 [42].

[31] Case C-20/03 *Burmanjer* [2005] ECR I-4133 [31]: 'it seems to follow from the information in the file transmitted to the Court that, if those rules did have such an effect [ie if they affected the marketing of products from other Member States to any greater degree than products from Belgium], it would be too insignificant and uncertain to be regarded as being such as to hinder or otherwise interfere with trade between Member States'. See also, in the sex discrimination context, Case C-167/97 *Ex p Seymour Smith and Perez* [1999] ECR I-623 [58]–[65].

[32] See A McGee and S Weatherill, 'The Evolution of the Single Market—Harmonisation or Liberalisation' (1990) 53 MLR 578, 589. They describe this as the 'playing away' problem.

On the other hand, where an enterprise is seeking only to provide services in another State, and is subjected to that State's rules as well as the rules of the State in which it is established, the dual burden imposed on the out-of-State service provider might well lead to a finding of discrimination.[33] The Court has held that 'the application of the host Member State's domestic legislation to service providers is liable to prohibit, impede or render less attractive the provision of services by persons or undertakings established in other Member States to the extent that it involves expenses and additional administrative and economic burdens';[34] but has not indicated explicitly (in large part because, under the *Dassonville* test, it does not need to address this point) whether this amounts to discrimination against out-of-State service providers. If it is held that out-of-State service providers suffer discrimination, it of course becomes impossible to square paragraph 18 of *Rush* with the *Keck* case.

Enterprises of transnational scope, which encounter a range of legal regimes in the various States in which they operate, are also candidates for discrimination. Transnational undertakings operating within the European market encounter particular difficulties and complexities resulting from having to take account of multiple national legal systems. The cumulative effect of the various national legal regimes to which they are subject can be said to create an extra burden. However, it is again possible to argue that there is no discrimination here. Whilst it is true that transnational enterprises face an extra burden, they are not treated any differently from enterprises of national scope as regards access to each of the Member States in which they operate. Accordingly, it may be that they are not subject to discrimination.

An acceptance of the *Keck* test, in preference to the *Dassonville* test, would have a significant impact on the range of labour law rules caught by the free movement provisions of the Treaty. Under *Dassonville*, almost all labour law rules would be caught and would therefore require justification. Under *Keck*, it is only those rules which prevent access to markets and those which have discriminatory effects which would be caught and would therefore require justification. There is, in the wake of the *Keck* case, a need for the Court to provide more guidance in relation to the circumstances in which discrimination against imported factors of production will be held to exist; for example by making it clear whether the imposition of national labour law rules amounts to discrimination against migrant workers, out-of-State service providers, or enterprises of national or transnational scope seeking to establish themselves in a particular Member State. However those issue are resolved, it is clear that national labour law rules, as a consequence of a move from *Dassonville* to *Keck*, would fall to be assessed differently, and that in some cases, they would no longer be caught by the free movement provisions of the Treaty.

---

[33] See eg Davies (n 8 above) 585, and 587–8.
[34] See Case C-164/99 *Portugaia Construções* [2002] ECR I-787 [18].

Choosing between the various possible tests for the barrier to free movement is, as stated in chapter 2 above, no easy task. Much is dependent on one's interpretation of the meaning of the integrationist, and ultimately also the European, project. My argument is that the extreme integrationist position adopted by the Court in the *Dassonville* case imposes too onerous a burden on Member States. They are put into a position where they have to attempt to justify national rules which may have no more than a marginal impact on integration. It also imposes too onerous a burden on the Court of Justice and national courts, which have to assess whether or not the arguments of the Member States should be allowed to prevail over the EU interest in free movement.

At the justification stage, the Court's task is first, to assess whether national rules serve a legitimate objective, and second, to apply a proportionality test. In the *Oebel* case, the Court upheld national rules restricting night work in bakeries, on the grounds that the national rules in question were 'a legitimate part of economic and social policy, consistent with the objectives of public interest pursued by the Treaty'.[35] Where the Court assesses whether national rules serve a legitimate objective, there is one limitation which may potentially be problematic in the labour law field. The Court has held that 'aims of a purely economic nature' cannot justify a barrier to the fundamental principles of free movement.[36] However, the Court has held that 'it cannot be excluded that the risk of seriously undermining the financial balance of the social security system may constitute an overriding reason in the general interest capable of justifying a barrier';[37] and also that 'the application by the host Member State of its minimum-wage legislation to providers of services established in another Member State pursues an objective of public interest, namely the protection of employees'.[38] It seems that there is a broad range of social and socio-economic arguments which Member States are able to deploy in order to justify various aspects of their labour law regimes.[39] Thus, the key to the final decision on justification is usually the application of the proportionality test.

---

[35] Case 155/80 *Oebel* [1981] ECR 1993 [12]. Weight was also attached to the fact that the rules were consistent with ILO Convention 20 of 1925.

[36] Case C-398/95 *SETTG v Ypourgos Ergasias* [1997] ECR I-3091 [23]; and Joined Cases C-49/98, C-50/98, C-52/98 to C-54/98 and C-68/98 to C-71/98 *Finalarte and ors* [2001] ECR I-7831 [39].

[37] Case C-158/96 *Kohll* [1998] ECR I-1931.

[38] *Portugaia Construções* (n 34 above) [22]. See also C-376/96 *Arblade and ors* [1999] ECR I-8453 [36].

[39] In Common Position adopted by the Council with a view to the adoption of a Directive on services in the internal market, 17 July 2006, Preamble, Recital 40, the Council states that the notion of overriding reasons relating to the public interest, which States may invoke in order to justify restrictions on the freedom to provide services, 'has been developed by the Court of Justice' and 'may continue to evolve'. It covers at least 18 grounds, all of which are listed in Recital 40, including the following: social policy objectives; the protection of workers, including the social protection of workers; the preservation of the financial balance of the social security system; and the prevention of unfair competition.

Here the task for the Court of Justice, or indeed the referring court,[40] is to assess not only the suitability and necessity of the measures in question,[41] but also whether the measures impose any greater restriction on free movement than is necessary for the achievement of the legitimate objectives in question. In the proportionality enquiry, as explained in chapter 3 above, values are ascribed to the legitimate objective of the State, and to the EU interest in establishing a market in Europe. It is not at all surprising that the intensity and form of the proportionality assessment have varied. Much depends on the extent to which the national measure adversely affects the integration project and on the value which the Court is prepared to ascribe to the legitimate objective of the State.[42] Much also depends on the extent to which the Court is prepared to investigate (or, perhaps, on the extent to which the Court expects Member States to demonstrate that they have investigated) whether there are any less restrictive means for the States to achieve their legitimate objectives.

The introduction of rights discourse may be relevant here. In the *Schmidberger* case an environmental group was granted permission by the Austrian authorities to demonstrate on the Brenner motorway, protesting against traffic levels in the Alps. An international transport undertaking brought an action for damages against Austria, claiming that Austria's breach of the free movement provisions of the Treaty had caused it loss. The Court held that:

... the fact that the competent authorities of a Member State did not ban a demonstration which resulted in the complete closure of a major transit route such as the Brenner motorway for almost 30 hours on end is capable of restricting intra-Community trade in goods and must, therefore, be regarded as constituting a measure of equivalent effect to a quantitative restriction which is, in principle, incompatible with the EU law obligations arising from Articles [28] and [29] of the Treaty, read together with Article [10] thereof, unless that failure to ban can be objectively justified.[43]

It then considered whether the restriction could be justified 'by considerations linked to respect of the fundamental rights of the demonstrators to freedom of

---

[40] In many cases, the Court of Justice has opted to leave the resolution of the proportionality enquiry to the referring court, which will often be in a better position to assess the suitability and necessity of the national measure in question in relation to its stated objectives. On the dialogue between national courts and the Court of Justice in the labour law context, see S Sciarra (ed), *Labour Law in the Courts: National Judges and the European Court of Justice* (Hart, Oxford 2001).

[41] In *Finalarte and ors* (n 36 above) [40] and [41], the Court held that 'whilst the intention of the legislature, to be gathered from the political debates preceding the adoption of a law or from the statement of the grounds on which it was adopted, may be an indication of the aim of that law, it is not conclusive'. 'It is, on the contrary, for the national court to check whether, viewed objectively, the rules in question in the main proceedings promote' the legitimate objective in question.

[42] The Court's statement in Case C-169/91 *Stoke-on-Trent* [1992] ECR I-6635 [15], that 'appraising the proportionality of national rules which pursue a legitimate aim under Community law involves weighing the national interest in attaining that aim against the Community interest in ensuring the free movement of goods', may have been provocative, but it sums up the task facing the Court rather well. Many have questioned whether this sort of balancing exercise is best undertaken by courts. In ch 5 below, I consider the extent to which the political institutions can and should provide clearer criteria to guide the judiciary.   [43] Case C-112/00 *Schmidberger* [2003] ECR I-5659 [64].

expression and freedom of assembly'.[44] The Court held that 'since both the Community and its Member States are required to respect fundamental rights',[45] 'the protection of those rights is a legitimate interest which, in principle, justifies a restriction of the obligations imposed by Community law, even under a fundamental freedom guaranteed by the Treaty such as the free movement of goods'.[46] The Court noted that both the free movement of goods and freedom of expression and assembly (as defined in Articles 10 and 11 ECHR) may be subject to derogations, and argued that 'in those circumstances, the interests involved must be weighed having regard to all the circumstances of the case in order to determine whether a fair balance was struck between those interests'.[47] Its conclusion was that 'the national authorities were reasonably entitled, having regard to the wide discretion which must be accorded to them in the matter, to consider that the legitimate aim of that demonstration could not be achieved in the present case by measures less restrictive of intra-Community trade'.[48]

Two important points emerge from the *Schmidberger* case; both related to the status of the freedoms of expression and assembly as fundamental rights. First, the fact that the freedoms of expression and assembly were fundamental human rights which the EU, as well as the Member States, were committed to observing, contributed to the value which the Court was prepared to ascribe to the legitimate objectives advanced by the Austrian Government.[49] The extent of the commitment of the EU and Member States to fundamental social rights—such as freedom of association and the right to strike—is, as shown in chapter 2 above, rather less obvious.[50] A consequence of this might be that fundamental social rights will not, at least until the EU makes a clear and unambiguous commitment to them, be accorded similar weight.[51] Second, the value attached to the protection of fundamental rights affects the way in which the proportionality test operates. If the Court were to apply the proportionality test with vigour, one would suspect that it would often hold that it is possible to achieve the legitimate objectives of the State by means that are less restrictive of free movement. A vigorous application of the proportionality test would therefore compromise national autonomy, and in cases such as *Schmidberger* would risk compromising national respect for fundamental rights. However, paragraph 93 of *Schmidberger* indicates that, at any rate where fundamental rights are at stake, the Court is prepared to accord a wide

---

[44] ibid [69].

[45] Authority for this proposition comes from the Court's case law on general principles of law, the Preamble to the Single European Act 1986, and Art 6 TEU; ibid [70]–[71].   [46] ibid [74].

[47] ibid [81].   [48] ibid [93].

[49] cf Case C-36/02 *Omega* [2004] ECR I-9609, especially [33]–[35].

[50] T Novitz, *International and European Protection of the Right to Strike* (OUP, Oxford 2003) ch 10; and Davies (n 12 above) 81–3.

[51] See eg *Albany International* (n 21 above) Opinion of AG Jacobs [131]–[194]. His opinion must now be read in the light of the provisions of the EU Charter of Fundamental Rights, on the uncertain effect of which, see T Hervey and J Kenner (eds), *Economic and Social Rights under the EU Charter of Fundamental Rights* (Hart, Oxford 2003).

discretion to the Member States and not interfere with the State's judgment that its legitimate objectives could not be achieved by measures less restrictive of intra-Community trade.[52] This is a positive move. However, a still more even-handed approach to proportionality would involve consideration of not only whether the legitimate objectives of the State could be achieved by means less restrictive of free movement, but also whether the integrationist objectives of the EU could be achieved by means less restrictive of national autonomy. One might expect the integrationist objectives of the EU to be scrutinized closely, and even to yield, when balanced against fundamental human rights protected at the national, and *a fortiori* at the EU, level.[53]

Conclusions

It is clear that the Court of Justice is committed to the pursuit of European integration. It has, in the main, interpreted the free movement and competition law provisions broadly, bringing a range of national rules within their ambit. It has also, again in the main, insisted that any restrictions on free movement imposed by national rules go no further than is necessary, applying the proportionality test relatively strictly. This stance has profound implications for domestic labour law. Almost all national provisions intended to protect workers are vulnerable as a result of a tension between what can be presented as the EU interest in integration and the national interest in labour regulation.

But a moment's reflection indicates that the tension is not straightforward. The EU's interest in integration is, as chapter 2 above makes clear, not an interest in integration for integration's sake; it is an interest in the (rather ill-defined) economic and social meta-objectives of the integration project. And it is at least possible that legitimate national regulation of the labour market is enacted with (some of) the same objectives in mind. This insight is significant. There may, in fact, not be a tension between the objectives of the integration project and those of national level labour market regulation. If national labour law rules do not have a significant

---

[52] See J Morijn, 'Balancing Fundamental Rights and Union Freedoms in Union Law: *Schmidberger* and *Omega* in the Light of the Union Constitution' (2006) 12 European Law Journal 15; and A Biondi, 'Free Trade, A Mountain Road and the Right to Protest: European Economic Freedoms and Fundamental Individual Rights' (2004) 1 European Human Rights Law Review 51.

[53] In this context, see also Council Regulation 2679/98 of 7 December 1998 on the functioning of the internal market in relation to the free movement of goods among the Member States [1998] OJ L337/8. The Regulation attempts to make it easier to deal with major obstacles to trade. Of most interest to labour lawyers is Art 2, which provides that 'this Regulation may not be interpreted as affecting in any way the exercise of fundamental rights as recognised in Member States, including the right or freedom to strike. These rights may also include the right or freedom to take other actions covered by the specific industrial relations systems in Member States'. It is at least arguable that the Regulation (which was referred to in the Opinion of the Advocate General but not in the judgment) influenced the Court's approach in *Schmidberger*, even though it was only adopted after the protests in *Schmidberger* took place.

adverse effect on the market-building endeavour, and if they advance European economic and social objectives, then in particular in view of the arguments from legitimacy advanced in chapter 3 above, it seems sensible to conclude that they should be allowed to survive.

There are essentially two strategies which the Court may be able to use so as to ensure this result. They may, and I would argue should, complement each other. The first is internal to the integrationist rationale, and involves a reconsideration of the test for the barrier to free movement. It is, as chapter 2 demonstrates, consistent with the dictates of the integrationist rationale for the Court to prefer the *Keck* test to that adopted in the *Dassonville* case. Were the Court to adopt the *Keck* approach, it would enable it to rule that many national labour law rules fall outside the ambit of the free movement provisions.[54] The second involves the relationship between the integrationist, economic, and social rationales. Specifically, it calls for a different approach at the justification stage. The argument advanced here is that the Court should be open to a variety of arguments at the justification stage and should adopt an even-handed approach to proportionality, endeavouring to discover whether a fair balance was struck between the various interests at stake. Both strategies involve the Court in the making of political or ideological choices. Despite the arguments encountered in chapter 3 above, I contend that the making of these choices need not put the legitimacy of the Court at risk. On the contrary, my argument is that the legitimacy of the European project is endangered if the Court fails to make these decisions and thereby fails to uphold the federal balance within the European Union.

However, the Court need not be left to make these decisions alone. There are, as we shall see in chapter 5 below, a range of ways in which the political institutions are able to intervene. They, like the Court, are able to take a position on the questions of what action may, or must, be taken under the integrationist rationale, and of the way in which the integrationist, economic, and social rationales may best be balanced. As we shall see, the relationship between the Court and the political institutions, and the relationship between the various political institutions involved in the making of labour law at the EU level, has not always been harmonious. Perhaps unsurprisingly, views on the proper scope of the integrationist rationale in the labour law field have differed, as have views on the relationships between the three rationales for intervention.

---

[54] The Court may, eg through its definition of the distortion of competition and other key concepts, also be able to ensure that labour law regulation falls outside the ambit of the competition and state aids provisions of the Treaty.

5

The Interventions of the
Political Institutions

Introduction

This chapter examines the interventions of the political institutions. Their approach is, of course, important in its own right, and it also provides an interesting perspective from which to view the negative integration case law of the Court. The political institutions have not sought to harmonize the labour law rules of the Member States, but have instead intervened in domestic labour law in ways which afford flexibility to the Member States and indeed the social partners. Their interventions illustrate the evolving relationship between various conceptions of three rationales. They also illustrate the extent to which the principles of subsidiarity and proportionality have operated so as to constrain the institutions. My discussion endeavours to show whether the interventions of the institutions are properly trained on integrationist, economic, and social objectives, and whether they demonstrate sufficient adherence to the principles of subsidiarity and proportionality.

Categorizing the interventions of the political institutions is not an easy task. My initial instinct was to distinguish between traditional and new approaches to governance.[1] Traditional governance at the European level is associated with the enactment of binding standards, capable of creating rights which are enforceable before national courts. It is associated with the Commission's right of legislative initiative and with participation within the legislative process by the Council of Ministers, the European Parliament, and a number of advisory committees. New approaches to governance differ in two respects. First, they tend not to involve the enactment of binding rules, but may instead involve the adoption of guidelines. Second, a more diverse set of actors is involved. Policy-making is no longer seen as the preserve of the Commission, European Parliament, and Council of Ministers, but instead new governance envisages and encourages the participation of a range of both private and public actors operating at the European and also the national and sub-national levels. But there is no clear dividing line between traditional and

[1] J Scott and D Trubek, 'Mind the Gap: Law and New Approaches to Governance in the European Union' (2002) 8 European Law Journal 1.

new approaches. Interventions may be traditional in some respects and new in others. More importantly, traditional approaches differ in a range of ways. Although a case can be made that the most traditional European governance strategy is the harmonization of the laws of the Member States, it is also consistent with the traditional approach for a legislative instrument to establish minimum standards upon which Member States are able to build their own more ambitious structures, or for it to create only a much looser framework with which a range of Member State solutions might comply.

I have chosen to adopt an approach the focus of which is on the extent to which EU rules constrain the autonomy of the Member States; or, to put this another way, afford flexibility to the Member States. The extent to which EU interventions in the labour law field constrain autonomy, or encourage diversity, is of key importance in relation to the operation of the three rationales and in relation to the application of the principles of subsidiarity and proportionality.

The structure of this chapter is as follows. The first section outlines the nature of the relationship between the negative integration case law of the Court and the interventions of the political institutions. The second reflects on the fact that the institutions have not harmonized or approximated the labour laws of the Member States. Typically, within a certain framework, EU interventions afford some flexibility to the Member States. This flexibility may, as the third subsection makes clear, arise in the context of minimum standard setting measures from which only upwards derogation is possible, or more flexible framework measures. It may also, as the fourth subsection explains, arise in the context of the open method of coordination. The intention throughout the chapter is to explore the extent to which particular modalities of intervention are able to realize the various objectives of the EU and the Member States.

The Relationship Between Negative Integration and the Interventions of the Political Institutions

All EU intervention in domestic labour law must be founded on an appropriate legal basis, and must respect the principles of subsidiarity and proportionality. It is perhaps trite, but nevertheless important, to state that the political institutions must also respect the Treaty. It is possible, for example, to challenge the validity of an act of the institutions on the grounds that it infringes the free movement provisions of the Treaty.[2] Where the institutions act under integrationist legal bases, the

---

[2] See Case C-51/93 *Meyhui* [1994] ECR I-3879 [11]: 'It is settled law that the prohibition of quantitative restrictions and of all measures having equivalent effect applies not only to national measures but also to measures adopted by the Community institutions.' The case law has, however, indicated that the Community legislature may attach conditions to, and determine the limits of, the rights and advantages which it accords in order to ensure free movement; Case C-56/01 *Inizan* [2003] ECR I-12403 [23], in the context of Art 42 EC.

Court is able to insist that their interventions contribute towards the establishment and functioning of the market. Where the institutions act under economic or social legal bases, the Court is able to insist that their interventions first, contribute towards the realization of economic and social objectives, and second, do not compromise the single market. EU intervention may either 'serve the economic demands of the single market' or 'merely interface with' them.[3]

In any assessment of the validity or legality of an act of the political institutions which involves the making of political, economic, and social choices, the Court tends, as seen in chapter 3 above, to allow the institutions a fairly broad discretion. In chapter 3, I criticized the Court for the deference it shows towards the institutions in its assessments of the principles of subsidiarity and proportionality. My concern was that in allowing the institutions a broad discretion it was ascribing insufficient value to the interests of the Member States and thereby failing to fulfil its role in striking the appropriate balance between the federation and its component entities.[4]

The interests at stake are rather different where the Court's task is to assess whether EU intervention under integrationist legal bases serves the economic demands of the single market. Recent cases have concerned EU rules which restrict tobacco advertising,[5] the sale of certain tobacco products,[6] and the sale of certain food supplements.[7] They are all, essentially, cases about the way in which the integrationist rationale should be conceptualized. In each situation, there were differences between the laws of the Member States and public health arguments for regulation to which the legislature decided to respond. Since the *Tobacco Advertising* case, the Court has affirmed the legality of the measures in all the cases which have come before it. The Court has concentrated on an analysis of the outer limits of Article 95 EC,[8] but has also, as necessary, dealt with arguments based on the infringement of Article 28 EC, the principles of subsidiarity and proportionality, the duty to give reasons, the fundamental property rights of traders, and the principle of non-discrimination. While I have some doubts concerning the approach which the Court adopts in its analysis of the barrier to free movement and the distortion of competition,[9] and while I would prefer to see an analysis of the principles of subsidiarity and proportionality which affords more weight to the interests of the Member States,[10] I consider it sensible for the Court to afford the political institutions a measure of discretion in their determination of how best to build the

[3] M Dougan, 'Minimum Harmonization and the Internal Market' (2000) 37 CML Rev 853, 860.

[4] See also K Lenaerts, 'Constitutionalism and the Many Faces of Federalism' (1990) 38 American Journal of Comparative Law 205.

[5] Case C-376/98 *Germany v Parliament and Council* [2000] ECR I-8419 (*Tobacco Advertising*).

[6] Case C-491/01 *BAT (Investments) Ltd* [2002] ECR I-11453 (*Tobacco Labelling*); Case C-434/02 *Arnold André* [2004] ECR I-11825; and Case C-210/03 *Swedish Match* [2004] ECR I-11893.

[7] Joined Cases C-154/04 and C-155/04 *Alliance for Natural Health* [2005] ECR I-6451.

[8] The Court points out that Art 95(3) EC itself explicitly requires that 'a high level of protection of human health should be guaranteed'; ibid [31].   [9] See ch 2 above.

[10] See pp 93–101 above.

market in Europe, in particular where integrationist objectives interface with other legitimate objectives (in these cases, public health concerns).[11]

Where the institutions intervene not under integrationist legal bases, but, for example, under the social provisions of the Treaty, the potential for tension is even more marked.[12] While EU intervention under the social provisions of the Treaty need not serve the demands of the single market, the requirement that the institutions must not infringe the free movement or competition law provisions of the Treaty remains.[13] In this situation, we are therefore dealing not only with the question of how the integrationist rationale should best be conceptualized, but also with the relationship between the integrationist and the economic and social rationales. The questions raised here, as Dougan puts it, 'create enough space to support the covert continuation of hostilities between rival agendas for the ongoing development of the Community's regulatory activities'.[14] In these situations, which call for interpretation of the Treaty, the Court must play a key role. Once again though, it is appropriate that the Court shows a degree of deference to the political institutions.

The relationship between the Court and the political institutions is an intriguing one. It is, of course, the Court's task to interpret the Treaty, and to ensure that the political institutions do not infringe the Treaty.[15] The traditional view is therefore that the political institutions should defer to the Court's interpretation of the dictates of the integrationist rationale. But this view may be criticized on the ground that it is too simplistic. This is not only because of the complexity of the assessments involved and the lack of clear criteria to guide the Court in these assessments; it is also, more fundamentally, because of the essentially cooperative nature of the market-building endeavour.[16] Neither the Court nor the political institutions are able

[11] For a flavour of the approach of the Court, in the course of its assessment of whether the Community measure was disproportionate (ie whether it restricted free trade more than necessary in relation to the objective of the protection of human health) see *Alliance for Natural Health* (n 7 above) [68]: 'In those circumstances and in view of the need for the Community legislature to take account of the precautionary principle when it adopts, in the context of the policy on the internal market, measures intended to protect human health ... the authors of Directive 2002/46 could reasonably take the view that an appropriate way of reconciling the objective of the internal market, on the one hand, with that relating to the protection of human health, on the other, was for entitlement to free movement to be reserved for food supplements containing substances about which, at the time when the directive was adopted, the competent European scientific authorities had available adequate and appropriate scientific data capable of providing them with the basis for a favourable opinion, whilst giving scope, in Article 4(5) of the directive, for obtaining a modification of the positive lists by reference to scientific and technological developments'.

[12] I know of no cases in which the legality of measures adopted under the social provisions of the Treaty have been challenged on the basis that they infringe either the free movement or the competition law provisions of the Treaty. In the environmental context, see Case C-341/95 *Safety Hi-Tech* [1998] ECR I-4355.

[13] eg Art 137(4) EC states that the provisions adopted pursuant to this Article 'shall not prevent any Member State from maintaining or introducing more stringent protective measures *compatible with this Treaty*' (author's emphasis).   [14] Dougan (n 3 above) 865–6.

[15] See Arts 220 and 230 EC. Ultimately, of course, it is open to the political institutions to amend the Treaty, and thereby to ensure the primacy of their preferred approach over that of the Court.

[16] See eg M Egan, *Constructing a European Market* (OUP, Oxford 2001).

to build the market alone. The market-building endeavour requires the intervention of the political institutions alongside the intervention of the Court.[17]

My suggestion is that the Court not only does, but also should, allow the interventions of the political institutions to colour its views of the nature of the market-making endeavour. The nature of the European market depends crucially on the balance between negative and positive integration. Thus, as explained in chapter 3 above, the principle of proportionality cannot demand that the EU should only embark on a positive integration strategy in those areas in which negative integration is not able to achieve the EU's integrationist objectives. The political institutions are entitled to decide that they should intervene, even in areas where obstacles to the establishment and functioning of the market could be eliminated by the Court, so that they may better achieve their various objectives. In my view, it is incumbent on the Court to ensure that its conception of the integrationist rationale, and its view of the relationship between the three rationales, is not too far removed from the view of the political institutions. The Court should intervene if it is convinced that the interventions of the political institutions are manifestly inappropriate, but it should also take guidance from the political institutions on the evolving relationship between various conceptions of three rationales. An example may help to illustrate this point.

One of the most controversial disputes at the intersection of internal market and labour law involves the posting of workers in the framework of the provision of services.[18] It is clear that the freedom to provide services under Article 49 EC includes the right of the service provider temporarily to post workers to another State. But what system of labour law should apply to posted workers? The application of host State labour law rules (ie the rules of the State in which they are posted) may, notwithstanding the *Rush* case,[19] infringe the freedom to provide services. Under the *Dassonville* test, it is (or, ought to be) clear that there is at least a potential effect on market access. Even under the alternative *Keck* test, the application of host State

---

[17] See eg Directive 2006/123/EC of 12 December 2006 on services in the internal market [2006] OJ L376/36, Preamble, Recital 6: Barriers to the free movement of services 'cannot be removed solely by relying on direct application of Articles 43 and 49 of the Treaty, since, on the one hand, addressing them on a case-by-case basis through infringement procedures against the Member States concerned would, especially following enlargement, be extremely complicated for national and Community institutions, and, on the other hand, the lifting of many barriers requires prior coordination of national legal schemes, including the setting up of administrative cooperation. As the European Parliament and the Council have recognised, a Community legislative instrument makes it possible to achieve a genuine internal market for services'.

[18] See eg Commission Communication 'Guidance on the posting of workers in the framework of the provision of services' COM(2006)159, 4 April 2006.

[19] See Case C-113/89 *Rush Portuguesa* [1990] ECR I-1417 [18]: 'Community law does not preclude Member States from extending their legislation, or collective labour agreements entered into by both sides of industry, to any person who is employed, even temporarily, within their territory, no matter in which country the employer is established.' In Cases 62 and 63/81 *Seco* [1982] ECR 223; Case C-43/93 *Vander Elst* [1994] ECR I-3803; and Case C-272/94 *Guiot* [1996] ECR I-1905, the relevant paragraphs read 'Community law does not preclude Member States from extending their legislation, or collective labour agreements entered into by both sides of industry relating to minimum wages, to any person ... '.

labour law rules may be held to amount to discrimination against out-of-State ser-vice providers. However, the application of home State labour law rules (ie the rules of the State in which the service provider is established) may undermine the host State's system of labour law.[20]

In the aftermath of the *Rush* case, the political institutions responded to this conundrum by enacting the Posted Workers Directive.[21] The Directive offers a guarantee to posted workers that, during the period of their posting, the employer will respect certain protective rules of the host State (ie the State in which they are posted).[22] Given that the Directive was enacted under what are now Articles 47(2) and 55 EC, legal bases which are intended to facilitate the freedom to provide ser-vices, it should, as a primary aim, serve the economic demands of the single mar-ket. Yet this is not what the Directive appears to do.[23] Barnard argues that the Directive was enacted 'in order to preserve the local system of wage setting and collectively negotiated, levy-based "social funds" in the German construction industry'.[24] And the Commission now accepts that the aim of the directive is to reconcile 'companies' rights to provide transnational services under Article 49 EC', and 'the rights of workers temporarily posted abroad to provide them'.[25]

My suggestion is that the adoption of the Posted Workers Directive should send a message to the Court about the importance which the political institutions attach to the integrity of national labour law systems. Specifically, in the context of the provision of services, the political institutions have come to a conclusion that labour law rules must be a matter for the host State. The political institutions seem unprepared to allow even posted workers, who by definition are only in the host State for a temporary period,[26] to undermine the integrity of the host State's labour law regime. This message has been underscored in the political debate which greeted the Commission's proposals for a Directive on services in the internal market.[27] The key feature of the so-called Bolkestein directive, named after the

---

[20] The longer the period of the posting, the greater this effect; see P Davies, 'Posted Workers: Single Market or Protection of National Labour Law Systems?' (1997) 34 CML Rev 571, 602.

[21] Directive 96/71/EC of 16 December 1996 concerning the posting of workers in the framework of the provision of services (the Posted Workers Directive) [1997] OJ L18/1.

[22] ibid Art 3(1). See also Art 3(10) which permits host states, *in compliance with the Treaty*, to broaden the scope of protection beyond the matters listed in Art 3(1).

[23] The rationale for the Directive is discussed in Davies (n 20 above). His view, which I share, is 'that the counter-intuitive proposition that the Directive does advance the interests of the home-State employer can be defended, but only with difficulty, and that the primary beneficiaries of the Directive are in fact the systems of labour regulation of the host States'. He remarks that the ECJ, in the *Rush* case, dealt the host States 'most of the aces', so 'they naturally played their cards so as to produce a Directive which was highly protective of domestic labour regulation'.

[24] C Barnard, 'EC "Social" Policy' in P Craig and G De Búrca (eds), *The Evolution of EU Law* (OUP, Oxford 1999) 479, 503–4.   [25] COM(2006)159 (n 18 above) 2.

[26] Case C-215/01 *Schnitzer* [2003] ECR I-14847.

[27] See Commission proposal for a Directive on services in the internal market, COM(2004)2, 5 March 2004; and Commission amended proposal for a Directive on services in the internal market, COM(2006)160, 4 April 2006. For a strong critique of the Commission's amended proposal, see Editorial Comments, 'The services directive proposal: Striking a balance between the promotion of the internal market and preserving the European social model?' (2006) 43 CML Rev 307.

Commissioner in charge of internal market affairs when the original proposal was presented, was the country of origin principle, according to which a service provider is subject only to the law of the country in which he is established.[28] However, the country of origin principle was accompanied by a series of derogations. In the case of the posting of workers, the proposal ensured coherence with Directive 96/71 by exempting all matters coming under the Posted Workers Directive from the application of the country of origin principle. The result was that, even under the original proposal, the existing Community *acquis* on the posting of workers was unaffected.[29] The European Parliament introduced significant amendments to the proposed directive, including the deletion of the country of origin principle.[30] These have, in large part, been accepted by the Commission and now the Council. It is now even clearer that the Directive does not affect 'labour law ... which Member States apply in accordance with national law which respects Community law', 'the social security legislation of the Member States', or 'the exercise of fundamental rights as recognised in the Member States and by Community law'.[31]

It is, of course, too early to know how the Court might respond to the Directive on services in the internal market. The Directive, like the Posted Workers Directive, is based on Articles 47(2) and 55 EC. It should therefore serve integrationist objectives.[32] The Court can be expected, should the opportunity present itself, to scrutinize the Directive closely (especially Articles 16 to 18) in order to ascertain whether it makes it easier for persons to provide services within the EU. If it decides that it does not, arguing for example that the legal consistency of the proposal has been compromised by the amendments of the European Parliament,[33] it may go so far as to annul (certain provisions of) the Directive.

In relation to the provisions on labour law, the position ought to be more straightforward. Since the adoption of the Posted Workers Directive, the Court has been prepared to take its provisions into account when interpreting the Treaty

---

[28] See also Case C-76/90 *Säger* [1991] ECR I-4221, the leading case in the field of the freedom to provide services.

[29] Arts 24 and 25 merely proposed the scrapping of certain administrative obligations concerning posting, and the reinforcement of administrative cooperation between the Member States; COM(2004)2 (n 27 above).

[30] 'The Parliament's proposed restrictions are based on the fear of a "race to the bottom" and social dumping'; Editorial Comments (n 27 above) 310. These concerns correspond exactly with fears about the potential negative effects of untrammelled regulatory competition, and with conception V of the distortion of competition.

[31] See Directive 2006/123/EC (n 17 above), Art 1(6) and (7). Art 3 provides that 'if the provisions of this Directive conflict with a provision of' the Posted Workers Directive, the latter 'shall prevail'.

[32] See W Streeck, 'Neo-Voluntarism: A New European Social Policy Regime?' (1995) 1 European Law Journal 31, 42: 'Examples abound of European social policy legislation that serves, not to create uniform social rights or obligations for participants in the European labour market, but to protect the viability of Member States as formally sovereign political entities ... While typically such legislation is accompanied by impressive integrationist rhetoric, it is in reality concerned with protective insulation of national regimes and the political stability of the nation-state.'

[33] See Editorial Comments (n 27 above) 308.

provisions on the freedom to provide services.[34] There has been no sign of a retreat from *Rush*.[35] The Directive on services in the internal market serves only to reinforce the existing legal position in relation to labour law. The Court should take heed of the consistent interventions of the political institutions, and reaffirm its holding in the *Rush* case.

What would be welcome is the provision of a more convincing rationale for *Rush*. In the *Rush* case the Court did not make it clear whether the imposition of host State labour law rules does not create an obstacle to service providers, or (more likely) whether it does create an obstacle, but that it is an obstacle which is justified. The Posted Workers Directive provides no assistance here. The Preamble to the Directive merely recites the Court's formulation in paragraph 18 of *Rush*.[36] The Preamble to the Directive on services in the internal market is more promising. It links the removal of obstacles to the development of service activities between Member States to the achievement of the task laid down in Article 2 EC,[37] and, in particular, to the growth and competitiveness agenda and the Lisbon strategy.[38] It goes on to state that it is 'important to achieve an internal market for services, with the right balance between market opening and preserving public services and social and consumer rights',[39] and provides that the Directive 'should not preclude the application by a Member State of rules on employment conditions. Rules laid down by law, regulation or administrative provisions should, in accordance with the Treaty, be justified for reasons relating to the protection of workers and be non-discriminatory, necessary and proportionate, as interpreted by the Court of Justice, and comply with other relevant Community law'.[40]

Thus, it seems that the view of the political institutions is that the imposition of host State labour law rules may create an obstacle to the freedom to provide services, but that any such obstacle is likely to be justified. Given the evident concern of the political institutions to liberalize service provision within the EU and to establish a genuine internal market in services by removing barriers to the development of service activities,[41] arguments for restricting the scope of the free movement of services provisions are not likely to be well received. In any event, the approach of the political institutions is consistent with the approach of the Court, which has not indicated that it is willing to extend the *Keck* test to the freedom to provide services. Even if, in accordance with my preferred analysis of the integrationist rationale, the Court were to extend the *Keck* test to services, labour

---

[34] See eg Case C-60/03 *Wolff and Müller* [2004] ECR I-9553.

[35] Instead, the case law on the posting of workers in the framework of the provision of services has focused on the measures which host States are able to take in order to guarantee that no abuses have taken place; see COM(2006)159 (n 18 above).

[36] Posted Workers Directive (n 21 above) Preamble, Recital 12.

[37] Directive 2006/123/EC (n 17 above) Preamble, Recital 1.   [38] ibid Recitals 2 and 4.

[39] ibid Recital 4.

[40] ibid Recital 82. On the relationship with the Posted Workers Directive, see Recitals 86 and 87.

[41] See also Commission Report on the State of the Internal Market for Services, COM(2002)441, 30 July 2002.

law rules would still be caught by the free movement provisions to the extent that they were held to discriminate against out-of-State service providers. Thus, it seems that the best rationale for *Rush* may be one which accepts that the application of host-State labour law rules to out-of-State service providers may be problematic from the integrationist perspective, but that it is justified so long as it is non-discriminatory, necessary, and proportionate. Those seeking to defend the integrity of national systems of labour law are left with the hope—or rather the expect-ation—that in the light of the interventions of the political institutions, the Court will accord significant weight to the interests served by national-level regulation of the labour market and will continue to hold that such regulation may be justified.

The above example is intended to illustrate that the evolving relationship between various conceptions of three rationales is not a matter for the Court alone. The political institutions also play a significant part in defining the contours of the European project.[42] While there are, of course, differences between the approaches of the Member States within the Council, and between the approaches of the Commission, the European Parliament, and the various social partner organ-izations involved in EU intervention in domestic labour law, it is nevertheless pos-sible to distinguish in two important respects between the approach of the Court and that of the political institutions. First, the political institutions do not tend to adopt the Court's view that mere differences between the laws of the Member States are problematic. This, in my opinion, reinforces the argument in chapter 2 above, to the effect that the *Keck* test should be preferred to that in the *Dassonville* case, and that conception III of the distortion of competition should be preferred over either conception I or II. Second, the focus of the political institutions, at least since Maastricht, has been on the relationship between the economic and social objectives of the EU rather than on the market-building endeavour. The evolving and contested relationship between the economic and the social will be critically important to the future direction of EU labour law.

The Harmonization (or Approximation) of National Labour Law Regimes

The negative integration case law of the Court, discussed at length in chapters 2 and 4 above, leads to the conclusion that differences between national labour law regimes are problematic. Disparities between national provisions are capable of affecting market access and so are caught by the *Dassonville* test for the barrier to free movement. Disparities may also discriminate against mobile factors of pro-duction—especially out-of-State service providers—and so may also be caught by

[42] There are, of course, many other examples which one could provide. The dynamic between the Court and the political institutions is particularly interesting in relation to Union citizenship and the mutual recognition of qualifications; neither of which are considered in any detail in this book.

the *Keck* test. The fact that national labour law rules are caught by the free movement provisions does not mean that they will be condemned by the Court. National labour law rules may be justified. As we have seen, the Court has not, in the main, subjected national labour law rules to serious scrutiny and has therefore tended to hold that they may indeed be justified.

Since the *Cassis de Dijon* case, under the so-called 'new approach to harmonization',[43] the political institutions have intervened on integrationist grounds in areas in which national regulation is liable to hinder free movement, but is also justified; ie in those areas in which negative integration is not able to eliminate barriers to trade. If this approach were to be adopted in the labour law field, one would expect the institutions to intervene to tackle those problematic differences between national labour law regimes which cannot be eliminated by the negative integration case law of the Court.

It is therefore striking that the political institutions have not sought to intervene in domestic labour law in order to eliminate disparities between the various national regimes. The Commission has stated that 'the total harmonization of social policies is not an objective of the Community or the Union';[44] and there were no proposals for the harmonization of any aspect of labour law in the Social Policy Agendas of 2000 or 2005.[45] Harmonization is explicitly ruled out in Article 129 EC, and was not referred to in the Agreement on Social Policy attached to the TEU. Although Article 136 EC refers to the harmonization of living and working conditions and the harmonization of social systems, Article 137(2)(a) EC specifically excludes 'any harmonisation of the laws and regulations of the Member States', and Article 137(4) EC makes it clear that provisions adopted pursuant to Article 137 EC 'shall not prevent any Member State from maintaining or introducing more stringent protective measures compatible with this Treaty'.[46] The interventions of the institutions are, as we shall see, consistent with the maintenance of disparities between national labour law systems; or to put this rather more provocatively, with the continuation of a state of affairs which is, from the Court's perspective, problematic in integrationist terms. The fact that the institutions have not harmonized the social policies of the Member States may be explained in at least two ways.

---

[43] See Case 120/78 *Rewe-Zentral v Bundesmonopolverwaltung für Branntwein* [1979] ECR 649 (*Cassis de Dijon*); and Commission White Paper on Completing the Internal Market, COM(85)310, 14 June 1985.

[44] See Commission Medium Term Social Action Programme 1995–97, COM(95)134, 12 April 1995, 2.

[45] Commission Communication, 'Social Policy Agenda' COM(2000)379, 28 June 2000; and Commission Communication on the Social Agenda, COM(2005)33, 9 February 2005.

[46] It is interesting that many commentators are reluctant to forfeit the language of harmonization. Slot, eg, identifies 'optional', 'partial', and 'minimum' harmonization alongside 'total' harmonization; PJ Slot, 'Harmonisation' (1996) 21 ELR 378, 382–8; Dougan refers to 'minimum' harmonization; Dougan (n 3 above); and Deakin refers to 'reflexive' harmonization; S Deakin, 'Two Types of Regulatory Competition: Competitive Federalism versus Reflexive Harmonization. A Law and Economics Perspective on *Centros*' (1999) 2 Cambridge Yearbook of European Legal Studies 231.

One account suggests that, contrary to appearances, the desire or aspiration of the EU is to harmonize the labour law rules of the Member States. Harmonization has not, however, occurred, quite simply because the relevant actors have gradually come to appreciate that there is no realistic chance of attaining political consensus on a harmonized system of labour law,[47] in particular as Europe has evolved from a Community of six relatively homogeneous Member States, towards today's much more heterogeneous Union of twenty-seven. According to this account, today's more flexible approaches are the product of irreconcilable differences between the Member States and represent no more than second-best solutions to the problems facing the Union. Those pointing to the advantages of diversity and seeking to promote differentiation within the framework of the EU are simply doing their best to make a virtue out of political necessity.

An alternative account shifts attention to the political institutions' views of the market-building endeavour. The analysis of the integrationist rationale in chapter 2 above illustrates that the creation of a single European market is not straightforward: 'At its highest level of abstraction, the question is surely whether the objective of economic integration, as first pronounced in 1957 and subsequently reaffirmed, really requires an approximation of national provisions in the social sphere in particular, to the point where the regulatory structure of the Community resembles that of a single State.'[48] Simitis and Lyon-Caen argue that 'Community experience to date supports the thesis that no such approximation is necessary'.[49] Chapter 2 shows that the integrationist rationale may be conceptualized so that mere differences between the laws of the Member States are not, without more, regarded as problematic. This conclusion casts doubt on the Court's approach. It may be that the political institutions take a different view of the dictates of the integrationist rationale and are prepared to countenance the maintenance of diversity between national labour law systems, confident that the differences do not put the functioning of the internal market at risk.

Both of these accounts have some merit. Many Member State governments would no doubt welcome an EU in which the policies of all States converged towards their chosen system of labour law. Among the supranational actors involved in the policy-making process, many would no doubt regard the harmonization of social systems as 'a fine idea'; and it may be that harmonization is 'usually mentioned with nostalgia'.[50] But I agree with Simitis and Lyon-Caen that the harmonization of national labour law rules is unnecessary. One of the main aims of this book is to cast doubt on the desirability of uniformity in the labour law field

---

[47] A retreat from harmonization towards flexibility is evident in the worker participation law of the Community; see P Syrpis, *The Rationales for European Community Social Policy: An Analysis of EC Worker Participation Law* (D Phil thesis, Oxford 2000) chs 6–8.

[48] S Simitis and A Lyon-Caen, 'Community Labour Law: A Critical Introduction to its History', in P Davies *et al* (eds), *European Community Labour Law: Principles and Perspectives; Liber Amicorum Lord Wedderburn* (Clarendon, Oxford 1996) 1, 5. [49] ibid.

[50] ibid 13.

and to illustrate the advantages of managed diversity between national systems of labour law.

The remainder of this chapter examines the various ways in which the institutions have intervened in domestic labour law. I discuss not only the economic and social, but also the integrationist arguments which are, and may be, made in support of EU intervention. I also consider the extent to which such intervention may be vulnerable to the principles of subsidiarity and proportionality.

Minimum Standard Setting and Other More Flexible Approaches

Many of the measures adopted at European level in the social field have involved not harmonization, but the setting of minimum standards. If the aim of European intervention is social (ie to improve the position of workers) this seems an eminently sensible approach. The EU intervenes so as to guarantee that workers across Europe will benefit from a certain level of social protection but does nothing to prevent those Member States who are willing and able to do so from maintaining or introducing higher standards. It is, however, much less obvious that this approach is beneficial from the perspective of either the integrationist or the economic rationale.

Many of the other interventions in the labour law field have been even more flexible, affording significant autonomy to the Member States (and often, to the social partners). The EU rules establish a framework, from which not only upward but also downward derogation is possible. The more developed the framework, the greater the intrusion on autonomy. In relation to these more flexible measures, it is not only the integrationist and economic, but also the social advantages associated with EU intervention which may be difficult to identify.

This section identifies the meaning of minimum standard setting in the labour law context and examines the more flexible approaches which have been adopted. It then discusses the contribution which minimum standard setting and other more flexible approaches are able to make to the realization of the EU's integrationist, economic, and social objectives, and analyses the extent to which European intervention may be vulnerable to a vigorous application of the principles of subsidiarity and proportionality. A case study of the Working Time Directive is presented.

As we have seen, the social provisions of the Treaty, Articles 136 and 137 EC—like the old Article 118a, introduced by the Single European Act 1986 and now incorporated within Article 137 EC—refer not only to minimum standard setting, but also to harmonization. To the extent that this suggests that the political institutions are aiming to eliminate disparities between the labour law rules of the Member States, this causes unnecessary confusion. In accordance with Article 137(4) EC, none of the Directives adopted under Article 118a or Article 137 EC seeks to prevent any Member State from maintaining or introducing more stringent protective measures.[51] Legislation which sets minimum standards upon which Member States are free to build does not result in harmonization of social standards throughout Europe. It would only be otherwise if there were mechanisms in place either to discourage Member States from setting standards above the floor, or alternatively to encourage States to set standards at the same level, somewhere above the floor. Such mechanisms do not exist.

If a Member State chooses to maintain or introduce more stringent rules in the labour law field, these are interpreted to extend not only to domestic workers and enterprises but also to migrant workers and to foreign enterprises seeking to becoming established or to provide services in its territory.[52] The Court has also made it clear that the significance of the expression 'minimum requirements', 'is that Member States are authorised to adopt more stringent measures than those which form the subject-matter of Community action'.[53] Community action is not limited to the lowest common denominator, or to the lowest level of protection established by the Member States.[54] The institutions are therefore free, in the light of their various objectives, to choose the level at which the standards are to be set.[55]

All minimum standard setting measures include what is sometimes termed a 'more favourable provisions' clause, making it clear that States have the right to maintain or introduce more stringent protective measures. The Collective Redundancies Directive, first enacted under what is now Article 94 EC, provides that 'this Directive shall not affect the right of Member States to apply or introduce laws, regulations or administrative provisions which are more favourable to workers'.[56] There are similar clauses in the Transfers of Undertakings Directive,[57] also

---

[51] EU labour law measures based on integrationist legal bases, such as Arts 94 and 308 EC, also tend to involve either the setting of minimum standards or the establishment of a more flexible framework; see eg Council Directive 75/129/EEC of 17 February 1975 on the approximation of the laws of the Member States relating to collective redundancies [1975] OJ L48/29; and Council Directive 2001/86/EC of 8 October 2001 supplementing the Statute for a European company with regard to the involvement of employees [2001] OJ L294/22.

[52] Contrast eg the interpretation of Council Directive 89/622/EEC of 13 November 1989 on the approximation of the laws, regulations and administrative provisions of the Member States concerning the labelling of tobacco products [1989] OJ L359/1, in Case C-11/92 *Gallaher* [1993] ECR I-3545.

[53] Case C-84/94 *UK v Council* [1996] ECR I-5755 (*Working Time*) [17]. See also Case C-2/97 *SIP v Borsana* [1998] ECR I-8597.   [54] *Working Time* (n 53 above) [56].

[55] ibid Opinion of AG Léger [134]: 'the reference in Article 118a to "minimum requirements" does not mean that the Community's powers regarding the safety and health of workers are limited; on the contrary, it means that the Member States are at liberty to apply rules more stringent than those laid down at Community level'.

[56] Council Directive 75/129/EEC (n 51 above) Art 5. See also Council Directive 98/59/EC of 20 July 1998 on the approximation of the laws of the Member States relating to collective redundancies [1998] OJ L225/16, Art 5, which further provides that Member States' right 'to promote or to allow the application of collective agreements more favourable to workers' is also not affected.

[57] Council Directive 77/187/EEC of 14 February 1977 on the approximation of the laws of the Member States relating to the safeguarding of employees' rights in the event of transfers of undertakings, businesses and parts of businesses [1977] OJ L61/27, Art 7. See also Council Directive 2001/23/EC of 12 March 2001 on the approximation of the laws of the Member States relating to the safeguarding of employees' rights in the event of transfers of undertakings, businesses and parts of businesses [2001] OJ L82/16, Art 8.

enacted under what is now Article 94 EC, and in the Directive on the introduction of measures to encourage improvements in the Safety and Health of Workers at Work,[58] enacted under Article 118a. A number of minimum standard setting measures also include what is sometimes termed a 'non-regression' (or 'non-retrogression') clause, insisting that in the implementation of the EU measure there should be no reduction in the general level of protection. One example of an EU labour law measure with both 'more favourable provisions' and 'non-regression' clauses is the Working Time Directive, which is considered in more detail below. Article 15 states that 'this Directive shall not affect Member States' right to apply or introduce laws, regulations, or administrative provisions more favourable to the protection of the safety and health of workers or to facilitate or permit the application of collective agreements or agreements concluded between the two sides of industry which are more favourable to the protection of the safety and health of workers'. Article 23 states that 'without prejudice to the right of Member States to develop, in the light of changing circumstances, different legislative, regulatory or contractual provisions in the field of working time, as long as the minimum requirements provided for in this Directive are complied with, implementation of this Directive shall not constitute valid grounds for reducing the general level of protection afforded to workers'.[59] Other measures with both 'more favourable provisions' and 'non-regression' clauses are three Directives based on framework agreements concluded by the social partners, the Parental Leave, Part-time Work, and Fixed-term Work Directives;[60] the two anti-discrimination law Directives based on Article 13 EC; and the 2002 amendment to the Equal Treatment Directive.[61]

---

[58] Council Directive 89/391/EEC of 12 June 1989 on the introduction of measures to encourage improvements in the safety and health of workers at work [1989] OJ L183/1, Art 1(3): 'This Directive shall be without prejudice to existing or future national and Community provisions which are more favourable to protection of the safety and health of workers at work.'

[59] Council Directive 93/104/EC of 23 November 1993 concerning certain aspects of the organisation of working time [1993] OJ L307/18, has—after amendment by Directive 2000/34/EC of 22 June 2000, amending Council Directive 93/104/EC concerning certain aspects of the organisation of working time to cover sectors and activities excluded from that Directive [2000] OJ L195/41—now been consolidated; see Directive 2003/88/EC of 4 November 2003 concerning certain aspects of the organisation of working time (the Working Time Directive) [2003] OJ L299/9. Council Directive 94/33/EC of 22 June 1994 on the protection of young people at work contains an almost identical 'non-regression' clause; see [1994] OJ L216/12, Art 16.

[60] Council Directive 96/34/EC of 3 June 1996 on the framework agreement on parental leave concluded by UNICE, CEEP and the ETUC [1996] OJ L145/4, Cl 4; Council Directive 97/81/EC of 15 December 1997 concerning the framework agreement on part-time work concluded by UNICE, CEEP and the ETUC [1998] OJ L14/9, Cl 6; and Council Directive 1999/70/EC of 22 June 1999 concerning the framework agreement on fixed-term work concluded by UNICE, CEEP and the ETUC [1999] OJ L175/43, Cl 8; stating first that Member States and/or the social partners may maintain or introduce more favourable provisions; and second that implementation of the agreement shall not constitute valid grounds for reducing the general level of protection for workers in the field of the agreement.

[61] Council Directive 2000/43/EC of 29 June 2000 implementing the principle of equal treatment between persons irrespective of racial or ethnic origin [2000] OJ L180/22, Art 6; and Council Directive 2000/78/EC of 27 November 2000 establishing a general framework for equal treatment in

More flexible framework measures differ from minimum standard setting measures in that not only upward, but also downward derogation from the EU standard is possible. What distinguishes the emerging European social policy regime 'is its low capacity to impose binding obligations on market participants, and the high degree to which it depends on various kinds of voluntarism'.[62] EU rules make provision for Member States and/or the social partners to derogate from the EU standard. Following the 'undeniable success' of the European Works Council Directive,[63] the recent measures adopted in the worker participation field which provide workers, or their representatives, with rights to participate in the making of decisions in the enterprises in which they work, follow a similar pattern.[64] These Directives insist that a system for the information and consultation of workers is in place in the relevant enterprises. They include reference rules, which apply if the social partners at enterprise level so choose,[65] or in the event that they are unable to reach agreement. However, agreements between the social partners are not subject to the reference rules.[66] Hence, the practical arrangements for information and consultation vary from State to State and from enterprise to enterprise.

---

employment and occupation [2000] OJ L303/16, Art 8; and Directive 2002/73/EC of 23 September 2002 amending Council Directive 76/207/EEC on the implementation of the principle of equal treatment for men and women as regards access to employment, vocational training and promotion, and working conditions [2002] OJ L269/15, Art 8e, stating that 'Member States may introduce or maintain provisions which are more favourable to the protection of the principle of equal treatment than those laid down in this Directive'; and that 'the implementation of this Directive shall under no circumstances constitute grounds for a reduction in the level of protection against discrimination already afforded by Member States in the fields covered by this Directive'.

[62] Streeck (n 32 above) 45.

[63] Council Directive 94/45/EC of 22 September 1994 on the establishment of a European Works Council or a procedure in Community-scale undertakings and Community-scale groups of undertakings for the purposes of informing and consulting employees [1994] OJ L254/64, extended to the UK by Council Directive 97/74/EC of 15 December 1997 extending, to the United Kingdom of Great Britain and Northern Ireland, Directive 94/45/EC on the establishment of a European Works Council or a procedure in Community-scale undertakings and Community-scale groups of undertakings for the purposes of informing and consulting employees [1998] OJ L10/22. The Commission offers a positive assessment of the Directive in Commission Communication on Worker Information and Consultation, COM(95)547, 14 November 1995, 2. Contrast Lord Wedderburn, 'Consultation and Collective Bargaining in Europe: Success or Ideology?' (1997) 26 ILJ 1.

[64] Directive 2002/14/EC of 11 March 2002 establishing a general framework for informing and consulting employees in the European Community [2002] OJ L80/29. See further P Syrpis, 'Directive 2002/14: A Model of new governance in Europe' (September 2002) European Current Law xi. This Directive also includes a non-regression clause. Art 9(4) provides that 'implementation of this Directive shall not be sufficient grounds for any regression in relation to the situation which already prevails in each Member State and in relation to the general level of protection of workers in the areas to which it applies'. See also Directive 2001/86/EC (n 51 above) adopted under Art 308 EC.

[65] Note that, under all these Directives, the Member States have considerable freedom to determine the rules and principles through which the social partners, who have the power to negotiate the information and consultation procedure which is to apply in their enterprise, are selected. In relation to enterprises of transnational scope, competence is divided between the State in which central management is located, and the States in the territories of which particular establishments are situated; see further Commission Report on the Application of Directive 94/45/EC, COM(2000)188, 4 April 2000.

[66] These reference rules may operate as a benchmark for negotiators.

My discussion of minimum standard setting and more flexible framework measures starts with an analysis of their relationship with market integration. Under some conceptions of the integrationist rationale, both the measures adopted by the EU, and those subsequently adopted by the Member States, may be regarded as problematic. However, other conceptions of the integrationist rationale lend support to the adoption of minimum standard setting measures at EU level, though it is rather more difficult, if not impossible, to see the integrationist arguments in favour of more flexible measures. As so often, everything turns on one's interpretation of what the task of building a market in Europe entails.

There is no question that when they are based on the social provisions of the Treaty, measures which set minimum standards upon which Member States are free to build, and more flexible framework measures, are lawful. When, on the other hand, they are based on integrationist provisions such as Articles 94 and 95 EC, their legality may in the light of the *Tobacco Advertising* case be called into question.[67] Dougan argues that:

... taken at face value (as several commentators have suggested), the *Tobacco Advertising* judgment appears to say that secondary legislation which provides for minimum harmonization without also containing an explicit free movement clause does not actually contribute to the elimination of obstacles to free movement, is not genuinely concerned with the establishment and functioning of the Internal Market, and cannot validly be based on Article 95 EC.[68]

However, he feels able to conclude that:

... it seems fallacious to interpret the *Tobacco Advertising* judgment as authority for the blunt proposition that secondary legislation containing a minimum harmonization facility, but without also including an express free movement clause, cannot validly be adopted under Article 95 EC. After all, the effects of any such strict approach to the Court's reasoning would be disastrous for many of the Community's social initiatives.[69]

In this book, my intention is to draw attention to the latent tension between the integrationist reasoning of the Court and the social initiatives of the EU; not to predict that the Court will annul EU labour law measures. My argument is that the Court need not view mere disparities between the labour law rules of the Member States (which are inevitable where the EU adopts minimum standard setting and flexible framework measures) as problematic, and that were it to adjust its conception of the integrationist rationale, its case law would be more readily compatible with the approach of the political institutions in the social field.

---

[67] See Case C-376/98 *Germany v Parliament and Council* [2000] ECR I-8419 (*Tobacco Advertising*) [101]. See also P Syrpis, 'Smoke Without Fire: The Social Policy Agenda and the Internal Market' (2001) 30 ILJ 271, 277.

[68] M Dougan, 'Vive la Différence? Exploring the Legal Framework for Reflexive Harmonization within the Single European Market' in R Miller and P Zumbansen (eds), *Annual of German and European Law, Volume 1 (2003)* (Berghahn, New York 2004) 113, 152. No minimum standard setting measures in the labour law field have been interpreted to include a free movement clause, which would in effect oblige Member States to apply a standard no higher than the Community minimum to migrant workers, foreign enterprises, and out-of-State service providers.   [69] ibid 153.

The integrationist rationale may also limit the autonomy of Member States which choose to introduce their own differential standards. Given that national standards in the labour law field apply to migrant workers and to enterprises seeking to become established or to provide services in another State, the relevant national rules may—under the *Dassonville* case, certainly; and under the *Keck* case, to the extent that discrimination against mobile factors is held to exist—amount to barriers to free movement.[70] The key question is whether the national rules may nevertheless be justified. In the light of the combined effect of the *Rush* case, the Posted Workers Directive, and the fact that EU minimum standard and framework measures explicitly authorize Member States to enact their own standards, it is difficult to conceive of circumstances in which the Court would disapply the rules of the Member States in the labour law field, on the ground that they infringe the free movement provisions of the Treaty.[71]

Thus, it is possible—but only with difficulty—to accommodate minimum standard setting and flexible framework measures in the labour law field with the Court's conception of the integrationist rationale. However, if an alternative conception is adopted and it is accepted that certain disparities between national labour law rules are not problematic from the perspective of the integrationist rationale, it becomes possible to see minimum standard setting, and perhaps also more flexible framework measures, in a much more positive light. As suggested in chapter 2 above, conceptions IV and V of the distortion of competition provide a basis for the view that labour law intervention which admits of national diversity may contribute to the establishment and functioning of the market in Europe.

Under conception IV of the distortion of competition, the EU is able to act so as to establish the baseline rules of economic ordering for the European market. It is able to insist that competition within the European market is only fair or legitimate if it is in accordance with particular rules. In the labour law field, the objective may be to ensure that labour law standards do not reach 'unacceptably low' levels. If conception IV of the distortion of competition is adopted, minimum standard setting, rather than harmonization, is the appropriate policy response. According to the Commission, 'the establishment of a framework of basic minimum standards, which the Commission started some years ago, provides a basic bulwark against using low social standards as an instrument of unfair competition'.[72]

Under this conception of the distortion of competition, the level at which minimum standards are set is of significance. If EU minimum standards are set at too

[70] In relation to minimum standard setting, see M Dougan, 'Minimum Harmonization and the Internal Market' (2000) 37 CML Rev 853, 855: 'the applicable Community legislation sets a floor, the Treaty itself sets a ceiling and the Member States are free to pursue an independent domestic policy between these two parameters'.

[71] National rules will, of course, be held to be unlawful where they breach a Community minimum standard, or fall outside the parameters established by a Community framework measure. See eg Cases C-382 and 383/92 *Commission v UK* [1994] ECR I-2435; and Case C-173/99 *Ex p BECTU* [2001] ECR I-4881.

[72] Commission White Paper, 'European Social Policy—A Way Forward for the Union' COM(94)333, 27 July 1994, 5.

high a level they may exclude certain types of 'fair' (according to this definition) competition between States. The difficulty lies in the identification of the 'unacceptably low' labour standard. What some might see as an 'unacceptably low' standard, others might see as legitimate comparative advantage. The EU is on secure ground if it insists only on the core labour standards accepted by the ILO and the OECD.[73] In the European context, given the level of development of the Member States, it may be possible to develop a more extensive list of core standards, based on ILO and Council of Europe sources, the EU Charter of Fundamental Rights and the fundamental rights case law of the Court of Justice. The ability of the EU to establish more stringent baseline rules of economic ordering for the European market under this conception of the integrationist rationale would increase were the economic and social objectives of the Community and the Union to be spelled out more clearly. However, conception IV cannot give the institutions a free rein. The onus is on the institutions to show that standards are necessary for the establishment and functioning of the market; to show, in other words, that the market will fail to function properly without EU standards in place. It is possible, but difficult, to apply a similar analysis to more flexible framework measures. The argument would be that the framework is necessary to prevent 'unfair' competition, but that, within the parameters established by the institutions, all competition is 'fair'.

Conception V of the distortion of competition authorizes EU intervention where it can be shown that the quest for competitive advantage is destructive, inducing States to lower their labour standards to sub-optimal levels and precipitating a 'race to the bottom'. The EU may act where there is evidence either that States are lowering their standards in this way or that they are likely to do so.[74] Formulating appropriate policy responses is not at all straightforward. European intervention should prevent Member States from lowering social and employment standards to sub-optimal levels in an attempt to attract trade and investment. If this is the rationale for European intervention, total harmonization is not necessary. To the extent that it allows high-cost economies to impose certain costs on their low-cost competitors to the detriment of the latter,[75] it would, in fact, be damaging. It is also clear that minimum standard setting, without more, is not a sufficient response. The Commission has claimed that the establishment of a framework of basic minimum standards provides 'protection against reducing social standards to gain competitiveness'.[76] However, the limitations of the 'floor of rights' response

---

[73] If one of the aims of EU intervention is to prevent standards falling to unacceptably low levels, it is extremely difficult to account for the exclusions in Art 137(5) EC, in particular in relation to free association and the right to strike. See B Ryan, 'Pay, Trade Union Rights and Community Law' (1997) 13 International Journal of Comparative Labour Law and Industrial Relations 305; and T Novitz, *International and European Protection of the Right to Strike* (OUP, Oxford 2003).

[74] Particular attention must therefore be paid to those areas of labour law which are vulnerable to competitive pressures. Pay seems an obvious candidate. However, as a result of Art 137(5) EC, the competence of the Community does not extend to pay; see Ryan (n 73 above).

[75] E Whiteford, 'W(h)ither Social Policy?' in J Shaw and G More (eds), *New Legal Dynamics of European Union* (Clarendon, Oxford 1995) 111, 120.   [76] COM(94)333 (n 72 above) 5.

ought to be obvious. While EU minimum standard setting may operate so as to prevent low-standard Member States from lowering their standards to sub-optimal levels,[77] it does nothing to prevent higher-standard States from lowering their standards to sub-optimal levels which nevertheless remain at or above the floor.[78] It is here that non-regression clauses, which may be found both in minimum standard setting and more flexible framework measures, may be of assistance. They obstruct 'downward-directed competition',[79] seeking to prevent higher-standard Member States from reducing levels of protection when implementing a minimum standard setting Directive; though given that they are often 'without prejudice to the right of Member States to develop, in the light of changing circumstances, different legislative, regulatory or contractual provisions',[80] they are difficult to enforce.

While it is possible to analyse the integrationist effects of EU measures without engaging in a detailed analysis of their content, it is much more difficult to come to a judgment as to their economic and social effects. In order to evaluate the economic and social effects of any EU measure, it is necessary to consider its provisions in detail.[81] The focus of my analysis of economic and social effects is the Working Time Directive, a measure controversially adopted on the basis of Article 118a, which lays down minimum health and safety requirements for the organization of working time.[82] The Working Time Directive makes for an interesting case study for several reasons. First, its legality has been considered by the Court of Justice in the *Working Time* case.[83] Second, a proposal for the amendment of the Directive is currently before the Council of Ministers and European Parliament.[84]

---

[77] Note, however, that if the Community standard is set at too high a level, low-standard Member States may claim that it is impossible for them to set their labour standards at optimal levels, and that Community intervention is itself distorting competition.

[78] Note that high-standard States may be willing to maintain or improve their superior social standards once they are secure in the knowledge that their standards will not be undercut by too large a margin.

[79] See W Sengenberger, 'Labour Standards: An Institutional Framework for Restructuring and Development' in W Sengenberger and D Campbell (eds), *Creating Economic Opportunities: The Role of Labour Standards in Industrial Restructuring* (International Institute for Labour Studies, Geneva 1994) 39.   [80] See Directive 2003/88/EC (n 59 above) Art 23.

[81] See eg Bell's analysis of Directive 2000/43/EC (n 61 above) in M Bell, *Anti-Discrimination Law and the European Union* (OUP, Oxford 2002); Ashiagbor's analysis of the European Employment Strategy, in D Ashiagbor, *The European Employment Strategy: Labour Market Regulation and New Governance* (OUP, Oxford 2006); and, on a much smaller scale, Fredman's analysis of the Parental Leave, Part-time Workers, and Fixed-term Workers Directives, in S Fredman, 'Transformation or Dilution: Fundamental Rights in the EU Social Space' (2006) 12 European Law Journal 41, 46–8. Her conclusion (at 48) is that 'the overall pattern of recent directives is to subordinate fundamental rights at work to economic concerns'.

[82] See Directive 2003/88/EC (n 59 above). The original Directive of 1993 was based on Art 118a. The Directives of 2000 and 2003 were based on Art 137(2) EC. See Commission Report, 'State of Implementation of Directive 93/104/EC' COM(2000)787, 1 December 2000.

[83] *Working Time* (n 53 above).

[84] For the Commission's proposals, see Commission proposal for a Directive amending the Directive 2003/88/EC of 4 November 2003 concerning certain aspects of the organisation of working time, COM(2004)607, 22 September 2004; and Commission amended proposal for a Directive amending the Directive 2003/88/EC of 4 November 2003 concerning certain aspects of the organisation of working time, COM(2005)246, 31 May 2005.

And third, it admits of a number of derogations, affording some flexibility to both the Member States and the social partners. In this section I aim to illustrate the way in which the EU has attempted to strike a balance between the economic and the social, and also consider the extent to which economic and social arguments for EU intervention may be vulnerable to a vigorous application of the principles of subsidiarity and proportionality.

The Preamble to the Directive provides that 'the improvement of workers' safety, hygiene and health at work is an objective which should not be subordinated to purely economic considerations'.[85] This may be thought of either as a key principle, which commits the EU to respect the social over the economic, or as a mere rhetorical flourish. The Preamble goes on to state that 'account should be taken of the principles of the ILO with regard to the organisation of working time, including those relating to night work',[86] locating the social objectives of the Working Time Directive within the ILO framework. Despite these recitals, it is clear that economic considerations are relevant. Both Article 118a and the Preamble refer to the avoidance of constraints which 'hold back the creation and development of small and medium-sized undertakings'.[87] More importantly, the Preamble states that 'in view of the question likely to be raised by the organisation of working time within an undertaking, it appears desirable to provide for flexibility in the application of certain provisions of this Directive, whilst ensuring compliance with the principles of protecting the safety and health of workers'.[88] It is, therefore, said to be 'necessary to provide that certain provisions may be subject to derogations implemented, according to the case, by the Member States or the two sides of industry'.[89]

The substantive provisions of the Directive provide workers with minimum daily rest periods and breaks, a minimum weekly rest period, a maximum 48-hour working week, and a minimum period of at least four weeks' annual leave.[90] There are additional protections for night and shift workers. There is also a large dose of flexibility. Articles 17 to 22 provide for a series of derogations and exceptions. Most controversial of all is Article 22(1), which grants Member States the option of allowing individual workers to derogate from Article 6 (on the maximum working week).[91]

---

[85] Directive 2003/88/EC (n 59 above) Preamble, Recital 4. See also *Ex p BECTU* (n 71 above) [59].

[86] ibid Preamble, Recital 6.

[87] Art 118a(2), and Directive 2003/88/EC (n 59 above) Preamble, Recital 2. From the social perspective, it is difficult to see why what may be presented as workers' 'unalienable rights', should depend on the size of the firm in which they are employed; see also P Davies, 'Market Integration and Social Policy in the Court of Justice' (1995) 24 ILJ 49, 61.

[88] Directive 2003/88/EC (n 59 above) Preamble, Recital 15.   [89] ibid Preamble, Recital 16.

[90] ibid Arts 3–7. In relation to reference periods, see Arts 16 and 19. Art 19 provides for the provisions relating to the reference period for the application of Art 6 to be re-examined before November 2003.

[91] ibid Art 22(1). Art 22(1) permits a Member State not to apply Art 6, 'provided that it takes the necessary measures to ensure that no employer requires a worker to work more than 48 hours over a seven-day reference period ... unless he has first obtained the worker's agreement to perform such

In 2004, the Commission proposed an amendment to the Working Time Directive, re-examining the individual opt-out in Article 22(1).[92] It stated that 'it is necessary to modernise Community legislation on working time, with a view to responding better to new realities and demands'.[93] It indicated that any future proposal in this area should not only 'ensure a high standard of protection of workers' health and safety', but that it should also, bringing the rationale for the Directive more closely into line with the Lisbon Agenda, 'allow greater compatibility between work and family life', 'give companies and Member States greater flexibility in managing working time', and 'avoid imposing unreasonable constraints on companies, in particular SMEs'.[94] Following the first reading of the European Parliament, the reconciliation of work and family life and the increase in the rate of employment among women were given more prominence in the Commission's amended proposal.[95]

Failure to reach agreement on the reform of Article 22(1) has delayed the adoption of an amended Directive. On this point, the opinions of the key actors are divided. While the ETUC argued that the only acceptable option is the phasing-out, as soon as possible, of the individual opt-out, both UNICE and CEEP were in favour of maintaining the provision.[96] The Commission stated that 'experience gained in the application of Article 22(1) shows that the individual final decision not to be bound by Article 6 of the Directive can be problematic in two respects: the protection of workers' health and safety and the freedom of choice of the worker'.[97] It proposed a complex amendment to Article 22(1), essentially providing that in those Member States in which this is possible, individual opt-outs from Article 6 are to be authorized only by agreement between the social partners, and attaching clearer and more stringent conditions to the consent of the individual worker.[98] The European Parliament was more forthright. Its view was that 'the opt-out provision is in flagrant contradiction to the objectives and provisions of the Directive and with the fundamental principles of health and safety'. It 'contradicts all the evidence that indicates that working time without limits poses a serious risk to workers' health and safety, as well as to the reconciliation of work and

work'. There is an obligation on the Community institutions to re-examine Art 22(1) before November 2003. The Commission has stated that only the UK has made use of the Art 22(1) derogation; COM(2000)787 (n 82 above) 17.

[92] COM(2004)607 (n 84 above). The Commission proposal also re-examined the provisions relating to the reference period for the application of Art 6, and endeavoured to take accounts of the case law of the Court relating to the on-call duties of doctors. See Case C-303/98 *SIMAP* [2000] ECR I-7963; and Case C-151/02 *Jaeger* [2003] ECR I-8389.

[93] COM(2004)607 (n 84 above) Explanatory Memorandum [4].

[94] ibid Explanatory Memorandum [10]. The requirement to avoid unreasonable constraints on SMEs stems from Art 137(2) EC.

[95] COM(2005)246 (n 84 above) Preamble, Recitals 4, 5, and 7.

[96] COM(2004)607 (n 84 above) Explanatory Memorandum [6].

[97] ibid Preamble, Recital 9. cf the approach of the European Parliament, which amended Recital 9, stating that 'the individual final decision not be bound by Article 6 *is* problematic *and has led to abuses* in two respects ...' (original emphasis).   [98] COM(2004)607 (n 84 above).

family life'.[99] Its proposal was that the opt-out should cease to apply within three years. The Commission has indicated that it is unwilling to accept the Parliament's amendment but that it is prepared to explore a possible compromise on this question which is dividing the Parliament and the Council.[100]

As suggested in chapter 2 above, 'Third Way ideology' has now come to dominate EU thinking. All too often, the rhetoric of the institutions encourages one to believe that there is no potential for conflict between the economic and the social, and that high social standards must contribute to economic success. The regulation of working time, and more broadly the regulation of health and safety at work, seems to lend itself to a synthesis between the economic and the social.[101] Improvements in the working environment benefit not only workers and their families, but also employers. Reductions in working time may be associated both with increases in productivity and increases in employment.[102]

In the light of this, it is difficult to understand the range of derogations and exceptions provided for in the Directive. There are, however, economic and social arguments in favour of the provisions which provide for derogations by means of collective agreements, on the condition that equivalent or appropriate protection is granted to workers.[103] These provisions in effect represent a delegation of authority from the political institutions at European level to management and labour either at national, regional, or lower levels in accordance with national systems of bargaining. Undertakings benefit from increased flexibility, but at the same time workers benefit both from the procedural protections within national systems and from the substantive provisions of the Directive, which insist that the outcome of the agreement between the social partners must provide equivalent or appropriate protection for workers.[104] There are a number of advantages associated with affording flexibility to the social partners. Where labour standards are determined by agreement between management and labour, the standards which emerge may

---

[99] European Parliament First Reading, 11 May 2005.

[100] COM(2005)246 (n 84 above) 3.

[101] G Fels, 'An Economic View of the Social Charter' in W Däubler (ed), *Market and Social Justice in the EC—the Other Side of the Internal Market* (Bertelsmann Foundation, Gutersloh 1991) 173: 'binding and far-reaching standards for the entire EC [in the health and safety field] are ... not only morally essential, but economically meaningful'.

[102] See eg Case C-84/94 *UK v Council* [1996] ECR I-5755 (*Working Time*), Opinion of AG Léger [96], finding that some of the provisions of the Directive would have 'a positive impact on employment'; and Court judgment [30]: 'it cannot be excluded that the directive may affect employment'. See also Council Resolution of 18 December 1979 on the adaptation of working time [1980] OJ C2/1. Contrast G Lyon-Caen, 'The Evolution of Labour Law' in Lord Wedderburn *et al* (eds), *Labour Law in the Post-Industrial Era* (Dartmouth, Aldershot 1994) 101: 'Work always calls out for more work. Why should this cease to be true? The reduction of the length of the working day can be necessary to attenuate the misery of men, its arrangement to facilitate the management of enterprises; to make of it a means to create new employment remains a major illusion.'

[103] See Directive 2003/88/EC of 4 November 2003 concerning certain aspects of the organisation of working time (the Working Time Directive) [2003] OJ L299/9, Art 18.

[104] The interpretation of these terms is ultimately a matter for the Court of Justice and national courts.

be better tailored to the needs of employers and workers. Decision-making is brought closer to the citizen, in accordance with the broad principle of subsidiarity. However, if social relations are not to be left 'to the mercy of market conditions and economic power relations',[105] it is important that sufficiently strong safeguards are in place to protect the interests of workers. This may lead, for example, to calls for EU intervention in order to ensure that national systems of worker participation are adequate.[106]

It is much harder to find arguments in favour of the provisions which afford Member States the power to derogate from the standards in the Directive. Within certain limits, Member States have the option of excluding groups of workers from the protections established in the Directive, of extending the relevant reference periods, of making use of extended transitional periods, and, of course, of allowing individual workers to derogate from Article 6 on the maximum working week.[107] These derogations operate so as to undermine the objectives of the Directive. The (economic and) social arguments for rules imposing limits on working time lose their force where Member States derogate from such rules. So too do the integrationist arguments for the Directive, based on conceptions IV and V of the distortion of competition.

In the light of the difficulties involved in identifying the integrationist, economic, and social advantages of the Working Time Directive, it is interesting to consider the impact of the principles of subsidiarity and proportionality. I first consider the way in which the principles were used by the Court and Advocate General Léger in the *Working Time* case, the UK's challenge to the legality of the Directive.[108] I then consider the way in which a more vigorous application of the principles might influence the EU's agenda.

When defending the choice of Article 118a as the legal base for the Working Time Directive, the Court of Justice attempted to maintain a clear distinction between the 'social' Article 118a and the 'integrationist' Articles 94 and 95 EC. The Court insisted that a directive whose principal objective is the protection of the health and safety of workers by the imposition of minimum requirements for

---

[105] W Streeck, 'Neo-Voluntarism: A New European Social Policy Regime?' (1995) 1 European Law Journal 31, 49.

[106] See Lord Wedderburn (n 63 above); and P Syrpis, *The Rationales for European Community Social Policy: An Analysis of EC Worker Participation Law* (D Phil thesis, Oxford 2000) chs 5–8.

[107] Directive 2003/88/EC (n 103 above) Arts 17, 19, and 22. On the use of the derogations, see COM(2000)787 (n 82 above).

[108] In order to be able to hold that the Directive was properly based on Art 118a, the Court gave a broad interpretation to the terms 'health and safety'. See J Kenner, 'A Distinctive Legal Base for Social Policy? The Court of Justice Answers a "Delicate Question" ' (1997) 22 ELR 579, 584; and K Banks, 'L'Article 118a: Elément Dynamique de la Politique Sociale Communautaire' (1993) 29 Cahiers de droit européen 537, 540. Nevertheless, the Court annulled the second sentence of Art 5 of the Directive, as it held that 'the Council has failed to explain why Sunday, as a weekly rest day, is more closely connected with the health and safety of workers than any other day of the week'; see *Working Time* (n 102 above).

gradual implementation, should be based on Article 118a and not Article 94 or 95 EC.[109]

When it came to the part of the UK's challenge which referred to the principle of subsidiarity,[110] the Court held that 'once the Council has found that it is necessary to improve the existing level of protection as regards the health and safety of workers and to harmonize the conditions in this area while maintaining the improvements made, achievement of that objective through the imposition of minimum requirements necessarily presupposes Community-wide action'.[111] This rather bland formulation is, like the wording of Article 118a,[112] unhelpful. Although the imposition of minimum requirements, rather like the harmonization of rules, does indeed presuppose Community-wide action, it is not at all obvious that EU intervention (either harmonizing conditions in this area, or imposing minimum requirements, or indeed, creating a rather more flexible framework) is required in order to improve the health and safety of workers. Arguments to the effect that the Member States, acting alone, lack the capacity to adopt standards relating to health and safety, are unconvincing; especially given the fact that the Directive itself seems to afford each State the opportunity, albeit within certain limits, to devise its own system.

The Advocate General's Opinion sheds rather more light. In order to dispose of the UK's arguments relating to subsidiarity, and in marked contrast to his approach in relation to the plea that Article 118a was not the appropriate legal basis for the Directive, he chose to focus not on the social objectives of either Article 118a or the Directive, but on the fact that Article 118a employs the language of harmonization:

> Accordingly, in so far as harmonization is an objective, it is difficult to criticize the measures adopted by the Council to achieve it on the ground that they are in breach of the principle of subsidiarity. It would be illusory to expect the Member States alone to achieve the harmonization envisaged, since it necessarily involves supranational action.[113]

> In view of the fact that the objective provided for in Article 118a is harmonization, there is no doubt that the aim of the contested directive can be better achieved by action at Community level than by action at national level.[114]

---

[109] *Working Time* (n 102 above) [45]. See also Opinion of AG Léger [73]: 'The delimitation of the respective fields of application of Articles 100a [now 95] and 118a is ... based on the fundamental aim pursued. Article 100a [now 95] constitutes the appropriate legal basis whenever a harmonization measure has as its fundamental object the establishment of the internal market ... On the other hand, Article 118a serves as the legal basis for directives relating to the safety and health of workers which do not have as their fundamental object the establishment of the internal market and which accordingly do not relate either to the elimination of barriers to trade or to the introduction of conditions in which competition is free from distortions.'

[110] The UK did not rely on the breach of the principle of subsidiarity as a separate plea. The arguments based on subsidiarity arose in the context of the plea that the legal basis for the Directive was defective.   [111] *Working Time* (n 102 above) [47].

[112] Art 118a(1) reads as follows: 'Member States shall pay particular attention to encouraging improvements, especially in the working environment, as regards the health and safety of workers, and shall set as their objective the harmonization of conditions in this area, while maintaining the improvements made.'   [113] *Working Time* (n 102 above) Opinion of AG Léger [129].

[114] ibid Opinion of AG Léger [131].

I have already remarked on the confusion which may arise as a result of the combination of the language of harmonization with the language of minimum standard setting, which is to be found in the text of not only Article 118a but also Articles 136 and 137 EC. I have also indicated that the approximation or harmonization of laws should, notwithstanding the language in Article 118a, not be regarded as an objective of the EU. It is merely a subordinate instrument for achieving the objectives of the EU.[115] But even if one is prepared to overlook these points, the Advocate's General argument is weak because of the simple fact that the Directive does not harmonize the laws of the Member States.[116] Instead, it lays down minimum standards, and even then admits of an array of derogations.

The UK's arguments relating to the principle of proportionality were also rejected. In part, this was because the UK's arguments were based on what the Court held to be a misreading of the expression 'minimum requirements'.[117] The UK also argued that the desired level of protection could have been achieved by less restrictive measures involving 'fewer obstacles to the competitiveness of industry and the earning capacity of individuals';[118] a very particular take on the economic and social implications of the Directive. In response to these arguments, the Court held that the Directive did not go beyond what was necessary. In reaching this conclusion, it placed considerable weight on the existence of the various derogations.[119]

In my view, the Court's approach in the *Working Time* case was inadequate. A more vigorous application of the principles of subsidiarity and proportionality might have resulted in the annulment of the Working Time Directive. Much more importantly, it might also have paved the way for the development of a more coherent rationale for EU intervention in domestic labour law, contributing towards the legitimacy of the EU project.

The subsidiarity enquiry begins with an identification of the objectives of the proposed action. The objective of the Working Time Directive is, as the Court and Advocate General accepted throughout the *Working Time* case—except when dealing with subsidiarity—the protection of the health and safety of workers.[120] The reason why the Court and Advocate General sought to identify alternative objectives when dealing with the UK's subsidiarity argument, is that it is not at all

---

[115] See C-D Ehlermann, 'Harmonisation for harmonisation's sake?' (1978) 15 CML Rev 4.

[116] The only references to harmonization or approximation in the Directive, are in the Preamble, in the Recital which quotes from Articles 7, 8 and 19 of the 1989 Community Charter of the Fundamental Social Rights of Workers; Council Directive 93/104/EC of 23 November 1993 concerning certain aspects of the organisation of working time [1993] OJ L307/18, Preamble.

[117] See p 131 above.   [118] *Working Time* (n 102 above) [52].

[119] ibid [50]–[67]. See also Opinion of AG Léger [136]: 'It is necessary to determine whether the intensity of Community action taken by means of the directive goes beyond what is necessary to achieve the objective of protecting the safety and health of workers. That does not seem to me to be the case, in so far as it is possible to derogate from the temporal constraints imposed by the directive and adjust them in a number of ways.'

[120] The Directive itself does not include any convincing explanation of why action at Community level might be warranted in relation to the regulation of working time.

obvious that the EU is better able to set health and safety standards than are the Member States.[121] There are, for example, no transnational aspects which cannot be satisfactorily regulated by action by Member States and no indication that a lack of EU action would significantly damage Member States' interests.[122] There is also, notwithstanding the UK's argument to the effect that the Directive creates an obstacle to the competitiveness of industry,[123] little or no evidence that the imperatives of international competitiveness, or the pressures of EMU, limit the capacity of States to set health and safety standards at a sufficiently high level. Thus, the social rationale for EU intervention is likely to fail. It may, however, be possible to establish a case for EU intervention on the basis of the integrationist rationale. Contrary to the approach of the Court and its Advocate General, this need not involve (the language of) harmonization. As indicated above, conceptions IV and V of the distortion of competition may provide a rationale for EU minimum standard setting in the labour law field. In relation to working time, the argument that the collective quest for competitive advantage is capable of leading to distortions of competition is unlikely to succeed, unless it can be said that competitive pressures are likely to induce States to lower their health and safety standards to sub-optimal levels. The argument for intervention on the grounds that distortions of competition might arise as a result of 'unacceptably low' standards is more promising. If this is the basis for EU intervention, it will be important for the EU not to set the minimum standard at too high a level (otherwise, it will be accused of ruling out 'fair' competition), and also important for it not to allow derogations from the minimum (otherwise, it will be accused of allowing 'unfair' competition to persist). Ultimately, it is for the institutions, including the Court, to determine the parameters within which competition between legal orders is judged to be fair.

The proportionality enquiry is concerned both with whether European level action is suitable and necessary with reference to the stated objectives, and with whether it has an excessive effect on Member State autonomy. In the *Working Time* case the Court and Advocate General Léger concentrated on the intensity of, and necessity for, EU intervention, and as a result regarded the derogations in a positive light. However, as Advocate General Léger acknowledged in the *Working Time* case that 'an inherent feature of legislation on safety and health is that the degree of flexibility in its application should not be infinite, since it will otherwise

---

[121] Arguing along similar lines, in relation to the Parental Leave Directive, see C Jensen, J Madsen, and J Due, 'Phases and dynamics in the development of EU industrial relations regulation' (1999) 30 Industrial Relations Journal 118, 128: 'Why, the observer may well ask, did the labour-market parties conclude a joint agreement on parental leave? It was hardly necessary to meet any instrumental needs felt by the parties. Nor does there seem to have been any pressing reason for choosing parental leave schemes as an eminently suitable subject for regulation at European rather than national level. If the subsidiarity principle were to be taken seriously, it is difficult to see what has been achieved by regulating this matter at European rather than national level.'

[122] See Provision 5 of the Protocol on the Application of the Principles of Subsidiarity and Proportionality, added by the Treaty of Amsterdam.   [123] *Working Time* (n 102 above) [52].

cease to serve any purpose having regard to the objective for which it was adopted'.[124] One may very well wonder, with the European Parliament, whether the derogations contained within the Working Time Directive, in particular the individual opt-out, are consistent with the objective of the protection of the health and safety of workers. If it is held that they are not, the principle of proportionality may provide the Court with grounds to annul those provisions of the Directive; though the Court is likely to, and in my view should, afford the political institutions a broad discretion here.

Thus, it is possible to provide arguments for EU intervention in domestic labour law, which takes the form of minimum standard setting or other more flexible measures. The strongest rationale for such intervention is provided through conception IV of the distortion of competition, and depends on the EU institutions being prepared to establish stringent baseline rules of economic ordering for the European market. It is also possible to make a case for EU intervention in response to conception V of the distortion of competition, so as to prevent competitive deregulation in the labour law field. However, in order to establish a strong case for EU intervention, it is necessary to show that there is a likelihood of a 'race to the bottom', which may be rather difficult to prove in, for example, the context of the regulation of working time. It is also necessary for the EU institutions to intervene in such a way as to prevent competitive deregulation by both high- and low-standard Member States.

Economic and social arguments for intervention may be vulnerable to a vigorous application of the principle of subsidiarity. In order to establish a case for EU intervention under either the economic or the social rationale, it is incumbent on the institutions to show that the EU is better able to set standards than are the Member States. Where there is a transnational dimension, the challenge of subsidiarity will be easy to overcome. In the absence of such a dimension, the competence of the Community should be exercised only to the extent that it is possible to show that the capacity of States to intervene in the labour law field has been compromised by the imperatives of international competitiveness and the pressures of EMU, and that the Community is therefore better placed to advance given economic and social objectives.

The Open Method of Coordination

As explained in chapter 2 above, the open method of coordination (or OMC) is now deployed in a range of policy areas. This approach, which was termed the 'open method of coordination' at Lisbon in 2000,[125] has been used in relation to

---

[124] ibid Opinion of AG Léger [142].
[125] Lisbon European Council, Presidency Conclusions, 23 and 24 March 2000 [37].

the coordination of economic policies since 1992,[126] and the coordination of employment policies since 1997.[127] More recently, it has been deployed to coordinate national policies in the social inclusion, social protection, and pensions fields.[128] It has also been used in relation to health care, education, research and development, immigration, and enlargement.

There are substantial disagreements as to the circumstances in which the OMC may and should be used.[129] The Treaty context is important; and as we have seen, there is Treaty authority for the use of the OMC in the economic, employment, and social policy fields.[130] My view is quite simply that the OMC should be used to the extent that it contributes to the realization of the EU's integrationist, economic, and social objectives, and to the extent that its use is compatible with the principles of subsidiarity and proportionality. It may be used either alongside, or instead of, other forms of EU intervention.

Much of the literature on the OMC is overwhelmingly positive.[131] The OMC is said to be the answer to the governance conundrum in today's multi-level European Union; 'the Lazarus of European integration'.[132] It 'aims to co-ordinate the actions of the several Member States in a given policy domain and to create conditions for mutual learning that hopefully will induce some degree of voluntary policy convergence'.[133] It enables policy to be steered at the European level,[134] but at the same time is sensitive to local autonomy.[135]

---

[126] Art 99 EC. See D Hodson and I Maher, 'The Open Method as a New Mode of Governance: The Case of Soft Economic Policy Co-ordination' (2001) 39 JCMS 719.

[127] Luxembourg European Council, Presidency Conclusions, 12 and 13 December 1997 [3].

[128] See Commission Communication 'Working together, working better: A new framework for the open coordination of social protection and inclusion policies in the European Union' COM(2005)706, 22 December 2005. On the launch of the social OMC processes, see P Syrpis, 'Legitimising European Governance: Taking Subsidiarity Seriously within the Open Method of Coordination' (EUI Working Paper Law No 2002/10, Florence 2002) 43–53.

[129] See eg Commission, 'European Governance: A White Paper' COM(2001)428, 25 July 2001; and J Scott and D Trubek, 'Mind the Gap: Law and New Approaches to Governance in the European Union' (2002) 8 European Law Journal 1.

[130] See Arts 99, 128, and 137(2)(a) EC. See also Art I-15 TeCE.

[131] See <http://eucenter.wisc.edu/OMC/>, for an extensive bibliography of the official and academic literature on the OMC.

[132] See D Chalmers and M Lodge, 'The Open Method of Co-ordination and the European Welfare State' (ESRC Centre for Analysis of Risk and Regulation, Discussion Paper No 11, LSE June 2003). The OMC has also been said to go 'some way towards resolving the intractable problem of the legitimacy of policy-making in the EU'; Hodson and Maher (n 126 above) 722.

[133] Scott and Trubek (n 129 above) 4.

[134] The European Council has a strong 'guiding and coordinating role', 'to ensure more coherent strategic direction and effective monitoring of progress'; Lisbon European Council, Presidency Conclusions, 23 and 24 March 2000 [7].

[135] A 'fully decentralised approach will be applied in line with the principle of subsidiarity in which the Union, the Member States, the regional and local levels, as well as the social partners and civil society, will be actively involved, using variable forms of partnership'. 'Achieving the new strategic goal will rely primarily on the private sector, as well as on public-private partnerships.' Lisbon European Council, Presidency Conclusions, 23 and 24 March 2000 [38] and [41].

This section will examine the OMC in the aftermath of the relaunch of the Lisbon strategy in 2005.[136] The Broad Economic Policy Guidelines (BEPGs) and the Employment Guidelines have now been integrated into a single package whose focus is on growth and employment.[137] In addition, the OMC process on social inclusion and pensions has been streamlined.[138] A close examination of these two processes, both of which are at the heart of the Lisbon Strategy, confirms the suspicion that while OMC processes may be able to finesse the tension between central steering and local autonomy, they are not able to eliminate it. The integrated economic and employment policy guidelines attempt to steer national policies in particular ways and are based on a 'resolve to converge towards jointly set, verifiable, regularly updated targets'.[139] Within this context, local autonomy is compromised.[140] On the other hand, the nascent inclusion and pensions OMC is less prescriptive and more sensitive to local autonomy. Within the context of the OMC, as in relation to all other governance strategies, it is important to be clear about the rationales for European intervention and about the ways in which specific policy objectives may best be realized. As we shall see, all too little attention is paid to whether and how OMC processes enable the EU and the Member States to realize integrationist, economic, and social objectives. The absence of a conspicuous enquiry into the need for central intervention is particularly worrying.[141]

For the purposes of this analysis, it is instructive to isolate three distinct stages in the development of any OMC. Stage one involves the identification of an area in which there are problems to be solved, challenges to be met, or opportunities to be grasped. The relevant stakeholders at all levels are invited to debate the issues and to reach understandings.[142] Indicators and benchmarks are developed and, with reference to these, best practice may be identified. At this stage it is important to consider the way in which the problem is conceptualized, the identity of those involved, the way in which their discussions are structured, and whether each participant may learn from the others.[143] The key question here is whether the OMC

---

[136] See Brussels European Council, Presidency Conclusions, 22 and 23 March 2005 [4]; and Commission Communication to the Spring European Council, 'Working together for growth and jobs: A new start for the Lisbon Strategy', COM(2005)24, 2 February 2005.

[137] See Council Decision 2005/600/EC of 12 July 2005 on Guidelines for the employment policies of the Member States [2005] OJ L205/21 and Council Recommendation 2005/601/EC of 12 July 2005 on the broad guidelines for the economic policies of the Member States and the Community (2005 to 2008) [2005] OJ L205/28.   [138] COM(2005)706 (n 128 above) 3–4.

[139] Luxembourg European Council, Presidency Conclusions, 20 and 21 November 1997 [3].

[140] Arts 99 and 128 EC provide for recommendations to be issued to Member States whose policies are not consistent with the European guidelines.

[141] G Bermann, 'Taking Subsidiarity Seriously: Federalism in the European Community and the United States' (1994) 94 Columbia Law Review 331, 416.

[142] 'The development of organized and reciprocal learning processes to cope with a rapidly changing world is at the heart of the method'; C De La Porte, P Pochet, and G Room, 'Social Benchmarking, policy making and new governance in the EU' (2001) 11 Journal of European Social Policy 291, 293.

[143] Problems should be framed in such a way as to reduce negative externalities and to exploit synergistic opportunities, and sectoral and national boundaries should be destabilized; N Lebessis and

is able to provide a forum within which the relevant actors improve their understandings of the policy domain in question and their policy responses.[144] Stage two involves reaching mutual agreement, fixing common objectives, and developing guidelines at the European, national, and sub-national levels.[145] At this stage, attention shifts to the clarity of the objectives and guidelines and how they might best be implemented.[146] It becomes important to find ways to ensure that States comply with the objectives and guidelines when developing their policies.[147] Finally, stage three ensures that the objectives set in stage two remain subject to refinement in the light of evolving knowledge. The method is circular. The criteria according to which performance is assessed, are developed and redeveloped via a democratic regime.

Sciarra's distinction between cooperation and coordination is useful here. Although they can be thought of as 'parallel paths leading in the same direction', cooperation and coordination are 'separate legal instrumentalities'. Cooperation—which can be equated with stage one of the OMC—involves the encouragement and support of national actions, and the giving of precedence to national competencies. With coordination—which can be equated with stage two—the impetus comes from the EU.[148] However, Sciarra also makes the point that coordination 'focuses its integrational impulse at the periphery of the European legal system, rather than attempting to impose integration from the centre'.[149]

Stage one of any OMC, with its focus on dialogue, learning, exchange of information, and experience, does not involve the loss of national or local autonomy. This is not true of stage two. As objectives and guidelines are developed with ever greater specificity and precision,[150] policy is steered from the centre. As Szyszczak says, 'the framing of Community policy through Guidelines, indicators, and

J Paterson, 'Developing New Modes of Governance', in O De Schutter, N Lebessis, and J Paterson (eds), *Governance in the European Union* (OOPEC, Luxembourg 2001) 259, 276.

[144] The focus is on 'regime' rather than 'performance' legitimacy. See N Walker, 'The White Paper in Constitutional Context' in C Joerges, Y Meny, and J Weiler (eds), *Mountain or Molehill? A Critical Appraisal of the Commission White Paper on Governance* (RSC Jean Monnet Working Paper No 6/01, Florence 2001) 33, 36–7.

[145] 'While the OMC has recourse to benchmarking, it goes beyond this by defining European-level guidelines and identifying common challenges, even if the formulation of the response to the challenges remains the responsibility of member states'; De La Porte, Pochet, and Room (n 142 above) 293.

[146] The Barcelona European Council has stated that, in relation to the Lisbon Strategy, the focus 'must be on action for implementation, rather than on the annual elaboration of the guidelines'; Barcelona European Council, Presidency Conclusions, 15 and 16 March 2002 [49].

[147] The focus is on 'performance', rather than 'regime' legitimacy. See Walker (n 144 above) 33; and ch 3 above.

[148] S Sciarra, 'Integration through Coordination: The Employment Title in the Amsterdam Treaty' (2000) 6 Columbia Journal of European Law 209, 218.

[149] ibid 223. With this distinction in mind, Ball commented that in the employment context, 'it is possible to see the relationship between member states and the EC as moving beyond one of mere cooperation, to one of coordination, with the EC firmly taking the lead'; S Ball, 'The European Employment Strategy: The Will but not the Way?' (2001) 30 ILJ 353, 357.

[150] On the specificity of objectives, see G De Búrca, 'Reappraising Subsidiarity's Significance After Amsterdam' (Harvard Jean Monnet Working Paper No 7/99, 1999) 24–5.

benchmarking is not a soft, or neutral process, but shapes the framework within which national policies, and actors must work'.[151]

In line with my approach in the rest of this chapter, I have chosen to categorize OMC processes according to the extent to which national autonomy is constrained. The key variants between what may be termed 'hard' and 'soft' (or 'strong' and 'weak'; or 'teleological' and 'non-teleological') OMC processes, are the extent to which guidelines and objectives are specified at EU level and the extent to which legal or political steps are taken so as to ensure that national policies are in line with those guidelines and objectives.[152]

In 'hard' OMC processes, precise guidelines and objectives are set. Legal and/or political pressure is put on Member States, and other relevant actors, to comply with European guidelines. The objective of 'hard' OMC processes is to ensure that States comply with the guidelines. Often, the aim is policy convergence; but, given the nature of the OMC process, the point, rate, and even degree of convergence are determined by interaction between the various stakeholders and are subject to refinement or redefinition. There may, as we shall see, be integrationist, economic, and social advantages associated with adherence to the guidelines; but there may also be concerns that European intervention may be in breach of the subsidiarity and proportionality principles.

'Soft' OMC processes, in which objectives are not set at the centre with any degree of specificity, and in which the 'hegemonic imposition of a monolithic discipline' is avoided,[153] create opportunities for learning, innovation, and experimentation at national, regional, and local levels. In these heterarchical settings, it is possible for stakeholders at various levels, having studied the map created in the course of their iterative interactions, to choose not only their preferred route towards a given destination, but also their destination.[154] Such an OMC regime need not be seen as transitional, underdeveloped, or immature. The advantages here, which are centred on the facilitation of learning and the evolution of new knowledges, may be diminished, rather than enhanced, by the tendency for specific objectives and guidelines to be promulgated at the European level. Where

---

[151] E Szyszczak, 'Experimental Governance: The Open Method of Coordination' (2006) 12 European Law Journal 486, 500. She has also argued that 'States are no longer free to determine national policy but must work within officially recognised Community Guidelines which have taken on a normative status'; E Szyszczak, 'The Evolving European Employment Strategy' in J Shaw (ed), *Social Law and Policy in an Evolving European Union* (Hart, Oxford 2000) 197, 211. Similarly, Ashiagbor's assessment of the European Employment Strategy is that 'the "soft" coordination of the open method does in fact have quite a "hard" impact, placing powerful political pressure on Member States to comply with centrally designed policies, and constraining their policy choices'; D Ashiagbor, *The European Employment Strategy: Labour Market Regulation and New Governance* (OUP, Oxford 2006) 191.

[152] See also D Trubek and L Trubek, 'Hard and Soft Law in the Construction of Social Europe: the Role of the Open Method of Co-ordination' (2005) 11 European Law Journal 343, 356–9, distinguishing between the top-down and bottom-up effects of the OMC.

[153] See De La Porte, Pochet, and Room (n 142 above).

[154] See J Shaw, 'Relating Constitutionalism and Flexibility in the European Union', in G De Búrca and J Scott (eds), *Constitutional Change in the EU: From Uniformity to Flexibility?* (Hart, Oxford 2000) 331, 350.

there are specific objectives in place, the paradigms within which learning can be acquired are relatively fixed and there is little or no encouragement for them to be transcended. The danger is that thinking might ossify, rather than evolve. 'Soft' OMC processes do not raise subsidiarity or proportionality concerns. The autonomy associated with 'soft' OMC processes, may, however, be seen as problematic from the perspective of each of the three rationales; depending, as ever, on the way in which each rationale is conceptualized.

With this background, it is possible to examine the integrationist, economic, and social rationales for OMC processes in the labour law field; and to consider the extent to which 'hard' OMC processes may raise subsidiarity and proportionality concerns.

An integrationist rationale for the OMC

As we have seen many times, under some conceptions of the integrationist rationale, including those adopted by the Court in the main thrust of its free movement case law, disparities between national rules are problematic. To the extent that these conceptions are accepted, all the interventions of the political institutions in the labour law field, including those within the framework of the OMC, are themselves problematic, on the basis that they authorize, encourage, or tolerate the maintenance of some diversity between national systems. However, there are alternative conceptions of the integrationist rationale under which it may be possible to view the OMC in a more positive light.

If the coronation theory of monetary union is accepted, the convergence of national economic policies, in particular within the eurozone, may be said to be necessary from the perspective of the integrationist rationale. In the BEPGs, it is said that 'the economic performance of, and policies pursued by, individual euro area Member States affect common goods such as the euro's exchange rate, interest rates, price stability and the cohesion of the euro area. All this implies a need for effective policy coordination, both in the EU and in the euro area, to improve growth potential and performance'.[155] From this starting point, it is possible to see the coordination of employment and social, as well as economic, policies as 'a simple, but sensitive solution to the problem created by the spillover of economic and monetary union'.[156]

It is, as indicated in chapter 2 above, possible to make several distinct integrationist arguments for the coordination of employment and social policies; arguing either for convergence of national policies or for a variety of more flexible

---

[155] Recommendation 2005/601/EC (n 137 above) s A.2. The Commission has also, for example, stated that there are 'externalities between Member States' economic policies and between those policies and the single monetary policy', and thus, a 'major need for co-ordination'; Commission Communication on strengthening economic policy coordination within the euro area, COM(2001)82, 7 February 2001, 4.   [156] Szyszczak (n 151 above) 495.

approaches.[157] In my view, the strongest integrationist argument for the coord-ination of employment and social policies is based on the perceived need to pre-vent an aggravated risk of regulatory competition leading to a race to the bottom. It is this particular integrationist argument which is discussed here.

Labour law matters were excluded from the EMU agenda, and neither the ECB's monetary policy nor the BEPGs and the Stability and Growth Pact have a direct impact on domestic labour law. However, EMU is likely to have a number of indirect effects on domestic labour law. First, it has increased the interdependence of national economies. Fiscal irresponsibility in any one Member State is liable to affect the position of the euro, and with it, the economic outlook in all other Member States (and in particular, in eurozone States).[158] Second, national govern-ments, as an inevitable consequence of monetary union, are no longer able to make adjustments in exchange or interest rates, making it impossible for them to use those tools in order to react to local economic conditions and react to asymmetric shocks. Third, government spending is constrained by the operation of the BEPGs and the Stability and Growth Pact. The ability to intervene in the labour law arena, as Trubek and Trubek explain, has become limited: 'Because of the common cur-rency, national governments [can] no longer use monetary policy as a tool for job creation, and because of the Stability and Growth Pact, they [are] also constrained in their ability to use fiscal policy for the same ends.'[159] One area in which States retain their independence, is 'in respect of the regulation—or rather deregulation—of labour standards and wages'.[160] EMU increases the pressure on States to deregu-late in the labour law field, and leads to a situation in which the quest for competitive advantage is more likely to lead to sub-optimal labour standards.

However:

… any suggestion of shifting power to the EU supranational institutions to adopt a cen-tralised industrial policy, social policy or employment policy, to counter the powerful effects of its Economic and Monetary Union policy was never a serious prospect. Quite apart from the objections in principle, or on grounds of effectiveness, to centralising policies of this kind within such a large political entity, the strong cultural diversity of EU Member States and the distinctive national sensibilities underlying diverse social protection systems, labour

---

[157] See ch 2 above, pp 60–1.

[158] As a consequence of this, all States have an interest in ensuring that levels of spending (eg, on employment and social policies) remain within bounds. It is therefore possible to see the Lisbon Strategy as a mechanism which aims to ensure that all States maintain their fiscal discipline, while at the same time enabling them to find solutions to employment and social problems.

[159] Trubek and Trubek (n 152 above) 345.

[160] C Barnard, 'EC "Social" Policy' in P Craig and G De Búrca (eds), *The Evolution of EU Law* (OUP, Oxford 1999) 479, 507. See also A Herrmann, 'Converging Divergence: How Competitive Advantages Condition Institutional Change Under EMU' (2005) 43 JCMS 287, 287–8: 'The Maastricht convergence criteria not only make EMU membership conditional on comparatively low domestic inflation rates, they also notably restrict the autonomy of national governments to conduct independent fiscal, monetary and exchange-rate policy. Thus, the only opportunity for national policy-makers to bring inflation rates into line with the Maastricht convergence criteria, and to maintain low and stable inflation rates once their country has joined EMU, consists in securing non-inflationary wage increases.'

law institutions, educational and health systems, made consensus on moving towards a single EU policy in these areas politically inconceivable.[161]

Nevertheless, the States were willing to countenance and pursue coordination strategies.[162] Integrationist accounts may be able to explain the development of OMC processes in the employment and labour law fields, on the basis that the OMC may be able to encourage States not to engage in destructive competition. According to this integrationist account, the constraints and interdependencies inherent in market integration (and in particular, EMU), set the stage for enhanced EU involvement.[163] The aim of the OMC is not the harmonization, or even the convergence, of the employment and social policies of the States. Rather the aim is to reduce the pressure on States to deregulate, and thereby contribute to the improved performance of the European economy and to the preservation of the European social model (ie to the realization of the EU's economic and social meta-objectives). The crucial question is whether EU intervention in the employment and labour law fields via OMC processes is able to contribute to the establishment and functioning of the market in Europe in the face of the pressures towards deregulation; or, to put this in slightly different terms, whether it constitutes an appropriate response to conception V of the distortion of competition. As indicated above, formulating appropriate policy responses to conception V is not at all straightforward. European intervention should prevent Member States from lowering social standards in an attempt to improve competitiveness and attract trade and investment. Harmonization is not necessary or appropriate. Minimum standard setting can be no more than a partial response. The OMC, which may be regarded as a species of reflexive harmonization,[164] may be thought to offer a prospect of greater success. However, if the OMC is to succeed in preventing competitive deregulation in the labour law field, it is important that there are mechanisms within, or associated with, the OMC, which are able to ensure that States comply with EU guidelines and do not, for example, pay lip-service to EU guidelines while at the same time engaging in destructive competition.[165]

---

[161] G De Búrca, 'The Constitutional Challenge of New Governance in the European Union' (2003) 28 ELR 814, 827.

[162] Thus, 'the OMC has been introduced, or recommended, in a number of arenas where the modern demands of European integration require policy coordination, but where Community competence in the field is weak, non-existent, or quite blatantly outlawed'; Szyszczak (n 151 above) 488.

[163] See also Trubek and Trubek (n 152 above) 345.

[164] 'The proper goals of reflexive harmonization are rather: first, to permit the general thrust of common legal solutions to be tailored more precisely and appropriately to local needs and preferences within each Member State; and secondly, to enable the Community to maintain a healthy stock of legal ideas from which Member States may draw inspiration to meet the challenges posed by changes in scientific technology or market behaviour that create new regulatory dilemmas and require fresh policy solutions'; M Dougan, 'Vive la Différence? Exploring the Legal Framework for Reflexive Harmonization within the Single European Market' in R Miller and P Zumbansen (eds), *Annual of German and European Law, Volume 1 (2003)* (Berghahn, New York 2004) 124. On the relationship between the OMC and reflexive harmonization, see Ashiagbor (n 151 above) 220–6.

[165] It is also, of course, important that the guidelines are formulated in such a way as to enable States to resist the pressures to deregulate in the labour law field.

It seems doubtful in the extreme that the mechanisms within, or associated with, the OMC can ensure that national policy choices remain within permissible bounds.[166] The crisis over the Stability and Growth Pact has demonstrated just how difficult it is to take action against States whose economic policy choices diverge from those prescribed at EU level.[167] The OMCs in the employment and social fields have a much lower profile. The various National Action Plans, National Reform Programmes, and National Strategy Reports, in which Member States develop their policies in response to EU guidelines, receive little public scrutiny. Although the relaunch of the Lisbon Strategy has brought a renewed focus on the 'delivery' and 'implementation' of the Lisbon objectives,[168] enforcement mechanisms remain weak. While OMC processes may, as we shall see, be able to generate learning, widen the range of policy responses under consideration in each Member State and contribute to the development of new discourses, it is difficult to see how they are able effectively to constrain a government which calculates that it may obtain a competitive advantage by lowering its social standards. This is true not only in relation to 'soft' OMC processes, such as those in the social protection and inclusion fields, but also in relation to the 'harder' European Employment Strategy.[169]

In the first set of employment guidelines, it was said that 'it is crucial for the coherence and effectiveness of the approach as a whole that all Member States make use of the "guidelines" in analysing their own situation and framing their policy and that they establish their attitude to each of them in their national employment action plan'.[170] The current set of guidelines 'shall be taken into account' in the employment policies of the Member States.[171] Article 128(4) EC gives the Council the power to adopt recommendations on the implementation of Member States' employment policies. These draw attention to priority areas, and address specific recommendations to each Member State, stating that the State in question 'should give immediate priority to' particular policy areas.[172] The difficulty is that the EU is not able to ensure that either the guidelines or the recommendations are translated into policy. There are no sanctions for failure to comply.

---

[166] I recognize that there are also difficulties with implementation and enforcement in relation to more traditional forms of Community intervention, especially directives.

[167] See Case C-27/04 *Commission v Council* [2004] ECR I-4829.

[168] See eg Brussels European Council, Presidency Conclusions, 22 and 23 March 2005; and COM(2005)24 (n 136 above).

[169] Since 2000, the EES has included an employment target; see eg Decision 2005/600/EC (n 137 above) Guideline 17: 'Policies should contribute to achieving an average employment rate for the European Union (EU) of 70% overall, of at least 60% for women and of 50% for older workers (55 to 64) by 2010, and to reduce unemployment and inactivity'. Notwithstanding the existence of this target, and the fact that the employment rate across the EU remains disappointing, many Member States have yet to set their own national employment rate targets. Hence the Council's insistence, again in the 2005 Guidelines, that 'Member States should consider setting national employment rate targets'.

[170] Luxembourg European Council, Presidency Conclusions, 12 and 13 December 1997 [15].

[171] Decision 2005/600/EC (n 137 above) Art 2.

[172] In 2004, for example, the recommendations addressed to the UK related to ensuring that 'wage developments do not exceed productivity development'; ensuring that 'active labour market

The Preamble to the 2004 Recommendations states that the examination of Member States' National Action Plans for employment contained in the Joint Employment Report 2003–2004 shows that Member States and the social partners have given only 'limited responses' to the 2003 Recommendations.[173]

If the rationale for EU intervention is to prevent competitive deregulation in the labour law field, it seems essential that the OMC is combined with other policy instruments. Ashiagbor questions whether 'a form of governance which eschews centralized social policy norms can adequately ensure a core of social rights, below which no Member State can fall'.[174] Along similar lines, Fredman argues that 'ultimately, then, new paradigms need to be underpinned by clear and inderogable fundamental rights'.[175] If the aim is to avoid destructive competitive deregulation in the labour law field (or, indeed, to prevent standards falling to unacceptably low levels), it seems that the OMC can be no more than a partial response. The OMC may be able to help States to focus on necessary reforms and may contribute towards the development of a consensus on the necessary reforms.[176] However, unless it is combined with other policy instruments, the OMC cannot guard against the risk that States may compete against each other in destructive ways in an effort to attract trade and investment.

Economic and social rationales for the OMC

The integrationist rationale for the OMC, discussed above, places considerable emphasis on the need to constrain the policy choices of the Member States so as to eliminate distortions of competition. As we have seen, intervention may be called for if there is evidence that States are deregulating, or are likely to deregulate, their

---

policies and benefit systems prevent deskilling and promote quality in work'; improving 'the access to and affordability of childcare and care for other dependants, increasing access to training for low paid women in part-time work and taking urgent action to tackle the causes of the gender pay gap'; implementing 'national and regional skills strategies to provide better incentives for lifelong learning and thereby increasing productivity and quality in work'; and placing 'particular emphasis on improving literacy and numeracy of the workforce, the participation and achievement of 16–19 year olds, and low-skilled workers, especially those in poorly paid jobs'; Council Recommendation 2004/741/EC of 14 October 2004 on the implementation of Member States' employment policies [2004] OJ L326/47. For the UK's response, see the 2005 National Reform Programme, at <http://www.hmtreasury.gov.uk/media/E60/3D/lisbon_jobs131005.pdf>.

[173] Recommendation 2004/741/EC (n 172 above) Preamble, Recital 4. Notwithstanding this, there is evidence that compliance with the Employment Strategy is 'extremely high'; though it is difficult to know whether the policy convergence of recent years in the employment field can be attributed to the existence of the OMC; Ashiagbor (n 151 above) ch 6.   [174] Ashiagbor (n 151 above) 191.

[175] S Fredman, 'Transformation or Dilution: Fundamental Rights in the EU Social Space' (2006) 12 European Law Journal 41, 53.

[176] The 'need to confirm the place of social protection within the common values of the Union in the context of its enlargement' was given as one of the reasons why the modernization of social protection systems was 'more urgent than ever'; Commission Communication, 'A Concerted Strategy for Modernising Social Protection' COM(99)347, 14 July 1999, 3.

labour standards to sub-optimal levels in an attempt to attract trade and investment. My view is that to the extent that the objective of the EU is to prevent both high- and low-standard Member States from deregulating in the labour law field, it is necessary to combine the OMC either with minimum standard setting measures incorporating a non-regression clause, or with measures which guarantee fundamental social rights.

If one rejects these integrationist arguments, either because of a failure to be convinced by the market structure and structural policy perspective on the distortion of competition, or because of a lack of evidence that competitive deregulation (either in labour law in general or in a specific area of labour law) is occurring or likely to occur, one faces the challenge of making an economic or social argument for EU intervention via the OMC. The economic and social rationales are able to provide support for either 'hard' or 'soft' OMC processes. However, economic and social arguments for 'hard' OMC processes which operate so as to constrain the autonomy of the Member States may be vulnerable to the application of the principles of subsidiarity and proportionality.

An economic and social case for OMC processes in the employment and social protection and inclusion fields emerges to the extent that it can be said that EU intervention via the OMC in these fields contributes to the improved performance of the European economy and the preservation of the European social model. The OMC may be regarded as beneficial because of its contribution to both performance and regime legitimacy, or, to put this another way, both in terms of the substantive outcomes it generates and in terms of the regime from which these outcomes are generated.

As indicated in chapter 2 above, Third Way rhetoric is pervasive in today's EU. The rhetoric asserts that advancement in the economic, employment, and social arenas is necessary for the achievement of the Lisbon goals. At Lisbon it was said that 'people are Europe's main asset and should be the focal point of the Union's activities'.[177] The Commission began its 2005 Report on Social Protection and Social Inclusion with the statement that 'at its heart, the Lisbon strategy promotes the idea of a positive interaction between economic, employment and social policies'.[178] There is, moreover, consistent reference to the 'synergies' between economic, employment, environmental, and social policies,[179] to the fact that these policies are 'mutually reinforcing',[180] and to the 'positive interdependencies between competitiveness, employment and social security'.[181] 'While robust economic and employment growth is a vital precondition for the sustainability of social protection systems, progress in achieving higher levels of social cohesion is,

---

[177] Lisbon European Council, Presidency Conclusions, 23 and 24 March 2000 [24].

[178] Commission Communication, Joint Report on Social Protection and Social Inclusion, COM(2005)14, 27 January 2005, 3.   [179] Decision 2005/600/EC (n 137 above) Recital 4.

[180] See eg Stockholm European Council, Presidency Conclusions, 23 and 24 March 2001 [2].

[181] Brussels European Council, Presidency Conclusions, 23 and 24 March 2006, [41].

together with effective education and training systems, a key factor in promoting growth.'[182]

However, notwithstanding the soothing Third Way rhetoric, there are concerns that the OMC systematically privileges the economic over the social. The first issue is the relationship between the BEPGs and the other OMC processes. The OMC processes in the employment and social domains are said to be 'subservient to the ideologies, path-dependencies and structures of Economic and Monetary Union, as institutionalised in the Broad Economic Policy Guidelines (BEPG).[183] As such, [the OMC] is not a coherent strategy, for all its rhetoric, but a tactical response with limited manoeuvre to the new political economy of the Eurozone'.[184] Tight budgetary controls and the maintenance of price stability are key elements of the BEPGs and the Stability and Growth Pact.[185] These operate so as to foreclose redistributive options, and to limit the potential of the OMC processes in the employment and social fields. A range of policy options cannot be considered, simply because of the economic constraints imposed in the name of EMU: 'The policy "experimentation" which is the hallmark of the open method of coordination in fact permits diversity only within a framework firmly wedded to sound public finances, comprehensive economic reform and restructuring of labour markets.'[186]

The second issue is the content of the guidelines in the employment and social domains. Detailed analyses of the employment guidelines, which examine the meaning of terms such as 'employability', 'entrepreneurship', 'adaptability', and 'flexibility', suggest that the guidelines have an economic, rather than a social focus. Even the much-heralded commitment to full employment has been said to amount to no more than 'a heavily supply-side orientated policy which strongly echoes the workfare-inspired "Third Way" approach'.[187]

The emphasis of the streamlined OMC on social protection and social inclusion is, as one might expect, rather different:

'The overarching objectives of the OMC for social protection and social inclusion are to promote:

social cohesion, equality between men and women and equal opportunities for all through adequate, accessible, financially sustainable, adaptable and efficient social protection systems and social inclusion policies;

---

[182] COM(2005)14 (n 178 above) 3; and Commission Communication 'Working together, working better: A new framework for the open coordination of social protection and inclusion policies in the European Union' COM(2005)706, 22 December 2005, 4: The social protection and inclusion OMC 'should parallel and interact closely with revised Lisbon—"feeding in" to growth and employment objectives while Lisbon programmes "feed out" to advance social cohesion goals'.

[183] Art 128(2) EC provides that the Employment Guidelines 'shall be consistent with the broad guidelines adopted pursuant to Article 99(2)'.

[184] D Chalmers and M Lodge, 'The Open Method of Co-ordination and the European Welfare State' (ESRC Centre for Analysis of Risk and Regulation, Discussion Paper No 11, LSE June 2003) 2.

[185] S Deakin and H Reed, 'The Contested Meaning of Labour Market Flexibility: Economic Theory and the Discourse of European Integration' in Shaw (n 151 above) 71, 90–1.

[186] Ashiagbor (n 151 above) 241.   [187] ibid 171. See also Deakin and Reed (n 185 above).

effective and mutual interaction between the Lisbon objectives of greater economic growth, more and better jobs and greater social cohesion, and with the EU's Sustainable Development Strategy;

good governance, transparency and the involvement of stakeholders in the design, implementation and monitoring of policy.'[188]

But even this statement, which only outlines the objectives of the EU and Member States in the broadest terms, refers to financial sustainability, adaptability, and efficiency, and locates the social protection and social inclusion OMC process within the broader Lisbon framework with its focus on growth and jobs.

There are reasons to believe that Member States' freedom of manoeuvre in the labour law field is limited by the constraints of EMU and, more broadly, the pressures of globalization. As we saw in the above subsection on the integrationist rationale, this may lead to calls for EU intervention. The problem is that the Lisbon Strategy, as currently formulated, does not appear to enable States to resist the pressures to deregulate. The constraints of globalization, and of EMU and economic policy coordination, seem to apply in much the same way to employment and social policy made within the context of an OMC, as they do to policy made at the national level. Thus, under the Lisbon Strategy, the integrationist argument outlined above is weak, because the OMC does not prevent, but may even encourage, deregulation in the labour law field. Also, the balance between the economic and the social is, notwithstanding the Third Way rhetoric, systematically tilted in favour of the former.

Given that the Lisbon Strategy does not appear to enable States to resist competitive pressures more effectively than they otherwise would, one is left wondering what grounds there may be for supposing that policy made in the context of the OMC may be able to realize economic and social advantages. Some proponents of the OMC argue that the OMC context contributes towards enhancing the effectiveness of national policies.[189] OMC processes are said to operate so as to strengthen, rather than to undermine, 'the political legitimacy, institutional integrity and problem-solving capacity of [the] Member States'.[190]

It seems clear that there may be a range of advantages, linked to the regime dimension of legitimacy, associated with stage one of the development of any OMC process. A process of collective reflection may be able to widen the range of policy options under consideration in each Member State, contribute towards innovation, and perhaps foster mutual learning.[191] The supranational institutions

---

[188] These objectives were approved by the Brussels European Council, Presidency Conclusions, 23 and 24 March 2006 [70]. See also COM(2005)706 (n 182 above) 5.

[189] See eg Art 3(i) EC.

[190] F Scharpf, 'European Governance: Common Concerns vs. The Challenge of Diversity', in C Joerges, Y Meny, and J Weiler (eds), *Mountain or Molehill? A Critical Appraisal of the Commission White Paper on Governance* (RSC Jean Monnet Working Paper No 6/01, Florence 2001) 1, 8.

[191] For a rather modest example of the value which the Commission derives from the OMC, see COM(2005)706 (n 182 above) 3: 'The added value of the inclusion process has been to make clear

may be able to support the States in meeting common challenges, for example by formulating indicators which help to measure progress towards particular goals.[192] And, depending on the identity of those involved, the OMC may also offer the prospect of a Europe-wide forum for public communication.[193]

It has also been argued that the European Employment Strategy affords an opportunity to 'depoliticize' the unemployment problem and to address it in a longer-term perspective: 'Implicit in this orientation (as with EMU and its convergence criteria) is the belief that politicians need to be detached from their immediate national constraints and political contingencies. On the basis of common objectives set within a supranational framework they are most likely to develop a capacity to solve fundamental problems such as unemployment.'[194] There are three problems with this account. First, on a normative level, the desirability of depoliticization may be questioned. Second, on a descriptive level, the extent to which the OMC in the employment sphere frees participants from national constraints and political contingencies may be doubted. And third, it is not clear that the capacity to solve fundamental problems is enhanced by the setting of common objectives. It may be that a constructive exchange of views about shared policy objectives is helpful and that the formulation of specific objectives helps to focus attention on necessary reforms. However, there is also a danger, mentioned above, that thinking might ossify rather than evolve. The advantages associated with problem-solving and learning may be reduced in the course of the move from stage one to stage two of the OMC. And, unless it is possible to point towards advantages associated with EU intervention which operates so as to constrain the autonomy of the Member States, EU intervention may be vulnerable to a vigorous application of the principles of subsidiarity and proportionality.[195]

---

the multi-dimensionality of poverty and exclusion and the consequent need for full, joined-up policy responses'.

[192] See <http://ec.europa.eu/employment_social/employment_strategy/indicators_emco_en.pdf>, in relation to the Employment Strategy; and <http://ec.europa.eu/employment_social/social_inclusion/docs/2006/indicators_en.pdf>, in relation to the social protection and social inclusion OMC process.

[193] See Commission Communication to the Spring European Council, 'Working together for growth and jobs: A new start for the Lisbon Strategy', COM(2005)24, 2 February 2005, 4: 'We have to mobilise support for change. Establishing broad and effective ownership of the Lisbon goals is the best way to ensure words are turned into results. Everyone with a stake in Lisbon's success and at every level must be involved in delivering these reforms. They must become part of national political debate'.

[194] J Goetschy, 'The European Employment Strategy: Genesis and Development' (1999) 5 European Journal of Industrial Relations 117, 132.

[195] See also L Tsoukalis, 'The JCMS Lecture: Managing Diversity and Change in the European Union' (2006) 44 JCMS 1, 4, expressing concern that the EU has come to be seen as a scapegoat for many of the Union's ills, and that it is 'seen by citizens as having responsibility for things on which it has little power to deliver'.

Conclusions

One is left with a rather unclear picture. The OMC is heralded by many, who claim that it is able to contribute to the enhanced legitimacy of the EU. It is said that it offers benefits in terms of both performance and regime legitimacy and that it 'radicalizes subsidiarity'.[196] My discussion suggests that many of its benefits are unproven. In performance legitimacy terms, the OMC offers a policy prescription which privileges the economic over the social. In addition, it lacks the mechanisms which enable the EU to ensure that guidelines are translated into action at national and local levels. In regime legitimacy terms, it may offer certain advantages, but there are also problems, in particular as regards participation (for example of the European Parliament and the social partners) and accountability.[197] The result is that, as it stands, the Lisbon Strategy is at best no more than a partial response to the integrationist, economic, and social challenges facing the EU and its Member States. In my view, there are two possible routes forward.

According to the first approach, the Strategy is recast as a 'soft' process, in which objectives and guidelines are set only at the most general level. If sufficient attention is paid to the identity of those involved in the process and to the way in which their interactions are structured, there is a prospect that the OMC may offer a Europe-wide forum for public communication, and may, it is hoped, enable mutual learning to occur and lead to the development of a broad political consensus on how best to tackle some of the economic and social challenges facing Europe.[198] A process of this sort would be unobjectionable from the perspective of the principles of subsidiarity and proportionality and may lead to better policy outcomes.

The second approach is more ambitious. It relies on the argument, developed above, that in the wake of EMU there is an ever-increasing pressure on States to deregulate in the labour law field. This can be said to create a need for EU intervention. This intervention may be said to be either integrationist or social. The integrationist rationale for Community intervention is provided by the need to prevent distortions of competition (defined as per conception V) in the European market. The social rationale is more straightforward—it may be expressed simply as the desire to protect the interests of workers—but the existence of significant pressure on States to deregulate enables the EU to overcome the challenge of subsidiarity.[199] This approach calls for a 'hard' OMC process. If the intervention of

---

[196] D Hodson and I Maher, 'The Open Method as a New Mode of Governance: The case of Soft Economic Policy Co-ordination' (2001) 39 JCMS 719, 728.

[197] See eg Commission Communication, 'Taking Stock of Five Years of the European Employment Strategy', COM(2002)416, 17 July 2002, 20; and Chalmers and Lodge (n 184 above).

[198] See further O Gersternberg and C Sabel, 'Directly-Deliberative Polyarchy: An Institutional Ideal for Europe?' in C Joerges and R Dehousse (eds), *Good Governance in Europe's Integrated Market* (OUP, Oxford 2002).

[199] The argument is, quite simply, that given the existence of competitive pressures, the EU is in a significantly better position than are the Member States to achieve given social objectives.

the EU is to be able to realize these integrationist or social advantages, it is important that the guidelines display a genuine commitment to the social and that the
process finds ways of ensuring that States do not succumb to the pressures to
deregulate standards. This is, in my view, only possible if the OMC processes are
combined either with minimum standard setting measures or, preferably, with
measures guaranteeing fundamental social rights.

The strongest objection to this second approach may come from a vigorous
application of the principle of proportionality. The EU may well find it difficult to
justify seeking to impose its chosen integrationist, economic, and social policies
on States which do not share the same objectives. The proportionality enquiry
asks that the EU is sensitive to the interests of the Member States and that it goes
no further than is necessary (in terms of intrusion on the legitimate interests of the
Member States) in order to achieve EU objectives. The proportionality enquiry
involves ascribing values to the legitimate interests of the EU and the Member
States, and with these values in mind, determining whether the EU has gone
beyond what is necessary. The institutions appear to have little difficulty in justifying EU intrusion on national autonomy on the grounds that it is necessary to constrain the policy choices of the Member States in order to further the integrationist
objectives of the EU (and, in particular, to harmonize various aspects of the
national legal regime). It is also possible to justify EU intrusion on national autonomy on the grounds that this is necessary in order to further the economic or
social objectives of the EU. But in order for this to be possible, it is important that
the EU makes a clearer commitment to particular economic or social goals.

6

Conclusions

There are a number of objectives which EU intervention in domestic labour law might be able to serve. In this book, I have arranged these into three broad categories—the integrationist, economic, and social rationales. These three rationales do not point clearly towards particular policy prescriptions. I have argued that a close examination of where a commitment to each of the rationales may or must lead, coupled with a close examination of the relationship between the three rationales, helps to explains the chequered history of EU labour law, and also, perhaps more importantly, enables one to point towards ways forward for the EU in this contentious field.

The focus of this book has been on the integrationist rationale. There are several reasons for this: first, because the integrationist rationale has not been sufficiently explored in the existing labour law literature; second, because the dictates of market integration create the framework within which the economic and social objectives of labour law may be pursued, at both the EU and the domestic level; and third, because it is not at all obvious whether the establishment of a single market in Europe calls for harmonization of labour law regimes within the market area, or for other forms of intervention.

The Court of Justice's interpretation of the dictates of the market-making endeavour has, in my view, been rather simplistic. It has suggested that disparities between national laws are problematic; either because they constitute barriers to free movement or distortions of competition. However, with reference to the legitimate objectives of domestic labour law, the Court has tended to go on to hold that domestic labour law rules are justified. This approach succeeds in leaving some space for national autonomy and experimentation, but it institutionalizes a tension between the integrationist objectives of the EU and the economic and social objectives pursued by national regulation in the labour law field, which, in my view, need not exist.

There is an important difference between the way in which the Court and the political institutions conceptualize the integrationist rationale. In the labour law field, the political institutions have not sought to harmonize the laws of the Member States, but have instead intervened in a range of ways which afford a degree of autonomy to the Member States (and indeed the social partners). If the political institutions shared the conception of the integrationist rationale adopted by the Court, they would at least have attempted to act so as to eliminate those obstacles to the establishment and functioning of the market which could not, because of the existence of justifications for national labour law rules, be eliminated by the negative integration case law of the Court. They have not done so. Thus, one is faced with two contrasting visions of the integrationist rationale, one hostile and the other sympathetic to diversity.[1]

Both of these conceptions are plausible. It becomes possible to choose between these two rival conceptions of the integrationist rationale by considering the economic and social meta-objectives of integration, and the arguments from legitimacy which operate so as to make a case for the maintenance of local autonomy in accordance with the principles of subsidiarity and proportionality.

Acceptance of the view that integration is not pursued for its own sake, but in order to further the economic and social meta-objectives of the EU and its Member States, leads one to view national regulation in the labour law field, which may, after all, be enacted with these same objectives in mind, with sympathy rather than hostility. This sympathy is enhanced when one reflects on the relative legitimacy of labour law regulation, enacted on economic or social grounds, at national and EU level. Thus, my conclusion is that the integrationist rationale need not, and indeed should not, be conceptualized so that mere disparities between national labour law rules are identified as problematic.

If this analysis of the integrationist rationale is accepted, it creates an enhanced space for national regulation in the labour law field. The requirement that disparities between national labour law regimes be eliminated simply ceases to exist. Member States are instead afforded considerable freedom to intervene in pursuit of their chosen objectives. In this new context, the role of the EU is much changed. No longer does it work towards the elimination of disparities between national regimes, or view national regimes with suspicion simply on the grounds that they are divergent. Instead, it intervenes in a range of ways to ensure that the market in Europe is able to function properly, and to the extent that its interventions are compatible with the principles of subsidiarity and proportionality, to further economic and social objectives. As a result of the ever-increasing interdependence of the various national economies, in part precipitated by the market-building endeavour, the EU has a significant role to play, and the impact of the principle of subsidiarity is reduced.

---

[1] See also Dougan's approach. 'The Single Market should no longer be conceived purely as an exercise in economic integration. The ideal of free movement across a regulatory level playing-field has been compromised by the Community's commitment to pursue higher standards of social protection within the fabric of this very process of economic integration, and thus by the Treaty's need to furnish a legal infrastructure capable of accommodating differences in the capacity and willingness of the various Member States to agree a common welfare agenda. Against such a background, certain variations in national law, and the consequent possibility of certain persistent barriers to unrestricted free movement, should not be construed as inherently incompatible with the existence of a functioning Single Market.' M Dougan, 'Vive la Différence? Exploring the Legal Framework for Reflexive Harmonization within the Single European Market', in R Miller and P Zumbansen (eds), *Annual of German and European Law, Volume 1 (2003)* (Berghahn, New York 2004) 113, 160.

All too often, however, the political institutions have not succeeded in providing convincing arguments (based either on the integrationist, the economic, or the social rationale) for EU intervention. As chapter 5 above illustrates, it is rather difficult to identify convincing rationales for many of the interventions of the EU—especially for many of the flexible interventions of recent years. The integrationist arguments for intervention may, as in the case of the Working Time Directive, be incoherent. Economic and social arguments are combined in ways which, despite the rhetoric, systematically privilege the former over the latter.

I contend that convincing arguments for EU intervention do exist. These arguments rely on a precise identification of the rationale(s) for, or the objective(s) of, EU intervention; and on steps being taken to ensure that the institutions' method or modality of intervention is chosen in such a way as to ensure a significant contribution towards the realization of the objective in question.

If the integrationist rationale is not conceptualized so as to require the elimination of disparities between national labour law regimes, the harmonization of such regimes is not required. My preferred conceptions of the integrationist rationale do, nevertheless, call for the imposition of certain constraints on national policy choices in the labour law field. The institutions act so as to eliminate barriers to free movement. Under this head, they ensure that national labour law rules do not prevent access to markets, and that they do not discriminate against imported factors of production. They have a role to play in preventing distortions of competition. Under this head, the institutions may act against States whose standards are 'unacceptably low', and may also act so as to ensure that the collective quest for competitive advantage does not lead to deregulation in the labour law field. And they act to ensure that EMU operates successfully. When acting under the integrationist rationale, the institutions must ensure that they take heed of the principle of proportionality, and that they do not infringe national autonomy further than is necessary for the realization of their objectives.

The institutions are also able to act under the economic and the social rationales. Once integrationist arguments for the harmonization of the laws of the Member States are rejected, the relationship between the economic and the social assumes a much greater significance. The Treaty tells us little about the nature of this relationship. The Third Way rhetoric which has come to dominate the Lisbon Strategy may be soothing on the surface, but it too tells us little about the way in which the inevitable conflicts between the economic and the social are to be resolved. The result is that the European project lacks a normative compass, and that the EU lacks clear authority to intervene to pursue particular economic and social goals. Both legal and political processes have a role to play in building the consensus necessary to make a stronger commitment to particular economic and social objectives. If Europe is not to lose itself,[2] and if the social is not to be subsumed by the

---

[2] M Maduro, 'Europe's Social Self: "The Sickness Unto Death"', in J Shaw (ed), *Social Law and Policy in an Evolving European Union* (Hart, Oxford 2000) 325.

economic, it is important that Europe overcomes its legacy of 'ambivalence of the social',[3] and makes a clear commitment to the social rationale. A clear commitment to the social rationale would affect the European project in a number of ways. It would profoundly affect the nature of the market-building endeavour, for example allowing the EU to act with more confidence in ruling out competition based on unacceptably low standards, and in resisting the pressures towards competitive deregulation. It would enable a reorientation of the Lisbon Strategy so as to give a greater priority to the realization of social objectives. And it would have a significant effect on the operation of the principle of proportionality, enabling a greater value to be ascribed to the social goals of both the EU and its Member States.

In the aftermath of French and Dutch referenda rejecting the Treaty establishing a Constitution for Europe, the future of the EU is uncertain. The legitimacy of the European polity can no longer be taken for granted. It is vital that the EU regains the trust of its people. A clear commitment to the social rationale in the labour law field would contribute towards this goal.

---

[3] C Joerges, 'On disregard for history in the Convention Process' (2006) 12 European Law Journal 2, 3.

Bibliography

P Alston (ed), *The EU and Human Rights* (OUP, Oxford 1999)

—— (ed), *Labour Rights as Human Rights* (OUP, Oxford 2005)

F Amtenbrink, *The Democratic Accountability of Central Banks: A Comparative Study of the European Central Bank* (Hart, Oxford 1999)

—— and J De Haan, 'Reforming the Stability and Growth Pact' (2006) 31 ELR 402

M Andenas and S Kenyon-Slade (eds), *EC Financial Market Regulation and Company Law* (Sweet and Maxwell, London 1993)

J Armour, 'Who Should Make Corporate Law? EC Legislation versus Regulatory Competition' (2005) 58 Current Legal Problems 369

K Armstrong and S Bulmer, *The Governance of the Single European Market* (MUP, Manchester 1998)

D Ashiagbor, 'Economic and Social Rights in the European Charter of Fundamental Rights' (2004) 1 European Human Rights Law Review 62

—— *The European Employment Strategy: Labour Market Regulation and New Governance* (OUP, Oxford 2006)

S Ball, 'The European Employment Strategy: The Will But Not The Way' (2001) 30 ILJ 353

K Banks, 'L'Article 118a: Elément Dynamique de la Politique Sociale Communautaire' (1993) 29 Cahiers de droit européen 537

J Baquero Cruz, *Between Competition and Free Movement: The Economic Constitutional Law of the European Community* (Hart, Oxford 2002)

N Barber, 'The limited modesty of subsidiarity' (2005) 11 European Law Journal 308

R Barents, 'The Internal Market Unlimited: Some Observations on the Legal Basis of Community Legislation' (1993) 30 CML Rev 85

C Barnard, 'A Social Policy for Europe: Politicians 1:0 Lawyers' (1992) 8 International Journal of Comparative Labour Law and Industrial Relations 15

—— 'Social Dumping and Race to the Bottom: Some Lessons for the EU from Delaware?' (2000) 25 ELR 57

—— and J Scott (eds), *The Law of the Single European Market: Unpacking the Premises* (Hart, Oxford 2002)

M Bell, *Anti-Discrimination Law and the European Union* (OUP, Oxford 2002)

B Bercusson, 'The dynamic of European labour law after Maastricht' (1994) 23 ILJ 1

G Bermann, 'Taking Subsidiarity Seriously: Federalism in the European Community and the United States' (1994) 94 Columbia Law Review 331

—— 'Editorial: The European Union as a Constitutional Experiment' (2004) 10 European Law Journal 363

N Bernard, 'The Future of European Economic Law in the light of the Principle of Subsidiarity' (1996) 33 CML Rev 633

—— *Multilevel Governance in the European Union* (Kluwer, The Hague 2002)

L Betten, 'The Democratic Deficit of Participatory Democracy in Community Social Policy' (1998) 23 ELR 20

A Biondi, 'Free Trade, A Mountain Road and the Right to Protest: European Economic Freedoms and Fundamental Individual Rights' (2004) 1 European Human Rights Law Review 51

K Bradley, 'The European Court and the Legal Basis of Community Legislation' (1988) 13 ELR 379

W Buiter, 'Alice in Euroland' (1999) 37 JCMS 181

W Cary, 'Federalism and Corporate Law: Reflections on Delaware' (1974) 83 Yale Law Journal 663

D Chalmers and M Lodge, 'The Open Method of Co-ordination and the European Welfare State' (ESRC Centre for Analysis of Risk and Regulation, Discussion Paper No 11, LSE June 2003)

D Chalmers *et al, European Union Law* (CUP, Cambridge 2006)

G Close, 'Harmonisation of Laws: Use or Abuse of the Powers under the EEC Treaty?' (1978) 3 ELR 461

R Coase, 'The problem of social cost' (1960) 3 Journal of Law and Economics 1

—— *The Firm, the Market and the Law* (University of Chicago Press, Chicago 1988)

H Collins, 'Labour law as a Vocation' (1989) 105 LQR 468

P Collins and M Hutchings, 'Articles 101 and 102 of the EEC Treaty: Completing the Internal Market' (1986) 11 ELR 191

J Conaghan, R Fischl, and K Klare (eds), *Labour Law in an Era of Globalization: Transformative Practices and Possibilities* (OUP, Oxford 2002)

I Cooper, 'The Watchdogs of Subsidiarity: National Parliaments and the logic of arguing in the EU' (2006) 44 JCMS 281

P Craig, 'Constitutions, Constitutionalism, and the European Union' (2001) 7 European Law Journal 125

P Craig and G De Búrca (eds), *The Evolution of EU Law* (OUP, Oxford 1999)

—— and G De Búrca, *EU Law: Text, Cases and Materials* (3rd edn, Clarendon, Oxford 2003)

S Crosby, 'The Single Market and the Rule of Law' (1991) 16 ELR 451

C Crouch, *Industrial Relations and European State Traditions* (Clarendon, Oxford 1993)

D Curtin, 'The Constitutional Structure of the Union: A Europe of Bits and Pieces' (1993) 30 CML Rev 17

R Dahl, *A Preface to Economic Democracy* (Polity Press, Cambridge 1985)

L Daniele, 'Non-Discriminatory Restrictions to the Free Movement of Persons' (1997) 22 ELR 191

A Dashwood, 'The Limits of EC Powers' (1996) 21 ELR 113

—— 'The Relationship between the Member States and the European Union/European Community' (2004) 41 CML Rev 355

W Däubler (ed), *Market and Social Justice in the EC—the Other Side of the Internal Market* (Bertelsmann Foundation, Gutersloh 1991)

A Davies, 'The Right to Strike Versus Freedom of Establishment in EC Law: The Battle Commences' (2006) 35 ILJ 75

G Davies, 'Can Selling Arrangements be Harmonised?' (2005) 30 ELR 371

—— 'Subsidiarity: The Wrong Idea, in the Wrong Place, at the Wrong Time' (2006) 43 CML Rev 63

P Davies, 'Market Integration and Social Policy in the Court of Justice' (1995) 24 ILJ 49

—— 'Posted Workers: Single Market or Protection of National Labour Law Systems?' (1997) 34 CML Rev 571

—— and M Freedland, *Kahn-Freund's Labour and the Law* (3rd edn, Stevens, London 1983)

—— *et al* (eds), *European Community Labour Law: Principles and Perspectives; Liber Amicorum Lord Wedderburn* (Clarendon, Oxford 1996)

S Deakin, 'Two Types of Regulatory Competition: Competitive Federalism versus Reflexive Harmonization. A Law and Economics Perspective on *Centros*' (1999) 2 Cambridge Yearbook of European Legal Studies 231

—— 'Legal Diversity and Regulatory Competition: Which Model for Europe?' (2006) 12 European Law Journal 440

—— and F Wilkinson, 'Rights vs. Efficiency? The Economic Case for Transnational Labour Standards' (1994) 23 ILJ 289

G De Búrca, 'The Principle of Proportionality and its Application in EC Law' (1993) 13 Yearbook of European Law 105

—— 'Reappraising Subsidiarity's Significance After Amsterdam' (Harvard Jean Monnet Working Paper No 7/99, 1999) <http://www.jeanmonnetprogram.org/papers/99/990701.html>

—— 'The Drafting of the EU Charter of Fundamental Rights' (2001) 26 ELR 126

—— 'The Constitutional Challenge of New Governance in the European Union' (2003) 28 ELR 814

—— 'After the Referenda' (2006) 12 European Law Journal 6

—— and J Scott (eds), *Constitutional Change in the EU: From Uniformity to Flexibility?* (Hart, Oxford 2000)

—— and J Scott (eds), *The EU and the WTO: Legal and Constitutional Issues* (Hart, Oxford 2001)

G De Geest, J Siegers, and R Van den Bergh (eds), *Law and Economics and the Labour Market* (Edward Elgar, Cheltenham 1999)

P De Grauwe, *Economics of Monetary Union* (6th edn, OUP, Oxford 2005)

J De Haan, F Amtenbrink, and S Waller, 'The Transparency and Credibility of the European Central Bank' (2004) 42 JCMS 775

—— S Eijffinger, and S Waller, *The European Central Bank: Credibility, Transparency and Centralization* (MIT Press, Cambridge 2005)

C De La Porte, P Pochet, and G Room, 'Social Benchmarking, policy making and new governance in the EU' (2001) 11 Journal of European Social Policy 291

M De La Torre, 'The Law Beneath Rights' Feet' (2002) 8 European Law Journal 513

O De Schutter, N Lebessis, and J Paterson (eds), *Governance in the European Union* (OOPEC, Luxembourg 2001)

B De Witte, 'Legal Status of the Charter: Vital Question or Non-Issue' (2001) 8 Maastricht Journal 81

—— 'Simplification and Reorganization of the European Treaties' (2002) 39 CML Rev 1255

M Dougan, 'Minimum Harmonization and the Internal Market' (2000) 37 CML Rev 853

—— and E Spaventa (eds), *Social Welfare and EU Law* (Hart, Oxford 2005)

K Dyson (ed), *European States and the Euro: Europeanization, Variation and Convergence* (OUP, Oxford 2002)

—— and K Featherstone, *The Road to Maastricht: Negotiating Economic and Monetary Union* (OUP, Oxford 1999).

F Easterbrook, 'Antitrust and the Economics of Federalism' (1993) 26 Journal of Law and Economics 23

Editorial Comments, 'Are European Values Being Hoovered Away?' (1993) 30 CML Rev 445

—— 'Taking (the limits of) competences seriously' (2000) 37 CML Rev 1301

—— 'Whither the Stability and Growth Pact' (2004) 41 CML Rev 1193

—— 'What now?' (2005) 42 CML Rev 905

—— 'The services directive proposal: Striking a balance between the promotion of the internal market and preserving the European social model?' (2006) 43 CML Rev 307

M Egan, *Constructing a European Market* (OUP, Oxford 2001)

C-D Ehlermann, 'Harmonisation for harmonisation's sake?' (1978) 15 CML Rev 4

—— 'The Internal Market following the Single European Act' (1987) 24 CML Rev 361

E Ellis (ed), *The Principle of Proportionality in the Laws of Europe* (Hart, Oxford 1999)

N Emiliou, *The Principle of Proportionality in European Law* (Kluwer, Deventer 1996)

K Endo, 'Subsidiarity and its Enemies: To what extent is Sovereignty Contested in the Mixed Commonwealth of Europe?' (EUI Working Paper RSC No 2001/24, Florence 2001) 25

A Estella, *The EU Principle of Subsidiarity and its Critique* (OUP, Oxford 2002)

D Esty and D Geradin (eds), *Regulatory Competition and Economic Integration: Comparative Perspectives* (OUP, Oxford 2001)

U Everling, 'Reflections on the Structure of the European Union' (1992) 29 CML Rev 1053

M Everson, 'Adjudicating the Market' (2002) 8 European Law Journal 152

B Fitzpatrick, 'Community Social Law after Maastricht' (1992) 21 ILJ 199

—— 'Straining the Definition of Health and Safety' (1997) 26 ILJ 115

G Fox and B Roth (eds), *Democratic Governance and International Law* (CUP, Cambridge 2000)

S Fredman, 'The New Rights: Labour Law and Ideology in the Thatcher Years' (1992) 12 OJLS 24

S Fredman, 'Transformation or Dilution: Fundamental Rights in the EU Social Space' (2006) 12 European Law Journal 41

R García, 'The General Provisions of the Charter of Fundamental Rights of the European Union' (2002) 8 European Law Journal 492

K Gatsios and P Seabright, 'Regulation in the European Community' (1989) 5 Oxford Review of Economic Policy 37

O Gerstenberg, 'Expanding the Constitution Beyond the Court: The Case of Euro-Constitutionalism' (2002) 8 European Law Journal 172

A Giddens, *The Third Way* (Polity Press, Cambridge 1998)

M Gijzen, 'The Charter: A Milestone for Social Protection in Europe?' (2001) 8 Maastricht Journal 33

S Giubboni, *Social Rights and Market Freedom in the European Constitution—A Labour Law Perspective* (CUP, Cambridge 2006)

J Goetschy, 'The European Employment Strategy: Genesis and Development' (1999) 5 European Journal of Industrial Relations 117

Lord Goldsmith, 'A Charter of Rights, Freedoms and Principles' (2001) 38 CML Rev 1201

L Gormley, P Kapteyn, and P VerLoren van Themaat, *Introduction to the Law of the European Communities* (2nd edn, Kluwer, Deventer 1989)

J Gray, *False Dawn: The Delusions of Global Capitalism* (Granta, London 1998)

E Haas, *Beyond the Nation State* (Stanford University Press, Stanford 1964)

J Habermas, 'So, Why Does Europe Need a Constitution?' (RSC, Florence 2001)

C Harlow, 'Voices of Difference in a Plural Community' (Harvard Jean Monnet Working Paper No 03/00, 2000) <http://www.jeanmonnetprogram.org/papers/00/000301.html>

T Hartley, *The Foundations of European Community Law* (5th edn, OUP, Oxford 2002)

D Held, *Democracy and the Global Order: From the Modern State to Cosmopolitan Governance* (Polity Press, Cambridge 1995)

B Hepple, 'The Crisis in EEC Labour Law' (1987) 16 ILJ 77

—— 'Social Rights in the European Community: A British Perspective' (1990) 11 Comparative Labor Law Journal 425

—— 'The Implementation of the Community Charter of Fundamental Social Rights' (1990) 53 MLR 643

—— 'Social Values and European Law' (1995) 48 Current Legal Problems 39

M Herdegen, 'Price Stability and Budgetary Restraints in the Economic and Monetary Union: Law as the Guardian of Economic Wisdom' (1998) 35 CML Rev 9

A Herrmann, 'Converging Divergence: How Competitive Advantages Condition Institutional Change Under EMU' (2005) 43 JCMS 287

T Hervey, *European Social Law and Policy* (Longman, London 1998)

—— and J Kenner (eds), *Economic and Social Rights under the EU Charter of Fundamental Rights* (Hart, Oxford 2003)

D Hodson and I Maher, 'The Open Method as a New Mode of Governance: The Case of Soft Economic Policy Co-ordination' (2001) 39 JCMS 719

R Howse and M Trebilcock, 'The Fair Trade/Free Trade Debate: Trade, Labor, and the Environment' (1996) 16 International Review of Law and Economics 61

W Hutton, *The State We're In* (Jonathan Cape, London 1995)

—— *The World We're In* (Little, Brown, London 2002)

International Labour Office, 'Social Aspects of European Economic Cooperation' (1956) 74 International Labour Review 99 (the Ohlin Report)

O Issing, 'The Eurosystem: Transparent and Accountable or "Willem in Euroland"' (1999) 37 JCMS 503

C Jensen, J Madsen, and J Due, 'Phases and dynamics in the development of EU industrial relations regulation' (1999) 30 Industrial Relations Journal 118

C Joerges, 'Product Safety in the European Community: Market Integration, Social Regulation and Legal Structures' (1992) 39 Journal of Behavioural Sciences 132

—— 'On disregard for history in the Convention Process' (2006) 12 European Law Journal 2

—— and R Dehousse (eds), *Good Governance in Europe's Integrated Market* (OUP, Oxford 2002)

—— Y Meny and J Weiler (eds), *Mountain or Molehill? A Critical Appraisal of the Commission White Paper on Governance* (RSC Jean Monnet Working Paper No 6/01, Florence 2001)

A Jones and B Sufrin, *EC Competition Law: Text, Cases and Materials* (OUP, Oxford 2001)

J Kenner (ed), *Trends in European Social Policy* (Dartmouth, Aldershot 1995)

—— 'A Distinctive Legal Base for Social Policy? The Court of Justice Answers a "Delicate Question"' (1997) 22 ELR 579

—— 'The EC Employment Title and the "Third Way": Making Soft Law Work?' (1999) 15 International Journal of Comparative Labour Law and Industrial Relations 33

—— *EU Employment Law: From Rome to Amsterdam and beyond* (Hart, Oxford 2002)

C Kilpatrick, T Novitz, and P Skidmore (eds), *The Future of Remedies in Europe* (Hart, Oxford 2000)

T Koopmans, 'Guest Editorial: In Search of Purpose' (2005) 42 CML Rev 1241

M Kumm, 'Who is the Final Arbiter of Constitutionality in Europe?' (1999) 36 CML Rev 346

—— 'Constitutionalising Subsidiarity in Integrated Markets: The Case of Tobacco Regulation in the European Union' (2006) 12 European Law Journal 503

B Langille, 'Eight Ways to think about International Labour Standards' (1997) 31(4) Journal of World Trade 27

K Lenaerts, 'Constitutionalism and the Many Faces of Federalism' (1990) 38 American Journal of Comparative Law 205

A Lo Faro, *Regulating Social Europe: Reality and Myth of Collective Bargaining in the EC Legal Order* (Hart, Oxford 2000)

J-V Louis, 'The Review of the Stability and Growth Pact' (2006) 43 CML Rev 85

Lord McCarthy (ed), *Legal Intervention in Industrial Relations: Gains and Losses* (Blackwell, Oxford 1992)

A McGee and S Weatherill, 'The Evolution of the Single Market—Harmonisation or Liberalisation' (1990) 53 MLR 578

M Maduro, *We, The Court: The European Court of Justice and the European Economic Constitution* (Hart, Oxford 1998)

—— 'Europe and the Constitution: What if this is as Good as it Gets?' (Con WEB No 5/2000) <http://les1.man.ac.uk/conweb>

G Majone, 'The European Community Between Social Policy and Social Regulation' (1993) 31 JCMS 153

—— 'The Credibility Crisis of Community Regulation' (2000) 38 JCMS 273

GF Mancini, 'Labour Law and Community Law' (1985) 20 Irish Jurist 1

TH Marshall, *Citizenship and Social Class* (CUP, Cambridge 1950)

R Miller and P Zumbansen (eds), *Annual of German and European Law, Volume 1 (2003)* (Berghahn, New York 2004)

F Mongelli, 'What is European Economic and Monetary Union telling us about the Properties of Optimum Currency Areas?' (2005) 43 JCMS 607

J Morijn, 'Balancing Fundamental Rights and Union Freedoms in Union Law: *Schmidberger* and *Omega* in the Light of the Union Constitution' (2006) 12 European Law Journal 15

K Nicolaidis and R Howse (eds), *The Federal Vision: Legitimacy and Levels of Governance in the United States and the European Union* (OUP, Oxford 2001)

T Novitz, *International and European Protection of the Right to Strike* (OUP, Oxford 2003)

—— and P Syrpis, 'Assessing Legitimate Structures for the Making of Transnational Labour Law: The Durability of Corporatism' (2006) 35 ILJ 367

OECD, *The OECD Jobs Study* (OECD, Paris 1994)

—— *Trade, Employment and Labour Standards: A Study of Core Workers' Rights and International Trade* (OECD, Paris 1996)

A Ogus, *Regulation—Legal Form and Economic Theory* (Clarendon, Oxford 1994)

I Pernice (ed), *Harmonization of Legislation in Federal Systems* (Nomos Verlagsgesellschaft, Baden-Baden 1996)

P Pescatore, 'Some Critical Remarks on the Single European Act' (1987) 24 CML Rev 9

K Polanyi, *The Great Transformation* (Beacon Press, Boston 1944)

M Pollack, 'Creeping Competence: The Expanding Agenda of the European Community' (1994) 14 Journal of European Public Policy 95

N Reich, 'The November Revolution of the European Court of Justice: *Keck, Meng* and *Audi* Revisited' (1994) 31 CML Rev 459

—— 'Union Citizenship: Metaphor or Source of Rights' (2001) 7 European Law Journal 4

M Rhodes, 'The Social Dimension of the Single European Market: National versus Transnational Regulation' (1991) 19 European Journal of Political Research 245

—— 'The Social Dimension after Maastricht: Setting a New Agenda for the Labour Market' (1993) 9 International Journal of Comparative Labour Law and Industrial Relations 297

B Ryan, 'Pay, Trade Union Rights and European Community Law' (1997) 13 International Journal of Comparative Labour Law and Industrial Relations 305

F Scharpf, 'Balancing Positive and Negative Integration: The Regulatory Options for Europe' (RSC Policy Papers 97/4, Florence 1997)

—— 'The European Social Model: Coping with the Challenges of Diversity' (2002) 40 JCMS 645

S Sciarra, 'Integration Through Coordination: The Employment Title in the Amsterdam Treaty' (2000) 6 Columbia Journal of European Law 209

—— (ed), *Labour Law in the Courts: National Judges and the European Court of Justice* (Hart, Oxford 2001)

J Scott and D Trubek, 'Mind the Gap: Law and New Approaches to Governance in the European Union' (2002) 8 European Law Journal 1

W Sengenberger and D Campbell (eds), *Creating Economic Opportunities: The Role of Labour Standards in Industrial Restructuring* (International Institute for Labour Studies, Geneva 1994)

—— and D Campbell (eds), *International Labour Standards and Economic Interdependence* (International Institute for Labour Studies, Geneva 1994)

M Shanks, 'The Social Policy of the European Communities' (1977) 14 CML Rev 375

J Shaw, 'The Interpretation of Union Citizenship' (1998) 61 MLR 293

—— (ed), *Social Law and Policy in an Evolving European Union* (Hart, Oxford 2000)

—— and G More (eds), *New Legal Dynamics of European Union* (Clarendon, Oxford 1995)

S Simitis, 'Dismantling or Strengthening Labour Law: The Case of the European Court of Justice' (1996) 2 European Law Journal 156

PJ Slot, 'Harmonisation' (1996) 21 ELR 378

S Smismans, *Law, Legitimacy, and European Governance: Functional Participation in Social Regulation* (OUP, Oxford 2004)

F Snyder, *New Directions in European Community Law* (Weidenfeld and Nicolson, London 1990)

Spaak Report, Political and Economic Planning (1956) Planning No 405

E Spaventa, 'From *Gebhard* to *Carpenter*: Towards a (Non-)Economic European Constitution' (2004) 41 CML Rev 743

E Stein, 'International Integration and Democracy: No Love at First Sight' (2001) 95 American Journal of International Law 489

W Streeck, 'Neo-Voluntarism: A New European Social Policy Regime?' (1995) 1 European Law Journal 31

M Streit and W Mussler, 'The Economic Constitution of the European Community—"From Rome to Maastricht"' (1995) 1 European Law Journal 5

C Summers, 'Models of Employee Representational Participation' (1994) 15 Comparative Labor Law Journal 1

J Sun and J Pelkmans, 'Regulatory Competition in the Single Market' (1995) 33 JCMS 67

A Supiot, 'The dogmatic foundations of the market' (2000) 29 ILJ 321

P Syrpis, *The Rationales for European Community Social Policy: An Analysis of EC Worker Participation Law* (D Phil thesis, Oxford 2000)

—— 'Smoke without Fire: The Social Policy Agenda and the Internal Market' (2001) 30 ILJ 271

—— 'Legitimising European Governance: Taking Subsidiarity Seriously within the Open Method of Coordination' (EUI Working Paper Law No 2002/10, Florence 2002)

—— 'Directive 2002/14: A Model of new governance in Europe' (September 2002) European Current Law xi

E Szyszczak, 'Future Directions in European Union Social Policy Law' (1995) 24 ILJ 19

—— 'Experimental Governance: The Open Method of Coordination' (2006) 12 European Law Journal 486

S Tierney, *Constitutional Law and National Pluralism* (OUP, Oxford 2004)

A Toth, 'Is Subsidiarity Justiciable?' (1994) 19 ELR 268

B Towers and M Terry (eds), *Industrial Relations Journal European Annual Review 1997* (Blackwell, Oxford 1998)

D Trubek and L Trubek, 'Hard and Soft Law in the Construction of Social Europe: the Role of the Open Method of Co-ordination' (2005) 11 European Law Journal 343

L Tsoukalis, 'The JCMS Lecture: Managing Diversity and Change in the European Union' (2006) 44 JCMS 1

University of Cambridge Centre for European Legal Studies, *The ECJ's Tobacco Advertising Judgment* (CELS Occasional Paper No 5, Cambridge 2001)

R Van den Bergh, 'The Subsidiarity Principle in European Community Law: Some Insights from Law and Economics' (1994) 1 Maastricht Journal 337

—— 'Subsidiarity as an Economic Demarcation Principle and the Emergence of European Private Law' (1998) 5 Maastricht Journal 129

D Vignes, 'The Harmonisation of National Legislation and the EEC' (1990) 15 ELR 358

I Ward, 'Beyond Constitutionalism: The Search for a European Political Imagination' (2001) 7 European Law Journal 24

P Watson, 'Social Policy after Maastricht' (1993) 30 CML Rev 481

S Weatherill, 'After *Keck*: Some Thoughts on how to Clarify the Clarification' (1996) 33 CML Rev 885

—— 'Better Competence Monitoring' (2005) 30 ELR 23

Lord Wedderburn, 'Workers' Rights: Fact or Fake?' (1991) 13 Dublin University Law Journal 1

—— *Labour Law and Freedom: Further Essays in Labour Law* (Lawrence and Wishart, London 1995)

—— 'Consultation and Collective Bargaining in Europe: Success or Ideology?' (1997) 26 ILJ 1

—— *et al*, *Labour Law in the Post-Industrial Era* (Dartmouth, Aldershot 1994)

J Weiler, 'Does Europe Need a Constitution? Demos, Telos and the German Maastricht Decision' (1995) 1 European Law Journal 219
—— *The Constitution of Europe* (CUP, Cambridge 1999)
—— 'A Constitution for Europe: Some Hard Choices' (2002) 40 JCMS 563
E Whiteford, 'Social Policy after Maastricht' (1993) 18 ELR 202
J Wouters, 'European Company Law: *Quo Vadis?*' (2000) 37 CML Rev 257
E Young, 'Protecting Member State Autonomy in the European Union: Some Cautionary Tales from American Federalism' (2002) 77 New York University Law Review 1612

Index